Good riddance! I know what to do.

How may I direct your call?

Would you like to leave a message?

Could I pick your brains?

Nothing sinks in.

It's being kicked around.

I need to rest my eyes.

He knows what he's saying.

What's Plan B?

현지인이 가장 많이 쓰는
영어 표현
1000

Winning & Living English

수잔튜즈데이 지음

I was born ready. Hang tough!

Someone called me from this number.

WINTIMES

About the Author **Susan Tuesday**

She is a former instructor and simulated language test designer (TOEFL/TOEIC/TEPS/SEPT) at some of Korea's largest language institutes. She also consulted on effective English presentations at Korea's most elite universities.

Apart from Korea, Susan has lived, worked and studied in Japan, Hong Kong, Taiwan, Britain, and other places around the world. She is currently a financial consultant in New York, and holds an MBA from Seattle University.

현지인이 가장 많이 쓰는
영어 표현 1000

ⓒ Susan Tuesday, 2007, Printed in Korea.

초판 1쇄 2014년 9월 26일 발행
초판 2쇄 2015년 2월 2일 발행
2판 1쇄 2016년 12월 22일 발행
2판 2쇄 2018년 4월 25일 발행

지은이 Susan Tuesaday
펴낸이 김성실
제작 한영문화사

펴낸곳 원타임즈   등록 제313-2012-50호(2012. 2. 21)
주소 03985 서울시 마포구 연희로 19-1
전화 02) 322-5463   팩스 02) 325-5607
전자우편 sidaebooks@daum.net

ISBN 979-11-85651-87-3 (13740)

책값은 뒤표지에 있습니다.

잘못된 책은 구입하신 곳에서 바꾸어드립니다.

이 도서의 국립중앙도서관 출판예정도서목록(CIP)은 서지정보유통지원시스템 홈페이지(http://seoji.nl.go.kr)와 국가자료공동목록시스템(http://www.nl.go.kr/kolisnet)에서 이용하실 수 있습니다.(CIP제어번호 : CIP2016029821)

'요요 현상 없는 영어'
Winning & Living English

단어 하나, 표현 하나를 배워도 '온전히 내 것'으로
만들어 써먹을 수 있는 영어 프로그램을 만들겠습니다.
모국어의 소중함을 망각하지 않고,
영어 배우기가 세계인과 소통하는 수단으로써
자리매김되도록 혼신을 다하겠습니다.

{ 대한민국 보통사람들을 위한 외국어 학습교재의 산실 }

INTRO 머리말

"Hello, Everyone! I'm Susan Tuesday."

:: 안녕하세요? 저는 한국을 너무 좋아하는 미국인, 수잔 튜즈데이랍니다. 한국사람과 문화에 매료되어 한국어를 배우기로 마음먹었고요 — 이제 한국어는 중급 정도의 실력이 되었지요! 사실, 전 MBA 출신으로 전공은 금융·경제 분야이지만, 한국과 아시아권에서 오랫동안 일하면서 자연스럽게 영어 교육에 관심을 갖게 되었습니다. 그동안 영어를 잘하고 싶어하는 한국 친구들도 많이 알게 되었습니다. 초등학생부터 대학생 그리고 직장인들을 대상으로 다양한 강의를 하면서 한국 친구들의 '영어 스트레스'에 대해서도 공감하게 되었습니다. 그래서 제가 한국어 처음 배울 때 심정으로 이 책을 쓰게 된 것입니다! **실제로 네이티브들이 매일같이 사용하는 '생생한 표현'을 1000문장 정도만 뭉텅이로 알고 있으면 자신감도 붙고 말도 하고 싶어지거든요!**

:: 언어가 달라도 보통 사람들이 살아가는 모습은 어디나 비슷합니다. 이 책에 나오는 표현들을 공부하다 보면 한국말과 아주 흡사한 것도 꽤 있다는 것을 발견하게 될 것입니다. 예를 들면 장애 요인이 생겨 일의 진행이 잘 안 될 때, 한국말로 '벽에 부딪혔다'고 하듯이 영어로도 hit a wall 또는 hit a roadblock이라고 해요. 또, 너무 추워서 '몸이 꽁꽁 얼어붙겠다'고 하지요? 영어표현도 I'm frozen stiff.예요. 저는 한국어를 배울 때 이런 점이 아주 흥미로웠고 기억에도 잘 남았습니다. 그래서 기회만 되면 자꾸 그 표현들을 써먹고 싶어졌죠. 내가 툭 던진 말을 한국 친구가 바로 알아들었을 때 엄청 기뻤죠! 영어도 별게 아니거든요. 여러분도 저와 똑같은 기쁨을 맛보실 겁니다!

Everybody's welcom!

:: 이 책에 담긴 대부분의 표현들은 일상적으로 자주 쓰이는 것은 물론이고, 여러분이 「프렌즈」나 「섹스앤더시티」 같은 인기 시트콤에서 자주 접하는 위트 넘치는 상황에서 뽑은 것도 있습니다. Wild and Crazy라는 Chapter에 나오는 표현들을 한번 음미해 보시기 바래요. 술 마시고 춤추고 노래하고 욕하고 화해하고… 뭐, 그런 게 다 우리 생활이잖아요? 생활 속에서 친구들과 어울리며 툭툭 던지는 말부터 입에 붙으면 자신감이 생깁니다!

Enjoy the book!

Design of this book

This book is constructed to be broad enough to cover the full range of communication situations, from the mundane to the extreme. By doing this, it succeeds in being truly multifunctional, acting as: A learning tool / A reference / A global bridge / An entertainment package.

가장 많이 쓰는 표현 1000, 레퍼런스 + 말하기 트레이닝북

How to use

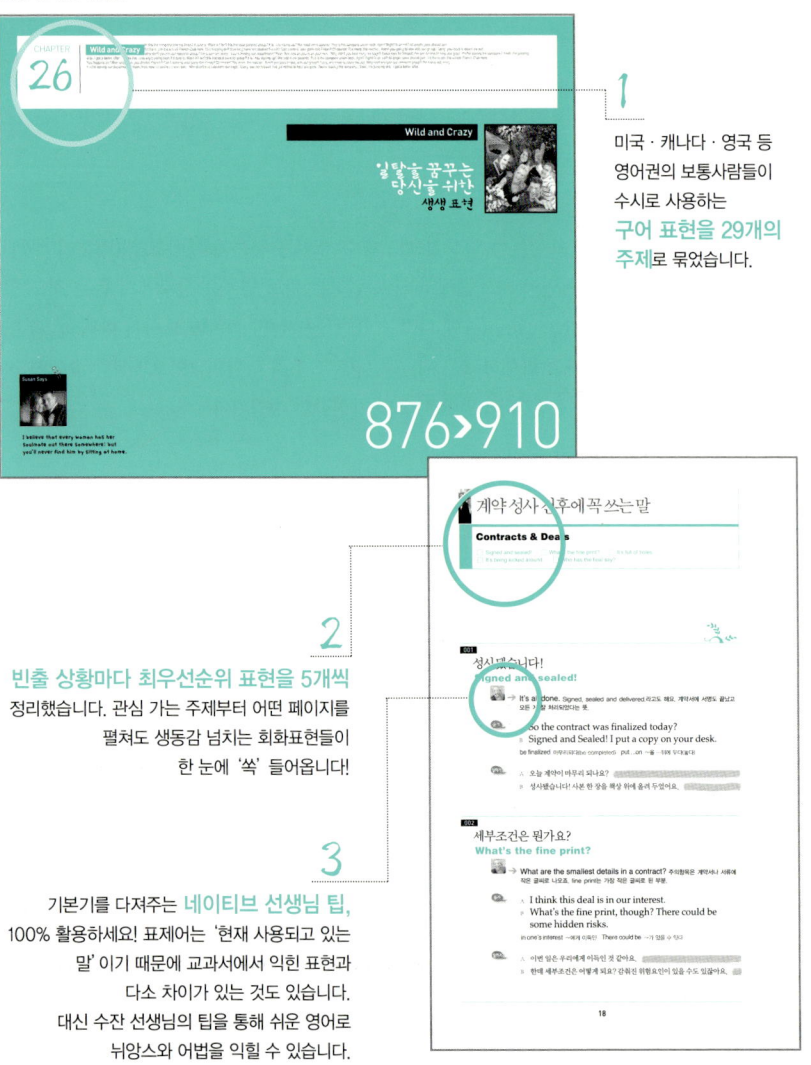

1
미국 · 캐나다 · 영국 등 영어권의 보통사람들이 수시로 사용하는 **구어 표현을 29개의 주제**로 묶었습니다.

2
빈출 상황마다 최우선순위 표현을 5개씩 정리했습니다. 관심 가는 주제부터 어떤 페이지를 펼쳐도 생동감 넘치는 회화표현들이 한 눈에 '쏙' 들어옵니다!

3
기본기를 다져주는 **네이티브 선생님 팁**을 100% 활용하세요! 표제어는 '현재 사용되고 있는 말'이기 때문에 교과서에서 익힌 표현과 다소 차이가 있는 것도 있습니다. 대신 수잔 선생님의 팁을 통해 쉬운 영어로 뉘앙스와 어법을 익힐 수 있습니다.

이 책의 구성

4 한글 번역은 '영어 말하기'의 수단으로 적극 활용하세요!
영어회화를 할 때 활용도가 높은 예문들도 몽땅 여러분 것으로 만드세요.
먼저 입에 '착' 붙을 때까지 반복해서 듣고 읽습니다. 그런 다음 한글만 보고 영어로 말해 보세요.

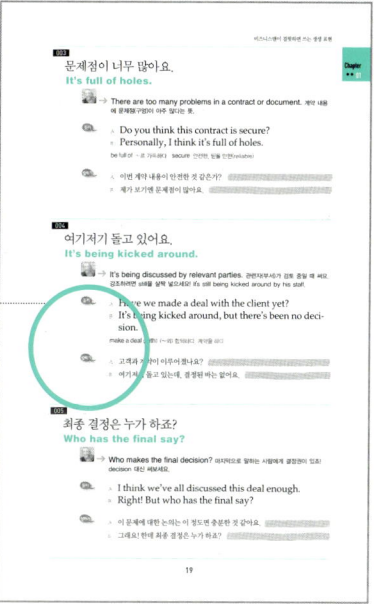

5 살아있는 영어, 보너스 카드!
'첫 대면부터 호감 가는 말문 트기'
'안녕하세요?'도 나이에 따라 달리 말한다!
'의례적으로 묻는 말'엔 이런 답변이 최고!

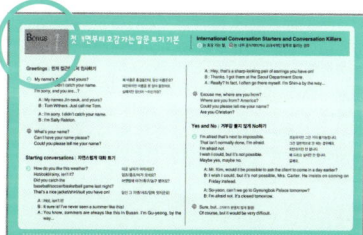

Tip
∷ 쉽게 '실천할 수 있는' 하루 영어습관 3가지

1. 매일 들르는 곳에 '영어'의 존재를 만든다.
   예) 화장실, 침실, 자동차 등 매일 '내가 있어야 할 장소'에 영어와 관련된 물건을 비치해 눈다.
2. 기간을 정하고 영어 관련 사이트를 방문한다.
   예) 오늘부터 한 달 동안, 하루 시작 또는 마감 전에 영어 관련 사이트를 방문해서 맘에 드는 코너에 참여한다.
3. 오늘 '내가 건진 영어'의 체크리스트를 만든다.
   예) 매일 내가 접했던 영어를 기록한다. 기억에 남는 단어, 표현, 청취 내용 등을 적거나 녹음해 둔다.

Chapter 1
Business Life

- 18 계약 성사 전후에 꼭 쓰는 말
- 20 모르면 낭패인 수익과 손실 표현
- 22 위기상황에 대처하는 말
- 24 일을 도모할 때 꼭 하는 말
- 26 협상할 때 누구나 쓰게 되는 말
- 28 생소한 물건이 '뭔지' 궁금할 때
- 30 사소한 말도 친근하고 세련되게!

Chapter 2
Campus Life

- 34 죽기보다 싫은 시험공부!
- 36 시험·성적 얘기에 빠지지 않는 말
- 38 난, 어떤 유형의 학생일까?
- 40 강의만 잘 들었어도!
- 42 대학생활에 대한 의견들
- 44 교수님들, 어떤 유형일까?
- 46 학창시절, 내가 얻은 것들

Contents
● 주제별로 고르고 고른 좋은 표현 1000

Is this the company bowling team? It sure is. Want in? Isn't this the local parents' group? It is. You signing up? We need more parents. This is the company union desk, right? Right! In or out? All employees should join. I'd like to join the school French Club here. You hopping on? How long have you studied French? Can I come to your party this Friday? Of course! The more, the merrier. Aren't you going to stay with our group? Sorry, you have to count me out. Why don't you join our research group? I'm a solo act, sorry. You're leaving our department? Yeah, from now on you're on your own. Why didn't you help carry our bags? Every man for himself; I've got no time to help you guys. You're leaving the company? Yeah, I'm jumping ship. I got a better offer. Is this the company bowling team? It sure is. Want in? Isn't this the local parents' group? It is. You signing up? We need more parents. This is the company union desk, right? Right! In or out? All employees should join. I'd like to join the school French Club here. You hopping on? How long have you studied French? Can I

Chapter 3
Emotions

- 50 화가 나면 나오는 말
- 52 황당한 상황을 당하면 나오는 말
- 54 기쁠 때 나도 모르게 나오는 말
- 56 미움이 넘칠 때 나오는 말
- 58 고대하던 일을 표현하고 싶을 때
- 60 소망을 얘기할 때 쓰면 좋은 말
- 62 별것 아닌 일에 툭 던지는 말

Chapter 4
Action and Reaction

- 66 할 일이 많을 때 으레 쓰는 말
- 68 피곤하고 지치면 저절로 나오는 말
- 70 방해꾼에겐 따끔하게 한마디!
- 72 힘든 상황에도 꿋꿋하게!
- 74 한바탕 공세를 취할 때 힘이 되는 말
- 76 깨끗이 물러설 때 던지는 한마디!
- 78 만전을 기하고 있을 때 하는 말

Contents

Chapter 5
Romance

- 82 사랑에 빠지면 누구나 쉽게 하는 말
- 84 사랑의 불씨가 꺼지면 내뱉는 말
- 86 구애할 때 흔히 쓰는 말
- 88 동거할까, 결혼할까?
- 90 헤어지는 연인들이 흔히 쓰는 말
- 92 관계 회복을 원할 때 쓰는 말
- 94 잘못된 만남의 징조들

Chapter 6
Ideas and Innovation

- 98 아이디어가 번뜩일 때 튀어나오는 말
- 100 자신 있게 해결책 말하기
- 102 분석과 검토 할 때 쓰는 말
- 104 기분 좋게 맞장구 칠 때 쓰는 말
- 106 제안할 때 쓰기 좋은 쉬운 말
- 108 견해를 피력할 때 흔히 쓰는 말
- 110 한쪽만 고려할 수 없을 때 하는 말

come to your party this Friday? Of course! The more, the merrier. Aren't you going to stay with our group? Sorry, you have to count me out. Why don't you join our research group? I'm a solo act, sorry. You're leaving our department? Yeah, from now on you're on your own. Why didn't you help carry our bags? Every man for himself; I've got no time to help you guys. You're leaving the company? Yeah, I'm jumping ship. I got a better offer. Is this the company bowling team? It sure is. Want in? Isn't this the local parents' group? It is. You signing up? We need more parents. This is the company union desk, right? Right! In or out? All emplo yees should join. I'd like to join the school French Club here. You hopping on? How long have you studied French? Can I come to your party this Friday? Of course! The more, the merrier. Aren't you going to stay with our group? Sorry, you have to count me out. Why don't you join our research group? I'm a solo act, sorry. You're leaving our department? Yeah, from now on you're on your own. Why didn't you help carry our bags? Every

Chapter 7
Starting and Stopping

- 114 행동을 개시할 때 으레 쓰는 말
- 116 긍정적으로 일하게 해주는 말
- 118 막간 휴식이 목마를 때 나오는 말
- 120 행동 복귀를 알리는 말
- 122 사고의 전환이 필요할 때 쓰면 좋은 말
- 124 속도가 생명일 때 하는 말
- 126 종료를 알릴 때 툭 던지는 말

Chapter 8
Calls and Calling

- 130 전화걸기
- 132 전화받기
- 134 통화 대기 요청
- 136 회답 전화걸기
- 138 전화 통화 불가
- 140 전화 건 사람 확인하기
- 142 메모 전달하기

Chapter 9
Health

- 146 복통 · 요통 · 근육통 등의 통증 말하기
- 148 머리가 맑지 못하면 나타나는 증세
- 150 술 마신 뒤에 오는 증상들
- 152 피곤하면 툭 내뱉게 되는 말
- 154 유행성 질병에 관해 자주 쓰는 말
- 156 내장기관에 탈이 났을 때 쓰는 말
- 158 목과 코가 아플 때 하는 말

Chapter 10
Time

- 162 입에 바로 붙는 기간과 빈도 표현
- 164 촉각을 표현하는 말
- 166 시간이 좀 걸릴 때 하는 말
- 168 시도 때도 없이 일어나는 일들
- 170 어쩌다 있는 일들
- 172 시작을 알리는 쉬운 말
- 174 종료 · 마감을 알리는 쉬운 말

Contents ● 주제별로 고르고 고른 좋은 표현 1000

Is this the company bowling team? It sure is. Want in? Isn't this the local parents' group? It is. You signing up? We need more parents. This is the company union desk, right? Right! In or out? All employees should join. I'd like to join the school French Club here. You hopping on? How long have you studied French? Can I come to your party this Friday? Of course! The more, the merrier. Aren't you going to stay with our group? Sorry, you have to count me out. Why don't you join our research group? I'm a solo act, sorry. You're leaving our department? Yeah, from now on you're on your own. Why didn't you help carry our bags? Every man for himself; I've got no time to help you guys. You're leaving the company? Yeah, I'm jumping ship. I got a better offer. Is this the company bowling team? It sure is. Want in? Isn't this the local parents' group? It is. You signing up? We need more parents. This is the company union desk, right? Right! In or out? All employees should join. I'd like to join the school French Club here. You hopping on? How long have you studied French? Can I

Chapter 11
Possibilities and Impossibilities

- 178 부탁을 쉽게 들어줄 때 하는 말
- 180 일을 감당하기 어려울 때 하는 말
- 182 절대로 있을 수 없는 일이 생기면
- 184 가능성을 딱히 장담하지 못할 때
- 186 일의 성사를 고무시키는 말
- 188 방안을 모색할 때 흔히 쓰는 말
- 190 장애물에 걸려 푸념하고 싶다면

Chapter 12
Trust and Reliance

- 194 믿음을 주는 쉽고 좋은 말
- 196 충성심을 보여주는 든든한 말
- 198 자신 있을 때 툭 던지는 말
- 200 오랜 우정을 전하는 친근한 말
- 202 믿을 수 있는 사람과 정보가 필요해!
- 204 팀워크를 고취시키는 쉽고 좋은 말
- 206 한결 같은 마음과 행보를 전하는 말

Contents

Chapter 13
Requests, Invitations & Denials

- 210　순간적으로 요청할 게 있다면
- 212　엄포를 놓아 지시해야 한다면
- 214　단호하게 거절할 때 툭 던지는 말
- 216　공손하게 요청할 때 쓰면 좋은 말
- 218　기분 상하지 않게 거절하기
- 220　최후통첩할 때 으레 쓰는 말
- 222　부담 없이 초대할 때 쓰는 말

Chapter 14
Warnings and Danger

- 226　상대에게 경고할 때 쓰는 말
- 228　위기 상황이 예감될 때 쓰는 말
- 230　경솔함을 꾸짖는 한마디!
- 232　협박이 필요할 때 흔히 하는 말
- 234　주의를 요할 때 쓰면 좋은 말
- 236　고통과 위험은 성공의 또 다른 얼굴
- 238　큰 실수를 따끔히 지적할 때

Chapter 15
Skepticism and Doubt

- 242　회의적인 생각이 들 때면
- 244　의견이 다를 때 툭 던지는 말
- 246　의구심이 들면 툭 던지는 말
- 248　냉소적인 말대꾸를 즐기려면
- 250　반대 의견을 전하는 쉬운 말
- 252　불신이 가득하면 튀어 나오는 말
- 254　확실한 증거를 요구할 때 쓰는 말

Chapter 16
Personal Enquiries

- 258　매일 하는 안부 인사, 생기발랄하게!
- 260　신경이 예민해져 있다면
- 262　의기소침해진 친구에게 한마디!
- 264　뭔가 불안해 보이는 상대에게 한마디!
- 266　화를 삭이지 못할 때 한마디!
- 268　호기심이 생길 때 하게 되는 말
- 270　가족의 안부를 묻고 싶다면

Chapter 17
Customer Service

- 274 고객에게 도움을 제안하는 말
- 276 고객을 마중할 때 쓰는 말
- 278 고객의 불편사항을 점검하는 말
- 280 고객을 대기시킬 때 하는 말
- 282 물건을 건네면서 하는 말
- 284 고객만족을 확인해 보는 말
- 286 고객의 요구를 들어주지 못할 때

Chapter 18
Enthusiasm and Encouragement

- 290 열광적으로 동조할 때 어울리는 말
- 292 상대방을 격려해주는 말
- 294 긍정적인 태도로 이끄는 말
- 296 깔끔한 동의가 맘에 들어!
- 298 상대방의 기를 살려주는 쉽고 좋은 말
- 300 성공과 칭찬, 누구나 듣고 싶은 말!
- 302 그대에게 아낌 없는 찬사를!

Contents ● 주제별로 고르고 고른 좋은 표현 1000

Is this the company bowling team? It sure is. Want in? Isn't this the local parents' group? It is. You signing up? We need more parents. This is the company union desk, right? Right! In or out? All emplo yees should join. I'd like to join the school French Club here. You hopping on? How long have you studied French? Can I come to your party this Friday? Of course! The more, the merrier. Aren't you going to stay with our group? Sorry, you have to count me out. Why don't you join our research group? I'm a solo act, sorry. You're leaving our department? Yeah, from now on you're on your own. Why didn't you help carry our bags? Every man for himself; I've got no time to help you guys. You're leaving the company? Yeah, I'm jumping ship. I got a better offer. Is this the company bowling team? It sure is. Want in? Isn't this the local parents' group? It is. You signing up? We need more parents. This is the company union desk, right? Right! In or out? All emplo yees should join. I'd like to join the school French Club here. You hopping on? How long have you studied French? Can I

Chapter 19
Surprise and Shock

- 306 너무 갑작스러워 감당하기 힘들 때
- 308 황당한 상황에 툭 내뱉는 말
- 310 인상 깊은 일이 벌어지면
- 312 이렇게 황당하고 실망스럽기는 처음이야!
- 314 경외감이 들 정도로 놀라울 때
- 316 평정심을 보여주고 싶을 때
- 318 참는 것도 한계가 있지!

Chapter 20
Money

- 322 돈에 대한 나의 생각은?
- 324 돈이 차고 넘친다면
- 326 돈이 떨어졌을 때 하게 되는 말
- 328 누가 돈을 낼 것인지 정할 때
- 330 돈 빌리고, 빌려줄 때 으레 쓰는 말
- 332 대박과 쪽박, 한두마디면 통해!
- 334 돈을 내 놓으라고? 그게 문제일 때

Contents

Chapter 21
Gossip and Rumor

- 338 세상의 비밀은 모두 알고싶어!
- 340 '소문난 잔치에 먹을 게 없다' 지만
- 342 일파만파 번지는 소문!
- 344 결국엔 들키게 될 거짓말
- 346 소문의 진상을 알고 보니
- 348 비밀, 너 딱 걸렸어?!
- 350 창피하고 굴욕스런 순간이 닥치면

Chapter 22
Responsibility and Management

- 354 결정의 순간이 찾아 오면
- 356 내 책임이 아니라고 강조하고 싶다면
- 358 책임소재를 밝힐 때 쓰는 말
- 360 책임감을 고취시키는 말
- 362 무책임을 따끔하게 질책하는 말
- 364 믿고 맡길 건지 고민 된다면
- 366 책임을 전가할 때 으레 쓰는 말

come to your party this Friday? Of course! The more, the merrier. Aren't you going to stay with our group? Sorry, you have to count me out. Why don't you join our research group? I'm a solo act, sorry. You're leaving our department? Yeah, from now on you're on your own. Why didn't you help carry our bags? Every man for himself; I've got no time to help you guys. You're leaving the company? Yeah, I'm jumping ship. I got a better offer. Is this the company bowling team? It sure is. Want in? Isn't this the local parents' group? It is. You signing up? We need more parents. This is the company union desk, right? Right! In or out? All emplo yees should join. I'd like to join the school French Club here. You hopping on? How long have you studied French? Can I come to your party this Friday? Of course! The more, the merrier. Aren't you going to stay with our group? Sorry, you have to count me out. Why don't you join our research group? I'm a solo act, sorry. You're leaving our department? Yeah, from now on you're on your own. Why didn't you help carry our bags? Every

Chapter 23
Foolishness and Wisdom

- 370 똑똑한 사람을 좋아하세요?
- 372 그런 '꼼수'에는 안 속아요!
- 374 해결책, 내 손 안에 있소이다!
- 376 머리는 좀 떨어지지만
- 378 어리석음, 그대를 어찌할꼬?!
- 380 꼬인 문제로 난감할 때
- 382 언변이 뛰어난 사람에게 한마디!

Chapter 24
Groups and Individuals

- 386 참여의사, 가장 쉽게 묻기
- 388 탈퇴의사, 가장 쉽게 말하기
- 390 단도직입적으로 '어느 편' 인가요?
- 392 협동심을 북돋아주는 말
- 394 팀워크 방해꾼에겐 따끔한 충고를!
- 396 강점과 약점, 긍정적으로 말하기
- 398 팀원들 사이에 생기는 사소한 일들

Chapter 25
Alcohol

- 402 나만의 술 주문 방식은?
- 404 나의 음주 스타일은?
- 406 술 마시는 장소도 가지가지!
- 408 취하면 누구나 튀어나오는 말
- 410 고약한 술버릇에 일침을 주는 말
- 412 분위기에 따라 달리 건배하기
- 414 술의 유혹으로부터 '말짱' 하려면

Chapter 26
Wild and Crazy

- 418 쉬운 말로 '작업' 걸기
- 420 한판 붙어 볼까?
- 422 게으름의 유혹에 빠지고 싶을 때
- 424 끝없는 욕망을 드러내는 쉬운 말
- 426 좌절과 절망도 쉬운 말로 담담하게
- 428 실수와 후회할 때 툭 던지는 말
- 430 용기와 자신감을 드러내는 말

Contents ● 주제별로 고르고 고른 좋은 표현 1000

Is this the company bowling team? It sure is. Want in? Isn't this the local parents' group? It is. You signing up? We need more parents. This is the company union desk, right? Right! In or out? All emplo yees should join. I'd like to join the school French Club here. You hopping on? How long have you studied French? Can I come to your party this Friday? Of course! The more, the merrier. Aren't you going to stay with our group? Sorry, you have to count me out. Why don't you join our research group? I'm a solo act, sorry. You're leaving our department? Yeah, from now on you're on your own. Why didn't you help carry our bags? Every man for himself; I've got no time to help you guys. You're leaving the company? Yeah, I'm jumping ship. I got a better offer. Is this the company bowling team? It sure is. Want in? Isn't this the local parents' group? It is. You signing up? We need more parents. This is the company union desk, right? Right! In or out? All emplo yees should join. I'd like to join the school French Club here. You hopping on? How long have you studied French? Can I

Chapter 27
Communication

- 434 납득 여부를 확인할 때 쓰는 말
- 436 궁금증을 설명해주고 싶다면
- 438 마지못해 동의할 때 쓰는 말
- 440 소통이 잘 안 될 때 튀어나오는 말
- 442 말하는 데 문제가 있나요?
- 444 피드백과 승인 받을 게 있다면
- 446 에둘러서 반대하는 말

Chapter 28
Weather

- 450 덥고 추운 날씨에 으레 쓰는 말
- 452 날씨의 변화를 예측할 때 쓰는 말
- 454 비오고, 눈오는 날이면 쓰는 말
- 456 극한의 날씨를 표현하고 싶다면
- 458 난, 어떤 계절과 날씨를 좋아하지?
- 460 날씨에 따라 건강 챙길 때
- 462 날씨에서 나온 유용한 생활표현

Contents

Chapter 29
Special Corners

466 요조숙녀는 이렇게 말하지!

468 칙칙폭폭! 10대의 인생 열차

470 가정주부의 '거룩한' 일상

472 샐러리맨의 고충이 느껴질 때면

Appendix

476 Bonus 1 :
첫 대면부터 호감 가는 말문 트기 기본

479 Bonus 2 :
세대별로 다른 일상 말투 따라잡기

480 Bonus 3 :
알아 두면 힘이 되는 영어의 의례적인 인사말

come to your party this Friday? Of course! The more, the merrier. Aren't you going to stay with our group? Sorry, you have to count me out. Why don't you join our research group? I'm a solo act, sorry. You're leaving our department? Yeah, from now on you're on your own. Why didn't you help carry our bags? Every man for himself; I've got no time to help you guys. You're leaving the company? Yeah, I'm jumping ship. I got a better offer. Is this the company bowling team? It sure is. Want in? Isn't this the local parents' group? It is. You signing up? We need more parents. This is the company union desk, right? Right! In or out? All employees should join. I'd like to join the school French Club here. You hopping on? How long have you studied French? Can I come to your party this Friday? Of course! The more, the merrier. Aren't you going to stay with our group? Sorry, you have to count me out. Why don't you join our research group? I'm a solo act, sorry. You're leaving our department? Yeah, from now on you're on your own. Why didn't you help carry our bags? Every

---

[일러두기]

당장 네이티브에게 말 걸고 싶어지는 실용적인 표현들!

회화표현은 이디엄과 달리 문화적 배경지식 없이도 바로 현장에서 한 문장처럼 써먹을 수 있기 때문에 특히 초보 학습자들에게 유용합니다. 늘 곁에 두고 자투리 시간이 생기면 읽고, 듣고, 말하기를 '실천' 하세요! 당장 TV 시트콤 대사가 한두 마디씩 들리고, 길거리에서 외국인을 만나면 '말 걸고 싶은 충동' 에 사로잡힐 테니까요!

이 책에 실린 표현들은 원어민들이 가장 즐겨 사용하는 말로 구어체 어법을 따른 것입니다.
1. 회화표현은 단독으로 사용해도 의미전달이 가능합니다.
2. 회화표현은 문장의 처음, 중간 또는 말미에 나올 수 있습니다.
3. 회화표현은 오는 위치에 따라 시제나 성·수의 일치가 적용될 수 있습니다.

예) **That's news to me**, Sumi. 수미야, 난 몰랐던 일인데.
Kang-ho's China trip is **news to me** because he said he never had time.
강호의 중국여행은 의외야. 그가 시간이 없다고 했거든.
You don't like the job but **that's news to me**. 일이 맘에 들지 않는다고, 그런지 난 몰랐네.

CHAPTER 01

Business Life

Is this the company bowling team? It sure is. Want in? Isn't this the local parents' group? It is. You sig[n]
I'd like to join the school French Club here. You hopping on? How long have you studied French? Ca[n]
Why don't you join our research group? I'm a solo act, sorry. You're leaving our department? Yeah, [I]
got a better offer. Is this the company bowling team? It sure is. Want in? Isn't this the local parents' group? It is. You signing up? We ne[ed]
You hopping on? How long have you studied French? Can I come to your party this Friday? Of course! The more, the merrier. Aren't you[?]
You're leaving our department? Yeah, from now on you're on your own. Why didn't you help carry our bags? Every man for himself; I've

Susan Says...

No person can stand alone in business. I make sure I put together the right team before I do anything.

Business Life

비즈니스맨이
걸핏하면 쓰는
생생 표현

001 ▸ 035

계약 성사 전후에 꼭 쓰는 말

Contracts & Deals

- [ ] Signed and sealed!
- [ ] What's the fine print?
- [ ] It's full of holes.
- [ ] It's being kicked around.
- [ ] Who has the final say?

001
성사됐습니다!
Signed and sealed!

 → **It's all done.** Signed, sealed and delivered.라고도 해요. 계약서에 서명도 끝났고 모든 게 잘 처리되었다는 뜻.

A So the contract was finalized today?
B Signed and Sealed! I put a copy on your desk.

be finalized 마무리되다(be completed)   **put ...on** ~을 …위에 두다(놓다)

A 오늘 계약이 마무리 되나요?
B 성사됐습니다! 사본 한 장을 책상 위에 올려 두었어요.

002
세부조건은 뭔가요?
What's the fine print?

 → **What are the smallest details in a contract?** 주의항목은 계약서나 서류에 작은 글씨로 나오죠. fine print는 가장 작은 글씨로 된 부분.

A I think this deal is in our interest.
B What's the fine print, though? There could be some hidden risks.

in one's interest ~에게 이득인   **There could be** ~가 있을 수 있다

A 이번 일은 우리에게 이득인 것 같아요.
B 한데 세부조건은 어떻게 되요? 감춰진 위험요인이 있을 수도 있잖아요.

비즈니스맨이 걸핏하면 쓰는 생생 표현

Chapter 01

003
문제점이 너무 많아요.
It's full of holes.

 → There are too many problems in a contract or document. 계약 내용에 문제점(구멍)이 아주 많다는 뜻.

A Do you think this contract is secure?
B Personally, I think it's full of holes.

be full of ~로 가득하다   secure 안전한, 믿을 만한(reliable)

A 이번 계약 내용이 안전한 것 같은가?
B 제가 보기엔 문제점이 많아요.

004
여기저기 돌고 있어요.
It's being kicked around.

 → It's being discussed by relevant parties. 관련자(부서)가 검토 중일 때 써요. 강조하려면 still을 살짝 넣으세요! It's still being kicked around by his staff.

A Have we made a deal with the client yet?
B It's being kicked around, but there's been no decision.

make a deal (with) (~와) 합의하다, 계약을 하다

A 고객과 계약이 이루어졌나요?
B 여기저기 돌고 있는데, 결정된 바는 없어요.

005
최종 결정은 누가 하죠?
Who has the final say?

 → Who makes the final decision? 마지막으로 말하는 사람에게 결정권이 있죠! decision 대신 써보세요.

A I think we've all discussed this deal enough.
B Right! But who has the final say?

A 이 문제에 대한 논의는 이 정도면 충분한 것 같아요.
B 그래요! 한데 최종 결정은 누가 하죠?

모르면 낭패인 수익과 손실 표현

Profit & Loss

- [ ] We're bleeding cash.
- [ ] It's like a giant ATM.
- [ ] What's our bottom line?
- [ ] It's a write-off.
- [ ] What's Uncle Sam's due?

006
현금을 까먹고 있어요.
We're bleeding cash.

 → We're losing money. '피' 같은 현금을 '흘리고' 있다니… 원어민들이 쓰는 생생한 '현장 표현' 이예요.

A Is your department profitable?
B No, we're just bleeding cash.

profitable 수익이 나는   cf. lucrative 수익성이 좋은

A 당신 부서는 수익성이 있나요?
B 아니오. 현금만 까먹고 있습니다.

007
현금을 쏟아내주죠.
It's like a giant ATM.

 → It's very profitable. It earns us a lot of money. 거대한 현금지급기(ATM) 같다니! 금방 부자가 되겠죠. 또 '젖소'에 비유해 cash cow라는 표현도 써요.

A Is your overseas sales department profitable?
B Sure! It's like a giant ATM.

cf. cash cow (꾸준한) 수입원   eg. This will be our cash cow.

A 해외판매부는 수익성이 있나요?
B 그럼요! 현금을 쏟아내주죠.

008
수지타산이 어떻습니까?
What's our bottom line?

 밑지고 팔 수는 없겠죠? 비용을 제하고 최소한 얻어야 할 수입의 '마지노선'이 얼마냐는 뜻. bottom line은 원래 회사 재무제표(financial report) 마지막 줄에 나오는 순 수익/손실 부분을 일컫는 말.

A What's our bottom line for this new product?
B It should be about 230 million US dollars this year.

about 약, 대략

A 이번 신제품의 수지타산이 어떻습니까?
B 올해 미화 2억 3천만 달러는 될 겁니다.

009
정리해야죠.
It's a write-off.

 It has no value left. 수익 가치가 없는 사업을 아예 '접는' 것을 말해요.

A Don't you think we can save that division?
B No, it's a write-off. Sell it to some other company.

save 구하다   write-off 말소, 실패작   division 부, 과, 사업부

A 그 사업부를 건질 수 있지 않을까요?
B 아니오. 정리하고, 다른 회사에 파세요.

010
(미국에) 낼 세금은 얼마인가요?
What's Uncle Sam's due?

 How much is due in U.S. taxes? Uncle Sam은 미국 정부에 대한 속칭.

A We should earn about $200 million this year.
B Sounds good, but what's Uncle Sam's due?

A 올해 수익이 약 2억 달러 정도 될 겁니다.
B 괜찮군요. 한데, 미국에 낼 세금은 얼마나 되죠?

위기상황에 대처하는 말

Dealing with Risk

- [ ] What's the downside?
- [ ] And at worst? / Give me worst-case.
- [ ] Assuming what?
- [ ] What's Plan B?
- [ ] Something smells fishy.

011

위험요인은 뭔가요?
What's the downside?

→ **Tell me about major risks.** 여기서 downside는 major risks란 의미예요.

A I'm sure that this whole venture will be a success!
B Maybe, but what's the downside?

I'm sure that ~을 확신하다, 장담하다   venture 모험적인 사업, 신규사업

A 이번 사업은 성공할 겁니다!
B 잘 된다면요. 한데, 위험요인은 뭔가요?

012

최악의 경우는?
And at worst? / Give me worst-case.

→ **What's the worst that could happen?** 사업가는 최악의 경우를 항상 대비하죠.

A I'm positive we'll see profits rise!
B Give me worst-case. What if they don't?

I'm positive(that) ~라고 확신하다(I'm sure that)   what if ~인 경우엔 어떻게 하나?

A 분명 수익이 늘 겁니다!
B 최악의 경우도 말해봐요. 수익이 늘지 않으면요?

비즈니스맨이 걸핏하면 쓰는 생생 표현

013
근거가 뭔데요?
Assuming what?

 → What are your major assumptions? 그렇게 말하는 근거를 대라고 '들이댈 때' 써요.

A We're going to decrease costs next year.
B Assuming what? Please give me some details.

be going to ~할 예정이다   decrease 줄이다   details 세부사항

A 내년에는 비용이 절감될 겁니다.
B 뭘 근거로요? 좀 자세히 말씀해주세요.

014
차선책은 뭡니까?
What's Plan B?

 → What's your backup plan in case of failure? 'A 안'이 실패할 경우를 대비해 'B 안'을 준비할 것!

A We'll make this a success by targeting young customers.
B What if they don't buy? What's Plan B?

make (it) a success 성공시키다   by+-ing (수단·방법) ~함으로써

A 이건 젊은층을 대상으로 하면 성공할 거야.
B 그들이 사지 않으면요? 차선책은 뭔가요?

015
미심쩍은 데가 있어.
Something smells fishy.

 → Something doesn't seem right with a plan/situation. 뭔가 미심쩍은 게 있을 때 써요. 여기서 fishy는 suspicious와 같은 뜻.

A Our factory was able to raise output again!
B Something smells fishy! Let me see those output numbers.

be able to (실제 능력) ~할 수 있다   raise 상승시키다

A 우리 공장 생산량이 또 증가했군!
B 뭔가 미심쩍은 데가 있어! 그 생산량 수치 좀 봐요.

일을 도모할 때 꼭 하는 말

Planning

- [ ] Who dreamt it up?
- [ ] It's back-of-the-envelope.
- [ ] Let's start from square one.
- [ ] It doesn't add up.
- [ ] What's your best guess?

016

누구 작품인가요?
Who dreamt it up?

→ Who made this dramatic plan? 긍정적인 뜻 말고 냉소적으로 돌려 말할 때도 써요.

A This plan is brilliant! Who dreamt it up?
B Terry, in the Engineering section.

brilliant 탁월한(excellent) **dream up** 창작하다, 생각해내다

A 이건 탁월한 기획이야! 도대체 누구 작품인가?
B 엔지니어 부의 테리가 했어요.

017

대충 적어본 겁니다.
It's back-of-the-envelope.

→ A plan drawn up without many details 번뜩 뭔가 떠올라서 우선 봉투 뒷면에 적어본 것에 비유한 말. 완성도가 떨어진다는 표현.

A This design looks great!
B Thanks, but it's just back-of-the-envelope.

A 이 디자인, 아주 근사해요!
B 고마워요, 우선 대충 해본 겁니다.

018
처음부터 다시 하죠.
Let's start from square one.

 square one은 맨 처음(very beginning)이란 뜻. Back to the square one도 좋아요!

A I don't know where this project went wrong!
B Let's start from square one, and review everything.

go wrong 잘못되다   eg. Everything went wrong!

A 이 프로젝트가 어디부터 잘못된 것인지 모르겠군!
B 처음부터 다시 하죠. 모두 다 검토해봐요.

019
말이 되지 않아요.
It doesn't add up.

 It doesn't make sense at all. 납득하기 힘든 상황에서 툭 튀어 나오는 말. They don't add up.도 함께 써요.

A What do you think of my suggestion?
B It doesn't add up. I want you to go back and rewrite it.

What do you think of~? ~에 대해 어떻게 생각해요?   I want you to 네가 ~하길 바래

A 내 제안서가 어떻습니까?
B 도통 말이 안 돼요. 검토하고 다시 써 와요.

020
잘 알아맞혀 보시겠어요?
What's your best guess?

 What would be most likely to happen? 짐작(guess)을 잘해서 맞혀보라는 뜻.

A We still haven't figured out our sales for the year.
B What's your best guess? $30 million?

figure out 알아내다, 해결하다

A 연간 매출을 아직도 모르겠어요.
B 잘 알아맞혀 보시겠어요? 3천 달러요?

협상할 때 누구나 쓰게 되는 말

Negotiations

- [ ] We hit a roadblock.
- [ ] They're talking past us.
- [ ] It's on the table.
- [ ] Push a little harder.
- [ ] Let's walk.

021
벽에 부딪혔어요.
We hit a roadblock.

→ roadblock은 시위 때 경찰이 치는 방어벽. 논의 자체가 힘든 상황일 때 써요.

A Are the talks going well?
B We hit a roadblock over a few items, I'm afraid.

be going well 잘 돼가다   talks 회담, 협의

A 그 협의는 잘 돼갑니까?
B 몇 가지 항목에 대해 벽에 부딪혔어요.

022
우리 의견이 먹히지 않아요.
They're talking past us.

→ The counterpart is not listening to what we say. 주장하는 바가 상대에게 '마이동풍'일 때 '답답한' 심정을 토로하는 말.

A Are you still negotiating the price with Bell Inc.?
B Yes, but they're still talking past us.

be still +-ing 여전히 ~하고 있는 중이다   negotiate 협상하다, 논의하다

A 아직도 벨 사와 가격협상 중인가요?
B 예, 한데 우리 의견이 먹히지 않아요.

023
안건으로 나왔어요.
It's on the table.

 → It's been made available for people to discuss. 공개적으로 검토할 수 있게 안건으로 상정되었다는 말.

A We offered Pratel Inc. free shipping?
B Yeah, it's on the table. No feedback yet.
free shipping 무료 선적 feedback 의견, 반응

A 프라텔 사에 무료선적을 제안했지요?
B 예, 검토 중일 텐데. 아직 반응은 없습니다.

024
좀 더 밀어 부쳐봐요.
Push a little harder

 → Try to convince. 설득되도록 더 애써 보라는 말.

A I'm not sure how I can persuade this client!
B You need to push a little harder, Richard.
I'm not sure how 어떻게 ~해야 할지 모르겠다 persuade 설득하다

A 이 고객을 어떻게 설득해야 할지 모르겠군.
B 리처드, 좀 더 밀어 부쳐봐요.

025
그만둡시다.
Let's walk.

 → Let's walk away from them. 여기서 walk는 더 논의할 필요도 없이 '박차고 나가자'는 뜻. 강경한 입장 표명이죠. 사과하지 않으면 그만두겠소! — You better apologize, or I'm walking!

A Don't you think this is a good offer?
B No, let's walk. We'll get better terms someplace else.
offer 제의, 제안 get better terms 더 나은 조건을 얻다

A 괜찮은 제안 같지 않나요?
B 아뇨, 그만 둡시다. 다른 곳에서 더 좋은 제안이 들어올 테니.

생소한 물건이 '뭔지' 궁금할 때

Business IT

- [ ] What's this gizmo? [ ] Show me the nuts and bolts. [ ] This works how?
- [ ] Don't tinker! [ ] It's out of juice.

026

이 기계는 뭔가요?
What's this gizmo?

→ **What kind of device or gadget is this?** gizmo는 잘 모르는 기계를 가리킬 때 가장 많이 쓰는 말. 특히 IT 제품에 많이 써요.

A What's this gizmo? A cell phone?
B Actually, it's an electronic dictionary.

actually 실은('그게 아니라'는 뜻)

A 이 기계는 뭔가요? 휴대폰인가요?
B 아뇨, 전자사전입니다.

027

자세히 설명해보세요.
Show me the nuts and bolts.

→ Show me details about a machine/appliance/software program.
제품 설명뿐만 아니라 일반적인 상황에도 자주 쓰는 말이죠.

A Please take a look at our newest software program.
B Show me the nuts and bolts. I want to see how it works.

how it works 작동 방식

A 폐사의 최신 소프트웨어 제품을 보시죠.
B 자세히 설명해주세요. 작동 방식을 알고 싶어요.

028
이렇게 작동하나요?
This works how?

 → How does this work? 직접 시도하면서 물어 볼 수 있는 말.

A See. This is a voice-activated lamp.
B Interesting. This works how?

voice-activated 음성인식으로 작동하는

A 자 봐요. 이건 음성으로 작동돼요.
B 흥미롭네요. 이렇게 하면 되나요?

029
건드리지 마세요.
Don't tinker!

 → Don't touch. 물건을 무작정 만져보려고 할 때 원어민들은 이렇게 툭 내뱉어요.

A Would you mind if I opened this up?
B Don't tinker! I'll show you how it opens.

Would you mind if ~해도 돼요? tinker 만지작거리다

A 이거 열어봐도 돼요?
B 건드리지 마세요! 어떻게 여는 건지 알려줄게요.

030
배터리가 다 됐어요.
It's out of juice.

 → There's no electricity. The battery's drained. 여기서 juice는 electricity를 말해요.

A Why isn't this appliance running?
B It's out of juice. You have to plug it in.

appliance 가전제품 run 작동하다(operate) have to ~해야 한다

A 가전제품이 왜 작동이 안 되죠?
B 배터리가 나갔어요. 전원에 연결하세요.

사소한 말도 친근하고 세련되게!

Up close & Personal

- [ ] What line of work are you in?
- [ ] I'm between jobs right now.
- [ ] Mind if I asked you something?
- [ ] You're still single, I bet!
- [ ] Doing well for yourself?

031

어떤 일을 하세요?
What line of work are you in?

 → **What do you do for a living?** 친밀감을 주면서 직업을 묻는 세련된 말.

- A What line of work are you in?
- B I'm in accounting.

  accounting 회계, 경리 cf. accountant 회계사

- A 어떤 일을 하세요?
- B 회계 쪽 일을 해요.

032

새 직장을 찾고 있어요.
I'm between jobs right now.

 → **I'm out looking. I'm looking for a job.** 원어민들은 '실직했다, 무직이다(I'm jobless.)'란 표현보다 이 말을 더 좋아해요. 긍정적인 어감의 말이 선호됩니다!

- A Are you working in Telcon Corp. still?
- B No, I'm between jobs right now.

- A 여전히 텔콘 사에 근무하세요?
- B 아뇨, 지금 새 직장을 찾고 있어요.

비즈니스맨이 걸핏하면 쓰는 생생 표현

Chapter 01

033
뭐 좀 물어봐도 될까요?
Mind if I asked you something?

 → Could I ask you something? 중학교 영어 단골 표현이죠! 이젠 마음껏 써보세요.

A Mind if I asked you something?
B Sure, go ahead Harold.

Mind if=Would you mind if   go (right) ahead 자, 어서 (해봐요.)

A 뭐 좀 물어봐도 될까요?
B 그럼요, 말해봐요, 해롤드.

034
아직 미혼이죠!
You're still single, I bet!

 → You're not married yet, are you? 기혼자라도 미혼처럼 보이고 싶은 심정! 특히 여성을 기분 좋게 해주는 말.

A Janice, you're still single, I bet! You look it!
B Actually, I've got a husband and two kids at home.

You look it! = You look single/young.

A 진희 씨, 아직 미혼이죠! 그렇게 보이는데!
B 실은, 남편과 두 아이가 있답니다.

035
먹고 살만 하시죠?
Doing well for yourself?

 → Are you earning a reasonable amount of money? 직접적으로 What's your salary?라고 묻는 건 실례일 수 있어요.

A Doing well for yourself?
B More or less. I could stand to earn more, actually.

more or less 어느 정도, 대체로   stand to do ~할 것 같다   eg. We stand to lose lots of money.

A 먹고 살만 하시죠?
B 그런대로요. 사실, 더 벌 수도 있어요.

CHAPTER 02

Campus Life

Is this the company bowling team? It sure is. Want in? Isn't this the local parents' group? It is. You sign I'd like to join the school French Club here. You hopping on? How long have you studied French? Ca Why don't you join our research group? I'm a solo act, sorry. You're leaving our department? Yeah, fr got a better offer. Is this the company bowling team? It sure is. Want in? Isn't this the local parents' group? It is. You signing up? We ne You hopping on? How long have you studied French? Can I come to your party this Friday? Of course! The more, the merrier. Aren't yo You're leaving our department? Yeah, from now on you're on your own. Why didn't you help carry our bags? Every man for himself; I've

Susan Says...

You've got to think fast if you want to get ahead.

Campus Life

학창시절,
안 쓰고는 못 베기는
생생 표현

036 > 070

죽기보다 싫은 시험공부!

Study

☐ I'm cramming.   ☐ I'm cracking the books.   ☐ Nothing sinks in.
☐ I pulled an all-nighter.   ☐ Could I pick your brains?

036

벼락치기 해야 돼.
I'm cramming.

 → I'm studying a lot at one time. cram은 '억지로 마구 채워 넣다'는 뜻. 의미가 금방 들어오죠!

A Come on. Let's go grab a beer!
B I'd love to, but I'm cramming for my Biology final.
Let's go grab+음식명 가서 ~먹자/마시자   biology 생물학   final(exam) 기말시험

A 자, 가서 맥주 한 잔 하자!
B 그러고 싶지만, 생물학 기말시험 벼락치기 해야 돼.

037

'열공' 할 거야.
I'm cracking the books.

 → 여기서 crack은 study와 같은 뜻. 학생들이 즐겨 쓰는 말은 따로 있어요!

A Let's go to the gym and work out.
B Not today. I'm cracking the books because I'm behind in my History class.
be behind in ~에서 뒤처지다, 밀리다   eg. I'm behind in my blogging.

A 체육관에서 가서 운동하자.
B 오늘은 안 돼. 역사과목이 뒤처져서, 열심히 공부해야 돼.

038
도통 이해되는 게 없어.
Nothing sinks in.

 I don't understand anything. 공부를 아무리 해도 머리에 남는 게 없다는 말(No knowledge "sinks in" to my brain).

A Do you understand these math problems?
B No, I've been studying a lot but nothing sinks in.

I've been+-ing ~해 오고 있다 eg. I've been learning English.

A 이 수학 문제가 이해가 되니?
B 아니, 열심히 하고 있는데 도통 이해가 안 돼.

039
밤샘 공부를 했어.
I pulled an all-nighter.

 I studied/sit up all night.

A You look so tired. What happened?
B I pulled an all-nighter to catch up in a class.

look tired/healthy 피곤해/건강해 보이다   catch up 따라잡다

A 아주 피곤해 보이는데, 무슨 일 있었니?
B 수업을 따라가려고 밤샘 공부를 했어.

040
네가 조언 좀 해줄래?
Could I pick your brains?

 Could I get advice from you? 친구의 두뇌(brain)를 빌리자는 표현이 재밌죠?

A Are you having trouble in this class?
B Yeah, could I pick your brains? Maybe you could help me.

have trouble in ~에 어려움이 있다

A 이 수업이 좀 힘드니?
B 그래, 네가 조언 좀 해줄래?

시험·성적 얘기에 빠지지 않는 말

Exams & Scores

☐ How'd you make out? ☐ Make the cut? ☐ What's it cover?
☐ Get what you expected? ☐ I outdid myself.

041

어떻게 나왔니?
How'd you make out?

 → How did you score on the test? 시험 결과를 묻는 말.

A How'd you make out on the last test?
B I got a "B", though I was hoping for an "A".

I was hoping for (유감)~를 희망했었는데 eg. I was hoping for a nice gift.

A 지난 시험 성적 어떻게 나왔어?
B B 받았어. A를 받았으면 했는데 말야.

042

커트라인은 통과했니?
Make the cut?

 → Did you score over the cut-off line? 이 때 make는 '통과하다' 는 뜻이에요.

A Did you make the cut to get into Law School?
B Yes I did, but just barely.

get into 들어가다, 입학하다(enter)   barely 가까스로

A 성적이 로스쿨에 들어갈 수 있게 나왔어요?
B 예, 아주 가까스로.

043
주로 어떤 게 나오나요?
What's it cover?

 → What's the main topic of a test. 여기서 cover는 '다루다, 취급하다'는 의미예요.

A You had this exam before, didn't you? What's it cover?
B Just a lot of literature, mainly.

mainly 주로, 대개(mostly/usually)

A 이 시험 본 적 있죠? 주로 어떤 게 나오나요?
B 주로 문학 문제가 많이 나와요.

044
예상한 대로 나왔어요?
Get what you expected?

 → Did you get what you hoped for? 시험 결과에 대해 묻는 것은 미국 얘들도 마찬가지!

A Get what you expected on the mid-terms?
B No, I did far worse!

worse bad의 비교급 far (비교급 강조) 훨씬 eg. I did far better!

A 중간고사 성적이 예상대로 나왔니?
B 아니, 훨씬 나빠!

045
기대 이상이었어.
I outdid myself.

 → I performed beyond my own expectations. 자신의 예상보다 성적이 좋았을 때 써요.

A How did you score on the last test?
B I outdid myself and got an "A".

outdo 능가하다, 뛰어나다(excel)

A 지난 시험 점수가 어땠어?
B 기대 이상으로 A를 받았어.

난, 어떤 유형의 학생일까?

Student Types

- ☐ That's the in-crowd.
- ☐ You dumb jock!
- ☐ He's a big man on campus.
- ☐ What a bookworm!
- ☐ She's a party animal.

046
그 패거리들이야.
That's the in-crowd.

 → **Popular group of students** 교내에서 유독 튀는 행동이나 복장으로 몰려다는 집단을 이렇게 말해요.

A Do you know those stylish students over there?
B Yes, that's the in-crowd. They always dress like that.

in-crowd 소집단, 패거리

A 저쪽에 멋진 애들이 누군지 아니?
B 응, 그 패거리들이야. 늘 저런 식으로 입고 다녀.

047
운동 밖에 모르는 멍청이!
You dumb jock!

 → jock은 미국 학생 속어로 운동선수(athlete)를 말해요. 특히 공부는 뒷전인 경우에 써요.

A Could you help me with my assignment?
B No, you dumb jock! You'd better study more.

help~ with ~이 …하는 걸 돕다   assignment 숙제, 과제

A 내 숙제 좀 도와주겠어?
B 싫어, 운동밖에 모르는 멍청이! 공부 좀 해라!

048

그는 교내 유명인사야.
He's a big man on campus.

 → 집안이 좋거나 부유한 애들은 학교에서도 튀게 마련. 그런 친구들을 말해요.

A Why does Ethan always walk around so proudly?
B He's the big man on campus. His father is a politician.

A 이단은 왜 늘 우쭐대며 다니는 거니?
B 교내 유명인사거든. 아버지가 정치인이잖아.

049

책벌레구나!
What a bookworm!

 → A person who studies constantly 한국말과 똑같죠!

A I'm going to the library again.
B What a bookworm! Why don't you have some fun sometimes?

have fun 재밌게 놀다, 즐기다

A 다시 도서관으로 가야겠어.
B 책벌레구나! 가끔은 즐기기도 하지 그래?

050

그 앤 파티광이야.
She's a party animal.

 → A person who enjoys only going to parties 파티라면 사족을 못 쓰는 친구들!

A Judy is just wasting her freshman year!
B Yes, she's a party animal.

A 쥬디는 대학 1년을 낭비하고 있어!
B 그래, 그 앤 파티밖에 몰라.

강의만 잘 들었어도!

Classes

- [ ] I'm doing a full load.
- [ ] I'm cutting.
- [ ] I'm taking time off.
- [ ] I've been called up.
- [ ] She's a career student.

051

최대한 수강을 많이 했어.
I'm doing a full load.

→ I'm taking the maximum number of classes. 들을 수 있는 강의는 모두 신청해서 공부한다는 말.

A How many courses do you have this semester?
B I'm doing a full load: 4 classes.

load (사람·기계 등) 작업량 eg. workload 업무량 semester 학기

A 이번 학기에 몇 개나 듣니?
B 최대한으로 수강 신청했어. 4과목 들어.

052

수업 빠질 거야.
I'm cutting.

→ I'm skipping class. 말 그대로 수업을 짤라(cutting) 버리고 '땡땡이' 피우겠다는 뜻.

A We'll be late for Calculus!
B You go on. I'm cutting today.

be late for ~에 늦다 Calculus 미적분(학)

A 미적분 강의에 늦겠어!
B 너희들이나 가. 난 오늘 수업 빠질 거야.

학창시절, 안 쓰고는 못 베기는 생생 표현

Chapter 02

053

휴학 중이야.
I'm taking time off.

 → I'm staying out of school temporarily. 1년간 휴학 중이라고 하려면? time 대신 a year를 넣으면 되요. I'm taking a year off.

A Won't you graduate next year?
B No, I'm taking time off, so my graduation will be delayed.

be delayed 연기되다(postponed), 지연되다

A 너, 내년에 졸업 아닌가?
B 아니야, 난 휴학 중이어서 졸업이 연기될 거야.

054

군대영장이 나왔어.
I've been called up.

 → I've been ordered to join the army/enter the service. 여기서 called up은 '군대 소집'을 말해요. military란 말이 없어도 군대간다는 뜻.

A Are you going to register this week?
B No, I've been called up, so I won't study next semester.

register 등록하다(enroll)

A 이번 주에 등록할 거지?
B 아니, 군대영장이 나왔어. 다음 학기에 없을 거야.

055

그앤 만년 학생이야.
She's a career student.

 → A student that seems to "study forever" without graduating 졸업을 미루고 캠퍼스에 계속 머무는 학생을 일컫는 말. 학생 신분이 그의 career가 된 셈이죠!

A I heard that Carrie's been studying 7 years!
B Yeah, she's a career student.

I heard (that) ~라고 하던데 eg. I heard you'd get married soon.

A 캐리는 7년 째 학교를 다니고 있나녀!
B 그래, 그녀는 만년 학생인 셈이지.

대학생활에 대한 의견들

Campus Life

- [ ] This campus is dead!
- [ ] What's to do besides study?
- [ ] Doesn't this place ever stop?
- [ ] Do they card?
- [ ] This place is for the birds.

056
이 대학은 활기가 없어!
This campus is dead!

 → There's no fun or activities on campus. 활기라곤 찾아 볼 수 없는 대학의 모습을 한탄하는 말.

A Doesn't your school ever have any festivals?
B No, the campus is dead!

A 교내 축제가 없니?
B 없어, 대학에 활기라고는 없어!

057
공부 말고는 대개 뭘 해요?
What's to do besides study?

 → Are there any activities at school apart from academics? 학업 외에 특별히 하는 게 있는지 물어볼 때 써요.

A What's to do besides study around here?
B There's a small pub on campus.

besides ~를 제외하고(apart from)

A 주변에 공부 말고 할 게 뭐 있어요?
B 교내에 작은 펍이 있죠.

058

조용히 하면 안 되겠니?
Doesn't this place ever stop?

 → Is this place always noisy/chaotic? 주변 환경이 매우 소란하다는 의미.

A Look! Another loud campus concert!
B Doesn't this place ever stop? I'm trying to study!

A 보라구! 또 교내 콘서트로 시끄럽군!
B 조용히 하면 안 되겠니? 난 공부를 해야 돼!

059

학생증을 가져가야 해요?
Do they card?

 → Is an ID necessary, especially for a concert/bar. 학생증 소지가 필요한지 물어 볼 때 써요.

A They just put a new pub on campus. Let's check it out.
B I don't have any ID. Do they card?

check it out (직접 가서) 확인해 보다, 둘러 보다

A 교내에 새로운 펍이 생겼대. 가보자.
B 학생증이 없는데, 그게 필요한가?

060

절간 같은 곳이야.
This place is for the birds.

 → There's nothing interesting on this campus 산새들이나 오기는 곳이라니? 젊음의 활기는 없고 한적하다는 말.

A Aren't you tired of our dull college?
B Yeah, this place is for the birds.

A 이곳의 한적한 학교생활이 지겹지 않니?
B 그래, 여긴 절간 같아.

# 교수님들, 어떤 유형일까?

Teacher/Professor Types

- [ ] He puts the class to sleep.
- [ ] She knows her stuff.
- [ ] He's from the Stone Age.
- [ ] He's the Ivory Tower type.
- [ ] She piles on the homework.

061
수업이 졸려요.
He puts the class to sleep.

→ **His class is too boring!** 따분한 수업엔 잠이 최고지!

A How was your Finance professor?
B He's smart, but he puts the class to sleep.

A 재무학 교수님의 수업은 어떠니?
B 똑똑하신데 수업은 졸려.

062
아는 게 많으세요.
She knows her stuff.

→ **The professor is very knowledgeable.** 폭 넓은 지식으로 수업이 유익하다는 말.

A What's the best thing about Dr. Wang's class?
B He's well-prepared for class and he knows his stuff.

well-prepared for ~에 대한 준비가 철저한

A 왕 박사님 강의에서 가장 좋은 점은 뭐니?
B 수업 준비가 철저하시고 아는 게 많으세요.

063

무척 고리타분하세요!
He's from the Stone Age.

 → He's an ultra-conservative or formal professor. 매우 보수적이고 고리타분한 교수님!

A Why don't you like Professor Wolf?
B His ideas are so old that he's from the Stone Age!

be from ~ 출신 이다   Stone Age 석기시대

A 울프 교수님을 왜 좋아하지 않니?
B 생각하시는 게 무척 고리타분해요!

064

상아탑 교수님이셔.
He's the Ivory Tower type.

 → A professor that excessively focuses on theory 사회와 교류가 적고 상아탑 이론에만 빠진 교수님!

A What do you think of Professor Reeves?
B He's the Ivory Tower type: distant from students.

distant from ~에서 떨어진, 먼

A 리브 교수님은 어떠셔?
B 상아탑 교수님이야. 학생들과 거리감이 있지.

065

과제를 엄청 내주셔.
She piles on the homework.

 → She gives us a lot of homework. 산더미처럼 쌓이게(pile) 과제를 내시는 분!

A What's wrong with Professor Lee?
B She really piles on the homework, so we have to work too hard!

A 이 교수님이 뭐가 문제라는 거야?
B 과제를 엄청 내주셔. '빡세게' 공부해야 돼!

학창시절, 내가 얻은 것들

School Experiences

- [ ] School opened doors.
- [ ] My degree isn't worth the paper!
- [ ] I got my MRS in school.
- [ ] A waste of 4 years!
- [ ] School made me what I am.

066

학교에서 성공기회를 찾았어요.
School opened doors.

→ Education gave me many chances in life. 학교에서 배운 게 성공의 밑거름이 되었다는 말.

A Don't you regret university sometimes?
B No, school opened doors for me.

Don't you regret ~ ? ~을 후회하지 않나요?

A 가끔 대학시절이 후회되지 않나요?
B 아뇨, 학교에서 성공기회를 찾았어요.

067

아무짝에도 쓸모 없는 학위!
My degree isn't worth the paper!

→ It is a useless degree. 학위에 대한 아주 부정적인 견해죠!

A Finally, we're graduates!
B I'm not glad. My degree isn't worth the paper!

worth ~의 가치가 있다   graduate 졸업생

A 드디어, 졸업이다!
B 난 기쁘지 않아. 아무짝에도 쓸모 없는 학위인 걸!

068
남편감을 건졌죠.
I got my MRS in school.

 → "MRS degree" is a pun on the word "Mrs". 대학생활에서 남은 거라곤 '남편감' 얻어서 Miss에서 Mrs로 된 것 뿐이란다!

A Did you learn a lot in college?
B No, but I got my MRS.

A 대학에서 많은 것을 배웠나요?
B 아뇨, 하지만 남편감을 얻었어요.

069
4년간 허송세월 했죠!
A waste of 4 years!

 → 말 그대로 시간만 아까웠다는 뜻이에요.

A How was your college?
B How was it? A waste of 4 years!

How was~? ~은 어땠어요? eg. How was your trip?

A 대학생활은 어땠어요?
B 어땠냐구요? 4년간 허송세월 했죠!

070
배움이 성공의 밑거름이 되었죠.
School made me what I am.

 → School made me successful. 아주 긍정적으로 대학생활을 한 경우죠!

A How did you become so successful, Director Trump?
B School made me what I am.

what I am 오늘의 나란 존재 cf. I'm not what I was.(과거의 내가 아니야.)

A 트럼프 이사님, 어떻게 성공하셨나요?
B 학교에서 배운 게 성공의 밑거름이 되었죠.

CHAPTER 03

Emotions

Is this the company bowling team? It sure is. Want in? Isn't this the local parents' group? It is. You signing u I'd like to join the school French Club here. You hopping on? How long have you studied French? Can I com Why don't you join our research group? I'm a solo act, sorry. You're leaving our department? Yeah, from no better offer. Is this the company bowling team? It sure is. Want in? Isn't this the local parents' group? It is. You signing up? We need You hopping on? How long have you studied French? Can I come to your party this Friday? Of course! The more, the merrier. Aren't y You're leaving our department? Yeah, from now on you're on your own. Why didn't you help carry our bags? Every man for himself; I'v

Susan Says...

Sexy, Smart and Cool: You need to be all three as an American career woman.

Emotions

감정을 나타내는
쉽고 재밌는
생생 표현

071 › 105

화가 나면 나오는 말

Anger

- [ ] Don't blow your top!
- [ ] Count to 10. / Take a deep breath.
- [ ] Why are you worked up?
- [ ] Hot under the collar
- [ ] If looks could kill!

071

너무 흥분하지 말라구!
Don't blow your top!

 → Please calm down! '머리 뚜껑' 이 날아가면 큰일나죠! 엄청 화난 사람에게 써요.

A I really can't stand rude people like that.
B Please don't blow your top, though.

can't stand 참을 수 없다   rude 무례한

A 저렇게 무례한 놈들을 정말 참을 수 없군.
B 제발 너무 흥분하지는 마세요.

072

열까지 세어요. / 심호흡을 해봐요.
Count to 10. / Take a deep breath.

 → Try to relax, either by counting slowly or breathing slowly. 한국말과 같아요!

A I'm so angry at Carl!
B Just take a deep breath. Don't do anything wild.

angry at/with ~에 화가 나다   wild 비 이성적인, 난폭한

A 칼에게 너무 화가 나!
B 숨을 깊게 들이쉬세요. 너무 흥분하지 말고.

감정을 나타내는 쉽고 재밌는 생생 표현

073
왜 그렇게 화가 난 거야?
Why are you worked up?

 → Why are you so angry? worked up은 angry와 같은 뜻.

A Why are you so worked up?
B Some guy pushed me down on the subway.

A 왜 그렇게 화가 났어?
B 지하철에서 어떤 사람이 날 밀었어.

074
화가 잔뜩 났어요.
Hot under the collar

 → Embarrassed or angry about something 당황하거나 화가 나서 얼굴이 벌개진 상태!

A Why do you argue with your husband all the time?
B I can't help it. I get hot under the collar because of what he says.

argue with ~와 언쟁하다　all the time 항상(always)　I can't help it. 어쩔 수 없다

A 왜 그렇게 남편과 다투세요?
B 어쩔 수 없어요. 그가 하는 말마다 날 화나게 해요.

075
보기만 해 봐라!
If looks could kill!

 → You are looking at someone with such anger that he/she might die. 죽이고 싶을 정도로 화났을 때!

A I'm really fed up with Matt's teasing me.
B I guess so! If looks could kill!

be fed up ~에 물리다, 지겨워지다

A 매트가 놀려대서 죽겠어.
B 그렇겠다! 보기만 해도 죽이겠네!

황당한 상황을 당하면 나오는 말

Shock

- [ ] I'm really blown away.   - [ ] My eyes got wide open.   - [ ] It made my head spin.
- [ ] It made me fall out of my chair!   - [ ] You need to sit down for this.

076
너무 황당했어요.
I'm really blown away.

→ 너무나 기막힌 일을 당했을 때 써요. 능동으로 It really blew me away.라고도 해요.

A Is it true that you lost your job?
B Yeah, it really blew me away.

lose one's job 실직하다

A 실직을 했다는 게 사실인가요?
B 그래, 너무 황당했었지.

077
눈이 번쩍 뜨이더군.
My eyes got wide open.

→ 놀라면 눈이 커지죠? big이 아니라 wide를 써요.

A Did you see that huge car crash?
B Yeah, my eyes got wide open. I'd never seen anything like that.

car crash 자동차 추돌 사고

A 그 대형 차 사고 봤어요?
B 예, 눈이 번쩍 뜨였어요. 그런 사고는 본 적이 없었거든요.

078
머리가 핑 돌더군요.
It made my head spin.

 → Too good to be true. 뜻밖에 횡재를 했다면? 머리가 핑 돌겠죠! 아, 방금 그런 일이 생겼다고요? 그럼, 현재진행형을 쓰세요!

A Is it true you've won the lottery?
B Yes, it's really making my head spin!

A 복권에 당첨됐다는 게 사실인가?
B 예, 머리가 핑 도는 게 어떨떨해요!

079
쓰러지는 줄 알았죠!
It made me fall out of my chair!

 → I was really shocked! 너무나 놀라면 쓰러지죠? 영어에선 '의자에서 떨어진다'고 말해요.

A Did that beautiful girl really send you a love letter?
B Yes, it made me fall out of my chair!

A 그 미녀가 네게 연애편지를 보냈다면서?
B 예, 쓰러지는 줄 알았어요!

080
우선 진정부터 하세요.
You need to sit down for this.

 → I'm going to tell you some shocking information. 미리 상대방을 진정시키는 말.

A What's going on?
B I've got something awful to tell you. You need to sit down for this.

A 무슨 일인가요?
B 안 좋은 소식이 있어요. 우선 진정부터 하세요.

기쁠 때 나도 모르게 나오는 말

Joy

☐ I was on cloud 9. ☐ You made my day! ☐ Couldn't be better!
☐ I'm on top of the world. ☐ I feel like a million bucks.

081

기분 최고였어.
I was on cloud 9.

→ 진짜 구름 위에 뜬 기분일 때! 왜 'cloud 9' 이냐고요? I really don't know!

A How was your honeymoon?
B I was on cloud for the entire trip.

for the entire trip 여행 내내

A 신혼여행은 어땠어요?
B 여행 내내 기분이 끝내줬어요.

082

너무 감사해요!
You made my day!

→ You made me really happy! 상대방 때문에 너무 행복할 때 써요!

A Just take the rest of the day off, Betty.
B Thanks, boss. You made my day!

take the day off 쉬다   the rest of ~의 나머지

A 오늘은 그만 쉬세요, 베티.
B 고마워요, 너무 감사해요!

083
최고예요!
Couldn't be better!

 → '이보다 더 좋을 수는 없다'는 표현, 잘 알고 계시죠?

A Are you feeling okay today?
B Couldn't be better!

feel OK/fine 좋다 cf. How are you feeling today? – I feel fine.

A 오늘은 어때요?
B 최고예요!

084
세상을 다 얻은 기분이에요.
I'm on top of the world.

 → I'm extremely happy! 온 세상이 내 것처럼 느껴질 때 써요.

A I hear your son just got into a top school!
B Yes, so now I'm on top of the world.

A 아드님이 최고 학교에 들어갔다면서요!
B 예, 이제 세상을 다 얻은 기분이에요.

085
부자가 된 기분이야.
I feel like a million bucks.

 → 부자가 되면 다 행복한 것인지는 모르겠지만… 아주 행복하다는 말.

A I heard you've got another boy!
B Why not? I feel like a million bucks!

feel like ~처럼 느껴지다

A 또 득남을 했다면서요!
B 그러게요? 부자가 된 것처럼 행복해요!

미움이 넘칠 때 나오는 말

Hatred

- [ ] He's better off dead!   [ ] Good riddance!   [ ] It makes me sick!
- [ ] I can't stand the sight of him.   [ ] How can you stand her?

086
그는 죽는 편이 나아!
He's better off dead!

 → I hate him so much that I'd like him dead. 이런 일이 없길!

A Won't you work with Perry anymore?
B He's better off dead! He stole my project from me!

not~ anymore 더 이상 ~이 아니다   better off ~하는 편이 낫다

A 이제 패리와 일하지 않을 거야?
B 그는 죽는 편이 나아! 내 프로젝트를 훔쳐갔거든!

087
거참 잘 됐네!
Good riddance!

 → I'm glad to be free of him. get rid of(~을 제거하다)란 숙어 알죠? riddance는 명사형. '없어진 게 아주 다행'이란 말.

A Rudy's leaving the company.
B Good riddance! He was always bothering me.

leave 떠나다, 그만두다   bother 성가시게 하다

A 루디가 회사를 그만둔데.
B 거참 잘 됐네! 항상 날 귀찮게 굴더니만.

088

너무 역겨워!
It makes me sick!

 어떤 사람이나 일이 내게 병을 준다면? 얼마나 싫겠어요!

A You don't like this movie?
B It makes me sick, because it's too violent.

A 이 영화 재미없니?
B 너무 역겨워, 지나치게 폭력적이잖아.

089

그를 보는 것조차 싫어.
I can't stand the sight of him.

 I don't want to see him anymore. 말 그대로 보기 싫은 사람에게 써요.

A We'll meet Darren tonight. Won't you come along?
B I can't stand the sight of that guy.

I can't stand ~을 참지 못하다

A 다린을 만날 건데, 같이 갈래?
B 난, 그 녀석 보는 것조차 싫어.

090

그녀를 어떻게 참아내요?
How can you stand her?

 I can't stand~가 '참을 수 없다' 니까 not이 빠지면 '참아주다' 가 되죠?

A I'm going to take Mr. Blakely to lunch. Join us?
B No. How can you stand him, even though he's a client?

take~ to lunch/dinner ~를 점심/저녁에 초대하다/데려오다

A 블레이크리 씨와 점심 같이 할 건데, 함께 갈래요?
B 아뇨, 아무리 고객이라도 그런 사람을 어떻게 참아요?

고대하던 일을 표현하고 싶을 때

Enthusiasm/Eagerness

- [ ] Can't be too soon
- [ ] Ready when you are!
- [ ] Ready to rock and roll
- [ ] All set!
- [ ] I was born ready.

091
어서 빨리 왔으면 좋겠네.
Can't be too soon

 → I can't wait. 좋은 일은 하루라도 더 빨리 왔으면 좋겠죠!

A A holiday begins next month.
B Can't be too soon, because I'm worn out from work.

be worn out ~로 지치다

A 다음 달이면 휴가가 시작되네.
B 빨리 왔으면 좋겠어요. 일로 너무 지쳤거든요.

092
난, 준비완료!
Ready when you are!

 → 말만 떨어지면 바로 '행동개시' 할 정도로 고대하는 일! 직역하면 난 준비가 끝났으니, 너만 준비하면 된다는 말.

A You seem all packed to go on our trip.
B Yes. Ready when you are!

all packed to do ~하려고 짐을 다 꾸리다

A 여행갈 짐을 다 꾸린 것 같네.
B 그럼요, 난, 준비완료입니다!

093
요이 땅! 만 하세요.
Ready to rock and roll

 → Let's get going.

A Are you ready to submit your work to the director?
B Yes, I'm ready to rock and roll.

be ready to+동사/for+명사 ~할 준비가 되다

A 이사님께 제출할 서류는 다 되었나요?
B 예, 준비완료입니다.

094
준비완료!
All set!

 → 게임 쇼에서 자주 듣는 말이죠. 일상 생활에도 자주 써요.

A Is dinner ready for all of us?
B Yes, the meal's all set.

A 저녁 준비 다 됐어요?
B 예, 식사준비가 다 됐습니다.

095
준비는 진작 다 됐죠.
I was born ready.

 → From the day I was born, I have been prepared for this. 태어날 때부터 준비가 된 일이라면?!

A Are you ready to apply for the space program?
B Sure! I was born ready.

apply for ~에 지원하다

A 우주항공 프로그램에 지원할 준비는 되었나요?
B 그럼요! 준비는 진작 다 됐죠.

소망을 얘기할 때 쓰면 좋은 말

Desire

- [ ] It means the world.
- [ ] Be careful what you wish for.
- [ ] Shoot for the moon.
- [ ] Sour grapes?
- [ ] Is that a must?

096
세상을 얻은 거나 진배없죠.
It means the world.

→ If I could have this, it would be like having the world. 이 일만 되면 '죽어도 여한이 없다'는 말.

A What's your biggest goal for the next year?
B I need a promotion! It means the world!

goal for ~에 대한 (구체적인) 목표   promotion 승진

A 내년 자네 목표는 뭔가?
B 승진이요! 그러면 세상을 얻은 거나 진배없어요!

097
잘 생각해서 소원을 비세요.
Be careful what you wish for

→ If you get your wish, it might harm you. 원하는 바를 얻고 나면 또 뭔가 문제가 생기죠? 함부로 소망을 말하지 말란 뜻.

A I want to get married one day!
B Be careful what you wish for. Married life also has many problems.

A 언젠가 결혼을 꼭 해야지!
B 잘 생각해서 소원을 비세요. 결혼 역시 많은 문제점이 있어요.

감정을 나타내는 쉽고 재밌는 생생 표현

Chapter 03

098
큰 꿈을 가져요.
Shoot for the moon

 → Hope for some great achievement. 별이 아니라 달을 향해 '꿈'을 쏘세요!

A Lionel says he wants to be a CEO.
B I know. He likes to shoot for the moon.

A 라이오넬은 CEO가 되길 원해요.
B 알아요. 그는 포부가 크죠.

099
시기하는 건가요?
Sour grapes?

 → Bitter and jealous? 이솝우화에 나오는 얘기죠. 자기 것이 못 될 바에야 '신포도'라고 여기는 게 낫죠.

A I don't care that I didn't win.
B Really? Or is that just sour grapes?

I don't care (that) ~는 개의치 않는다

A 승리하지 못해도 상관없어요.
B 정말이요? 혹시 시기심에서 그러는 건가요?

100
꼭 그래야 해요?
Is that a must?

 → 여기서 must(꼭 해야 할 것)는 명사예요.

A Let's take a vacation to Fiji this year.
B Is that a must? I'm too busy for a vacation nowadays.

too busy for ~하기에는 너무 바쁘다

A 올해는 피지로 휴가를 갑시다.
B 꼭 그래야 해요? 요즘 너무 바빠서 휴가는 엄두도 않나요.

별것 아닌 일에 툭 던지는 말

Indifference

☐ I couldn't care less. ☐ Whatever! ☐ It's all the same to me.
☐ Suit yourself ☐ No big deal

101
난 전혀 관심 없어요.
I couldn't care less.

→ That's none of my business. 강도 높게 무관심을 표현할 때 써요.

A Mary quit her job today!
B I didn't really like her, so I couldn't care less.

care less 덜 신경을 쓰다, 걱정하다

A 메리가 오늘 그만둔대요!
B 원래 그녀가 맘에 들지 않았으니, 내가 알 바 아니죠.

102
그게 어떻다는 거야!
Whatever!

→ 귀찮다는 듯이 한마디 툭 던지는 말.

A Honey, I'll be home late tonight.
B Whatever!

A 오늘 귀가가 늦을 것 같은데.
B 맘대로 하시구려!

103
아무거나 상관없어요.
It's all the same to me.

 → No difference to me. 어느 쪽을 딱히 선택할만큼 차이가 없을 때 써요.

A Would you like Italian or Japanese food for dinner?
B It's all the same to me.

all the same 매 한가지

A 저녁은 이탈리아식이 좋겠어요, 일식이 좋겠어요?
B 난 아무거나 상관없어요.

104
그렇게 하세요.
Suit yourself

 → Do as you please. 나는 개의치 말라는 뜻.

A I want to go shopping this afternoon.
B Suit yourself.

A 오후에 쇼핑갈 거예요.
B 그렇게 해요.

105
그게 뭐 대수인가.
No big deal

 → 한국말로도 그대로 쓰죠?

A Wow! That pop star is on TV again.
B That's no big deal to me.

A 아니! 저 가수가 TV에 다시 나오네요.
B 그게 뭐 대수인가.

CHAPTER 04

Action & Reaction

Is this the company bowling team? It sure is. Want in? Isn't this the local parents' group? I'd like to join the school French Club here. You hopping on? How long have you studied Why don't you join our research group? I'm a solo act, sorry. You're leaving our departme jumping ship. I got a better offer. Is this the company bowling team? It sure is. Want in? Isn't this the local parents' group? It is. You sign You hopping on? How long have you studied French? Can I come to your party this Friday? Of course! The more, the merrier. Aren't you You're leaving our department? Yeah, from now on you're on your own. Why didn't you help carry our bags? Every man for himself; I've

Susan Says...

In this outfit, I'm ready to take on the evening—or at least the evening dinner party.

Action and Reaction

이런 행동 ·
저런 행동에 쓰는
생생 표현

106>140

할 일이 많을 때 으레 쓰는 말

Busyness

- [ ] I'm up to my elbows.   [ ] I'm swamped with bills.   [ ] I'm knee deep (in).
- [ ] Busy as a bee.   [ ] I'm all tied up.

106
할 일이 태산이야.
I'm up to my elbows.

→ I've got plenty of work to do. up to my neck을 써도 같은 뜻.

A What about a game of tennis?
B No, I'm up to my elbows in a project I have to finish.

A 테니스 한 게임 어때요?
B 안돼요, 끝내야 할 프로젝트 일이 태산인 걸요.

107
청구서에 파묻히겠어.
I'm swamped with bills.

→ I'm full of bills. 서류, 일, 상황 등에 모두 써요. swamped는 홍수가 '확' 밀려오듯 뭔가 '쇄도하는' 상황을 말해요. be swamped with로 기억하세요.

A Do you save money for a rainy day?
B No, I'm swamped with bills.

save money for a rainy day 나중을 위해 저축하다

A 만약을 대비해 저축은 좀 하니?
B 아뇨, 청구서에 파묻혀 사는 걸요.

이런 행동 · 저런 행동에 쓰는 생생 표현

Chapter 04

108
할 일이 한 짐이야.
I'm knee deep (in).

 → 무릎까지 차오를 정도로 일이 쌓였다는 말.

A What's keeping you at the office?
B I'm knee-deep in paperwork.

A 뭐 때문에 사무실에 계속 있어요?
B 해야 할 서류 작업이 한 짐이야.

109
너무 바빠요.
Busy as a bee

 → 벌과 개미는 늘 바삐 움직이죠? 부지런함과 바쁨의 상징! Bees and Ants!

A Aren't you going to get a few moments' rest?
B Not now. I'm busy as a bee.

A 잠시만 쉬었다 하지 않을래요?
B 지금은 안 돼요. 너무 바쁘거든요.

110
스케줄이 꽉 찼어요.
I'm all tied up.

 → I'm not available. 도무지 짬이 나지 않는 상황에 써요. 월요일엔 도저히 시간이 안 나요. — I'm tied up on Monday.

A Can't you see a movie with me?
B Sorry, I'm all tied up right now.

A 나와 영화 보러 가지 않을래요?
B 미안해요, 지금은 짬이 나질 않네요.

피곤하고 지치면 저절로 나오는 말

Exhaustion

- [ ] I'm burnt/burning out. [ ] I'm on my last leg. [ ] I'm running on empty.
- [ ] I gave it everything I had. [ ] Until I drop

111
너무 지쳤어 / 지치는군.
I'm burnt/burning out.

몸이 타 버릴 정도면? 상상이 되죠! 특히 과중한 업무나 스트레스 또는 지나친 운동으로 피로가 누적된 경우에 써요. 지치게 하는 '원인'을 주어로 써도 됩니다. 이번 일이 날 너무 지치게 하는군. — This job is burning me out!

A How's your new job coming along?
B I think it's really burning me out.

A 새 직장은 어때요?
B 아주 녹초가 될 지경이에요.

112
피곤해 죽겠어요.
I'm on my last leg.

I'm so tired that I'm "near death". 마지막 남은 다리 하나로 몸 전체를 지탱한 다면… 죽지 못해 버틸 정도로 피곤하다는 뜻.

A You've been moving boxes all day.
B To be honest, I'm on my last leg.

to be honest(with) 솔직히 말해 eg. To be honest (with you), we've got another plan.

A 하루종일 상자들을 옮기고 계시네요.
B 실은, 피곤해서 죽겠어요.

113
배가 텅 빈 채 일해요.
I'm running on empty.

 → "like a car running out of gas" 휘발유 떨어져가는 자동차 같다는 비유.

A Why don't you have a biscuit and coffee?
B I could use that, because I'm running on empty.

A 비스켓과 커피 좀 먹을래요?
B 그래야겠어요. 배가 텅 빈 채 일했거든요.

114
죽을 힘을 다했어요.
I gave it everything I had.

 → 온 힘을 다 쏟아 부어 일한다는 말.

A You really ran a long way in that marathon!
B Yeah, I gave it everything I had.

A 마라톤 경기에서 아주 열심히 뛰더군요!
B 예, 죽을 힘을 다했어요.

115
녹초가 될 때까지
Until I drop

 → Keep doing until I fall down from exhaustion 지쳐서 쓰러질 때까지 하겠다는 말.

A Are you going to keep hiking all day?
B Yes! I'm going to hike until I drop.

A 하루종일 하이킹 할 건가요?
B 녹초가 될 때까지 할 거야.

방해꾼에겐 따끔하게 한마디!

Disruption

- ☐ Don't get in my way.
- ☐ You're cramping my style.
- ☐ Step aside, please.
- ☐ Get/Stay out of my hair
- ☐ Make yourself scarce

116
방해하지 마세요.
Don't get in my way.

 → 내가 하는 일안에 간섭하지 말라는 뜻.

A Are you in a hurry or something?
B Just don't get in my way. I have to rush home right now.

in a hurry 다급한, 서두르는

A 뭐 서두를 일이라도 있어요?
B 방해하지 마세요. 빨리 집에 가야 해요.

117
내 기분 망치지 말아요.
You're cramping my style.

 → You're interfering with my personal atmosphere. cramp는 방해하다, 막다(block)는 뜻.

A Can't I hang out with you?
B No, you'd cramp my style.

hang out (with) (~와) 어울리다

A 너희들과 함께 어울리면 안 되겠니?
B 안 돼, 넌 나와 기분이 맞지 않아.

118

비키세요.
Step aside, please.

 → Move out of the way.

A Why are you pushing me?
B Step aside, please – this lady needs a doctor.

A 왜 밀고 그래요?
B 비켜 주세요. 이 여자를 의사에게 데려가야 해요.

119

귀찮게 하지 마요.
Get/Stay out of my hair

 → You're bothering me. 머리를 헝클어지게 하듯 성가시다는 말.

A I need to talk to you about this.
B No, just get out of my hair. I'll talk to you later.

A 이 일에 대해 나와 얘기 좀 해요.
B 아뇨, 귀찮게 하지 말고, 나중에 얘기하죠.

120

얼쩡거리지 말아요.
Make yourself scarce

 → Don't stay around, please. 자꾸 내 앞에 나타나지 말라는 뜻. scarce는 hardly existing의 뜻.

A I'd like to stick around for a while.
B You'd better make yourself scarce instead.

stick around 근처에 있다   make oneself scare 떠나다, 물러가다

A 한동안 주변에 있을 겁니다.
B 얼쩡거리지 않는 게 좋아요.

힘든 상황에도 꿋꿋하게!

Resilience

- [ ] Bounce back
- [ ] I can go another round.
- [ ] I can take whatever's dished out.
- [ ] I'll tough it out.
- [ ] I'm still standing.

121
회복할 겁니다.
Bounce back

 → 공이 다시 튀겨 오르듯 나쁜 상황에서 벗어나겠다는 말. 사람이나 상황에 모두 써요.

A I heard the company stock collapsed last week.
B I'm not worried. It's sure to bounce back.

collapse 붕괴되다, 크게 떨어지다   be sure to 확실히 ~하다

A 지난주 회사 주가가 떨어졌다면서요.
B 걱정 안 해요. 회복할 테니까요.

122
더 해봐야죠.
I can go another round.

 → I'll keep trying. 좌절하지 않고 한 번 더 해보겠다는 말.

A Aren't you tired of failing in this project?
B I can go another round. It has to succeed sooner or later.

fail in ~에서 실패하다   sooner or later 조만간

A 이번 프로젝트 실패로 지치지 않았어요?
B 더 해 봐야죠. 조만간 성공할 테니까요.

123
아무리 힘들어도 할 거야.
I can take whatever's dished out.

 I'll endure anything. 못 먹을 음식이 나와도(dished out) 먹겠다, 즉 뭐든 참고 하겠다는 의지 표명!

A Mr. Ping is always pressuring you.
B I can take whatever's dished out, so I don't care.

A 핑 씨가 항상 스트레스를 주죠.
B 아무리 힘들어도 버텨야죠. 난 상관없어요.

124
버텨볼 겁니다.
I'll tough it out.

 tough it out은 굳건히 버티겠다(remain strong)는 뜻.

A Don't you want to quit driving for a while and rest?
B No, I'll tough it out for a few hours more.

A 운전을 멈추고 좀 쉴래요?
B 아니, 몇 시간만 더 버틸거야.

125
난 아직 끄떡없어요.
I'm still standing.

 I remain on my feet. 힘들어도 그냥 주저앉지 않겠다는 말.

A You got divorced last week, I heard.
B I'm still standing, though.
get divorced 이혼하다 cf. file for divorce 이혼 소송하다

A 지난주에 이혼했다면서요.
B 그래도 난 끄떡없어요.

한바탕 공세를 취할 때 힘이 되는 말

Attack

- [ ] I'm on the warpath.
- [ ] Wipe that smile off your face.
- [ ] I'll teach you a lesson.
- [ ] The gloves are coming off.
- [ ] I'll put you in your place.

126
공격할 준비가 됐어요.
I'm on the warpath.

 → I'm preparing for an attack. warpath는 인디언들이 적을 공격하기 전에 추었던 춤. 거기서 유래된 말이에요.

A That guy is making fun of you.
B He'll regret it. Now I'm on the warpath.

make a fun of ~을 조롱하다

A 저 녀석이 널 조롱하고 있어.
B 후회하게 해주지. 이제 내가 공격할 테니.

127
쓴맛을 보여주겠어.
Wipe that smile off your face.

 → I'll make you feel pain instead of humor. 지금은 웃지만 울게 해주겠다는 말.

A Ha! You failed again!
B Be careful, or I'll wipe that smile off your face.

wipe ~ off ~을 지워주다, 닦아 없애다

A 흥! 너 또 졌구나!
B 조심해, 그렇지 않으면 쓴맛을 보여줄 테니.

128
버릇을 고쳐주마.
I'll teach you a lesson.

 부정적인 뜻 외에 긍정적으로도 써요. That experience taught me a lesson.(그 일로 난 교훈을 얻었어요.)

A I think you're stupid.
B Keep talking, and I'll teach you a lesson.

A 넌 멍청이야.
B 어디 중얼거려봐, 버릇을 고쳐줄 테니.

129
한번 붙어보자.
The gloves are coming off.

 장갑 벗고 본격적으로 한번 '결전' 준비를 하겠다는 말.

A They took more of our market share.
B Okay, the gloves are coming off now! We'll get it back.

A 경쟁사에서 우리 시장을 더 잠식했어요.
B 그래, 이제 한번 붙어보자! 복수할 테니.

130
네 처지를 알게 해주지.
I'll put you in your place.

 I'll show you how low your real value is. '까불지 말라'는 뜻!

A My work's much better than yours.
B We'll find out. I'll put you in your place.
We'll find out. 결국엔, (진위를) 알게 되겠지.

A 내 기획안이 네 것보다 훨씬 나아.
B 두고 보면 알겠지. 네 처지를 알게 해주지.

깨끗이 물러설 때 던지는 한마디!

Retreat

- [ ] I give (up).
- [ ] I'll give you some room.
- [ ] Let's back up.
- [ ] I'll step down.
- [ ] I'll throw in the towel.

131
내가 포기하지.
I give (up).

 원어민들은 그냥 I give.라고도 해요.

A I'll choose tonight's movie!
B Okay, I give. What do you want to see?

A 오늘밤 영화는 내가 선택할래요?
B 좋아, 내가 포기하지. 뭘 보고 싶은데?

132
여유를 주겠소.
I'll give you some room.

 I'll allow you extra time and space to consider. 여기서 room은 시공간적으로 갖는 '여지, 여유'란 의미에요.

A You aren't going to force me to make a decision?
B No, I'll give you some room. Think about it.
force~ to do ~에게 …을 강요하다

A 억지로 결정하게 하는 것은 아니죠?
B 아뇨, 여유를 줄 테니, 생각해봐요.

133
한발 물러섭시다.
Let's back up.

 → 무작정 '전진 앞으로'는 곤란할 수 있죠. 일보 후퇴해서 재고할 때 써요.

A This plan looks really risky.
B Let's back up and rethink it, then.

A 이 계획은 정말로 위험해요.
B 그럼, 한발 물러서서 재고해보죠.

134
물러나겠소.
I'll step down.

 → I'll give up my rights or interests. 기득권을 포기하겠다는 말이죠.

A You aren't going to fight for your position?
B I'll step down if I need to.

fight for ~를 위해 싸우다, 애쓰다

A 직위를 고수하지 않을 건가요?
B 필요하다면 물러날 겁니다.

135
내가 백기를 들죠.
I'll throw in the towel.

 → I'll admit defeat. 복싱 경기에서 코치가 기권의 상징으로 상대 선수의 링을 향해 수건을 던지는 데서 나온 말.

A You should stop arguing with him.
B Right! I'll throw in the towel!

argue with ~와 논쟁하다

A 그와 논쟁하는 걸 그만둬요.
B 그래! 내가 백기를 들지!

만전을 기하고 있을 때 하는 말

Defense

- [ ] I'm prepared for the worst.   - [ ] I'm on full alert.   - [ ] I'm ready to rumble.
- [ ] I can take whatever's coming.   - [ ] She's like Teflon.

136
최악의 상황에 대비하고 있어요.
I'm prepared for the worst.

 → I'm prepared for the worst thing that could happen.

  A They're going to start firing staff!
B That's okay. I'm prepared for the worst.

fire 해고 하다   be prepared for ~에 대비하다

  A 회사에서 감원을 할 거래요.
B 괜찮아요. 난 최악의 상황에 대비를 하니까.

137
만전을 기하고 있어요.
I'm on full alert.

 → alert(경계)에 full이 붙었으니 '만전을 기한다'는 뜻이네요.

  A You might be sent overseas soon.
B I hope not, but I'm on full alert if that happens.

I hope not. 그렇지 않길 바래.(앞에 말한 내용과 반대 소망을 표현)

  A 당신은 곧 해외로 발령날지 몰라요.
B 그렇지 않길 바라지만, 만전을 기하고 있어요.

138
싸울 준비가 됐습니다.
I'm ready to rumble.

 여기서 rumble은 act, fight, compete와 같은 뜻이에요.

A Are you ready to play this soccer game?
B Yeah! I'm ready to rumble.

A 이번 축구 시합에 나갈 준비 됐나?
B 예! 싸울 준비가 됐습니다.

139
뭐든 감당할 수 있어요.
I can take whatever's coming.

 I'm ready for any approaching danger. '하나도 겁 안 난다'는 말.

A I might have some bad news for you.
B Okay, I can take whatever's coming.

A 좀 나쁜 소식이 있어요.
B 괜찮아요, 뭐든 감당할 수 있어요.

140
무쇠 같은 여자예요.
She's like Teflon.

 Nothing seems to harm or damage her/him. 테프론 코팅이 된 주방기기처럼 어떤 비판이나 어려움도 '달라붙지 않고' 비켜가는 사람! 그래서 온갖 스캔들에도 '건재한' 정치인을 a Teflon politician이라고 부르죠!

A Nothing ever seems to worry Martha.
B That's because she's like Teflon.

A 마사는 어떤 일에도 끄떡없는 것 같죠.
B 무쇠 같은 여자예요.

CHAPTER 05

Romance

Is this the company bowling team? It sure is. Want in? Isn't this the local parents' group? It is. You signing u~~p~~? I'd like to join the school French Club here. You hopping on? How long have you studied French? Can I co~~me~~? Why don't you join our research group? I'm a solo act, sorry. You're leaving our department? Yeah, from n~~o~~ better offer. Is this the company bowling team? It sure is. Want in? Isn't this the local parents' group? It is. You signing up? We need You hopping on? How long have you studied French? Can I come to your party this Friday? Of course! The more, the merrier. Aren't You're leaving our department? Yeah, from now on you're on your own. Why didn't you help carry our bags? Every man for himself; I

Funny how we smile when we speak to clients on the phone—even though they can't see our faces!

Romance

쉬운 영어로
사랑을 전하는
생생 표현

141 > 175

사랑에 빠지면 누구나 쉽게 하는 말

Falling in Love

- ☐ I'm lost in her.　　☐ He takes my breath away.　　☐ I'm swept away.
- ☐ He's the one.　　☐ I'm sweet on her.

141
그녀에게 빠졌어요.
I'm lost in her.

→ 완전히 '뿅' 갔다는 말. 남자와 여자 모두에게 써요.

　A I heard that you really like Jane.
　　B I'm really lost in her, especially when she smiles.
　　be lost in ~에 빠지다, 열중하다

　A 자네, 제인을 좋아한다면서.
　　B 그녀에게 정말 빠졌어요. 특히 미소 지을 때면요.

142
그가 내 마음을 사로 잡았어요.
He takes my breath away.

→ I'm so attracted to him. '숨을 쉴 수 없을 정도'로 사랑에 빠진 상태!

　A Have you ever seen a guy as handsome as Brad?
　　B He really takes my breath away just by looking at me.
　　as handsome as ~만큼 잘 생긴　**take~ away** ~를 뺏어가다

　A 브래드처럼 잘생긴 남자를 본 적 있니?
　　B 아니, 그를 쳐다보기만 해도 마음이 설레는 걸.

143
사랑의 바다에 푹 빠졌어.
I'm swept away.

 → I'm swept out into the "ocean of love." 얼마나 좋길래?! — He/She makes me feel a special love.

A How was your date last night?
B It was so romantic that I was swept away!

A 어젯밤 데이트는 어땠어요?
B 너무나 낭만적이어서 정신이 없었어요.

144
내 이상형이에요.
He's the one.

 → He the one that I've been looking for. 남녀 모두에게 써요.

A How do you feel about Paul?
B I've got a real feeling that he's the one.
I've got a feeling that ~라는 느낌이 든다

A 폴에 대해 어떻게 생각해요?
B 그가 내 이상형이라는 느낌이 들어요.

145
그녀가 정말 마음에 들어요.
I'm sweet on her.

 → I feel deep affection for her. 깊은 애정이 느껴진다는 말.

A Do you really like Sally?
B I must confess I'm sweet on her.
confess 고백하다 eg. Did he confess he'd killed her?

A 샐리를 정말 좋아해요?
B 그녀가 맘에 든다고 고백해야겠어요.

사랑의 불씨가 꺼지면 내뱉는 말

Falling out of Love

☐ The spark's gone. ☐ We've gone cold. ☐ There's nothing left between us.
☐ I'm seeing someone else. ☐ We're over/finished/through.

146

짜릿한 감정이 사라졌어요.
The spark's gone.

→ There is no more heat in our "fires of love".

A You've been married almost 20 years now!
B Yeah, but nowadays the spark's gone.

A 결혼한 지 20년이나 되셨죠!
B 그래요, 이젠 짜릿한 감정이라곤 없죠.

147

서로에게 냉담해졌죠.
We've gone cold.

→ We don't love each other anymore.

A You and Alice seem like a nice couple.
B It may look like that, but we've gone cold.
look like ~처럼 보이다

A 너와 앨리스는 잘 어울리는 것 같아.
B 그래 보이지만, 실은 서로 냉랭해.

148
우린 서로 아무 감정도 없잖아.
There's nothing left between us.

 남은 게 없다(nothing left), 즉 감정이 없다(no feelings)는 말.

A So you don't want to see me anymore?
B Sorry, but I really feel there's nothing left between us.

A 나와 그만 만나겠다는 거야?
B 미안해, 우린 서로 아무 감정도 없잖아.

149
다른 사람을 만나고 있어.
I'm seeing someone else.

 I'm dating someone else. 새로운 사랑이 찾아 오면 옛사랑은 식겠죠?

A You don't love me anymore?
B Sorry, I'm seeing someone else.

A 날 더 이상 사랑하지 않니?
B 미안해, 다른 사람을 만나고 있어.

150
우리는 끝났어.
We're over/finished/through.

 한국말과 똑 같아요!

A No one will ever love you like I do.
B I don't care. We're through.

A 나만큼 널 사랑해주는 사람은 없을 거야.
B 무슨 상관이야. 우린 끝났잖아.

구애할 때 흔히 쓰는 말

Courting/Flirting

- [ ] How about spending some time together? - [ ] Let's get to know each other. - [ ] Let's go out sometime.
- [ ] Let me show you around. - [ ] Let me treat you to lunch.

151
언제 함께 놀러 갈래요?
How about spending some time together?

 → '함께 시간을 보내자'는 것은? 연애기술에는 동서양이 별 차이가 없죠!

  A Jessica, how about spending some time together?
B Sure! I'd love to.

How about~? ~하는 게 어때요?

  A 제시카, 언제 함께 놀러 갈래요?
B 좋아! 그러고 싶어요.

152
서로 사귀어 봐요.
Let's get to know each other.

 → get to know는 꼭 연인 사이가 아니어도 새로운 사람을 사귈 때 자주 써요.

  A Let's get to know each other, Kelli.
B You're a nice guy, but I'm already engaged.

be engaged 약혼하다

  A 켈리, 우리 사귀어 봐요.
B 당신은 좋은 남자지만, 전 이미 약혼했어요.

153
우리 데이트하자.
Let's go out sometime.

 → Say this when you ask someone out.

A Let's go out sometime.
B No way! You're not my style at all!
No way! 말도 안 돼! 절대 안 돼!

A 우리 데이트하자.
B 말도 안 돼! 넌 내 타입이 아니야.

154
내가 구경시켜 줄게요.
Let me show you around.

 → 외지에서 온 사람에게 써 먹기 좋은 말이죠.

A You're new in Chicago, right? Let me show you around.
B I'm already dating someone, sorry.

A 시카고는 처음이죠? 내가 구경시켜 줄게요.
B 미안하지만, 지금 데이트하는 사람이 있어요.

155
점심 살게요.
Let me treat you to lunch.

 → 상황에 맞게 dinner, coffee, drinks를 써도 좋아요.

A Let me treat you to dinner this evening.
B Okay, what time do you want to go?

A 내가 오늘 저녁 살게요.
B 좋아요, 몇 시에 갈래요?

동거할까, 결혼할까?

Marriage/Cohabitation

- [ ] I'm getting hitched. [ ] I'm tying the knot. [ ] Make an honest woman out of her.
- [ ] Play house [ ] I live with my partner.

156

결혼해요.
I'm getting hitched.

→ I'm getting married. 결혼이란 '굴레'에 단단히 묶인다는 말.

A So have you been with Helen for a long time?
B Almost 5 years, so now we're finally getting hitched.

A 헬렌과 사귄 지 오래되었어요?
B 5년쯤 됐는데, 드디어 서로 맺어진 거죠.

156

혼인을 맺습니다.
I'm tying the knot.

→ 결혼이 두 사람을 하나로 맺어준다(tie the knot)는 의미에서 쓰는 말.

A Aren't you tired of just dating Mark?
B I'm tying the knot with him next month.

A 마크하고만 사귀는 게 지겹지 않니?
B 다음 달에 그와 혼인을 맺어요.

158
그녀를 아내로 맞을 거야.
Make an honest woman out of her.

 → 여자를 단지 데이트 상대가 아니라 진지하게 아내감으로 대한다는 의미예요.

A When are you going to make an honest woman out of her?
B We're discussing that nowadays.

A 언제쯤 그녀를 아내로 맞을 건가?
B 요즘 그 얘기를 하고 있습니다.

159
동거해요.
Play house

 → It's like pretending to be married in a house. 어릴 적 소꿉놀이 하듯 말이죠. Shack up이란 말도 써요.

A So you and Denise are married?
B No, we're just playing house.

A 너와 데니스는 결혼한 거니?
B 아뇨, 그냥 동거하고 있어요.

160
동거하는 사람이 있어요.
I live with my partner.

 → 동거하는 사람도 그냥 partner라고 해요.

A Do you live alone here?
B No, I live with my partner. We've been together for a year.

alone 혼자, 홀로   be/live together 함께 살다

A 여기서 혼자 살아요?
B 아뇨, 동거하는 사람이 있어요. 같이 산 지 1년 돼요.

헤어지는 연인들이 흔히 쓰는 말

Breaking up

- ☐ She dumped me.
- ☐ Time to move on
- ☐ Get rid of him
- ☐ Kick to the curb
- ☐ Give him the boot

161
그녀가 날 찼어.
She dumped me.

→ 마치 쓰레기 버리듯(dumping trash) 차 버렸다는 말.

A I don't see you with Annette anymore.
B She dumped me, that's why.

That's why. 그렇게 된 거야.

A 너와 아네트, 이제 데이트 안 하는구나.
B 그녀가 날 찼어. 그렇게 된 거지.

162
새 출발해야지.
Time to move on

→ I got over my old partner. 이별을 딛고 새 출발할 때 써요.

A Aren't you going to keep dating June?
B She's nice, but I think it's time to move on.

A 준과 계속 사귀지 않니?
B 좋은 여자지만, 이젠 각자 새 출발할 때가 됐어.

쉬운 영어로 사랑을 전하는 생생 표현

Chapter
•• 05

163

그와 헤어져.
Get rid of him

 → Don't meet him anymore. It's time for you to move on.

A Why don't you get rid of Ted? He's no good for you!
B I know, but I love him so much.

get rid of 제거하다   no good for ~에 도움이 안 된다

A 왜 테드와 헤어지지 않니? 너한테 도움이 안 되는데.
B 알아요, 그래도 난 그를 사랑해요.

164

갑자기 헤어졌어.
Kick to the curb

 → **Leave a partner suddenly** 길 모퉁이에서 발에 차인 깡통을 차 버리듯 갑자기 헤어진 경우에 써요.

A What happened, Carla? You look so down!
B Lee kicked me to the curb, that's why.

A 칼라, 무슨 일이야? 몹시 안 좋아 보여.
B 리가 날 갑자기 차 버렸어요.

165

그만 만나야겠어.
Give him the boot

 → 하도 급해서 신발을 한 짝만 신은 채로 쫓아낸다는 의미. 곧바로 헤어질 때 써요.

A Harry never seems to treat you right!
B That's true! I should just give him the boot.

treat ~ right ~를 잘 대해 주다

A 해리는 널 잘 대해주지 않아!
B 맞아요! 그를 그만 만나야겠어요.

관계 회복을 원할 때 쓰는 말

Reconciliation

- Let's patch things up.
- Take me back!
- Let's kiss and make up.
- Let's put it behind us.
- Let's start again.

166
관계를 회복해 봅시다.
Let's patch things up.

→ Let's fix our relationship. 헤진 옷에 천을 대어 수선하듯 '잘 해 보자'는 뜻.

A You really said a lot of cruel things to me.
B I'm sorry. Let's patch things up, okay?

cruel 잔인한 eg. Don't tease him about his weight – it's cruel.

A 내게 정말 심한 말을 했어요.
B 미안하오. 우리 관계를 회복해 봅시다.

167
날 용서해줘요!
Take me back!

→ Forgive me, and take me back! 다시는 안 그럴게요!

A I'm through with you!
B Please take me back! I'm sorry for what I've done.

be through with ~와 관계가 끝나다

A 당신과는 끝이에요!
B 제발 용서해줘요! 내가 한 일을 사과하오.

168
사랑으로 서로를 용서합시다.
Let's kiss and make up.

 → You just memorize this, and use it!

A I'm tired of arguing all the time, honey.
B Let's stop, and kiss and make up.

A 당신과 다투는 데 지쳤어요.
B 그만하고, 사랑으로 서로를 용서합시다.

169
지난 일은 잊어요.
Let's put it behind us.

 → 여기서 "it"은 안 좋았던 일(some negative incident)을 말해요.

A We've always argued in our relationship.
B I know, but let's put it behind us.

put ~ behind ~를 잊다, 묻어 두다

A 우린 늘 다투는 사이였어요.
B 알아요, 이제 지난 일은 잊읍시다.

170
다시 시작해봅시다.
Let's start again.

 → Can't we start all over again? 언제고 다시 시작할 수 있지 않을까요?

A I can't help it anymore. I want a divorce!
B I'll do better from now on. Let's start again.

A 더는 못 참겠어요. 이혼해줘요!
B 이제부터 잘 할게요. 다시 시작해봅시다.

잘못된 만남의 징조들

Bad Love

- ☐ You're a gold digger.   ☐ You're a player.   ☐ He's a caveman.
- ☐ She's a man eater.   ☐ You're a momma's boy.

171
당신은 돈만 밝혀요.
You're a gold digger.

 → A woman who only chases rich men 돈 많은 남자만 쫓는 여성을 빗댄 말.

A What do you think about Brenda?
B In my opinion, she's a gold digger.

A 브렌다에 대해 어떻게 생각해요?
B 내 생각엔 그녀는 돈만 밝히는 여자야.

172
당신은 바람둥이에요.
You're a player.

 → 남녀 모두(playboy/playgirl)에 다 써요.

A I can't stick to just one woman.
B I know; that's why you're a player.

stick to ~를 고수하다, 집착하다

A 한 여자만 사귈 수는 없어.
B 그렇겠죠. 당신은 바람둥이니까요.

쉬운 영어로 사랑을 전하는 생생 표현

Chapter 05

173
그는 야만인이야.
He's a caveman.

 예의범절이나 배려하는 마음이라곤 없는 남자!

A Why did you leave Tom?
B He's a caveman. He never had any manners around me.

A 왜 톰을 떠난거죠?
B 그는 야만인이에요. 도무지 날 배려할 줄 몰라요.

174
남자 잡는 여자죠.
She's a man eater.

 사랑 없이 남자를 만나며 즐기는 여자를 꼬집어 하는 말.

A Didn't you date Trudy for a while?
B She's a man eater. It wasn't enjoyable at all.
enjoyable 즐길 만한, 유쾌한 eg. Thank you for a most enjoyable evening.

A 한동안 트루디와 사귀지 않았나요?
B 남자 잡는 여자죠. 조금도 즐겁지 않았어요.

175
당신은 마마보이에요.
You're a momma's boy.

 여자는 daddy's girl이라고 해요.

A Before we go out, I have to call my mother.
B Let's break up. You're just a momma's boy.
break up 헤어지다, 깨지다

A 외출 전에 엄마에게 전화를 해야 해요.
B 그만 헤어져요. 당신은 마마보이에요.

CHAPTER 06

Ideas and Innovation

Is this the company bowling team? It sure is. Want in? Isn't this the local parents' g
I'd like to join the school French Club here. You hopping on? How long have you st
Why don't you join our research group? I'm a solo act, sorry. You're leaving our de
I'm jumping ship. I got a better offer. Is this the company bowling team? It sure is. Want in? Isn't this the local parents' group? It is. You
You hopping on? How long have you studied French? Can I come to your party this Friday? Of course! The more, the merrier. Aren't yo
You're leaving our department? Yeah, from now on you're on your own. Why didn't you help carry our bags? Every man for himself; I've

Susan Says...

You can rush through life, but you can't rush through putting on your makeup!

Ideas and Innovation

검토·분석·해결할 때
입에 달게 되는
생생 표현

176 > 210

아이디어가 번뜩일 때 튀어나오는 말

Inspiration
- ☐ I've got it! ☐ Eureka! ☐ Something just came to me.
- ☐ Something just popped into my head. ☐ I just had a stray thought.

176
좋은 생각이 있어요!
I've got it!

 → I received a sudden idea. 문득 아이디어가 떠올랐을 때 원어민들이 가장 많이 쓰는 말.

A How are you going to avoid the heavy weekend traffic?
B I've got it! I'll take a local flight!

avoid 피하다   eg. Can I avoid the test?

A 주말 교통체증을 어떻게 피할래요?
B 좋은 생각이 있어요! 항공편으로 갈게요.

177
알았다! 바로 이거야!
Eureka!

 → I have found it! I have discovered a solution! 아르키메데스가 외친 말이죠!

A Nothing seems to work! I give.
B Eureka! See now the engine starts!

seem to ~인 것 같다   work 작동하다   I give.=I give up.

A 어떻게 해도 작동이 되지 않아! 포기해.
B 알았다! 보라구, 이제 엔진이 작동돼!

검토·분석·해결할 때 입에 달게 되는 생생 표현

178
뭔가 떠올랐어요.
Something just came to me.

 → An idea occurred to me. something은 idea를 말해요.

A What are you typing so quickly?
B Something just came to me, so I want to input it right now.

A 뭘 그렇게 급하게 타이핑하고 있어요?
B 뭔가 떠올랐거든. 바로 입력을 해둬야지.

179
뭔가 머리에 떠올랐어.
Something just popped into my head.

 → An idea just entered my mind.

A Why are you leaving so suddenly?
B Something just popped into my head about our project.

suddenly 갑자기   pop (into) 불쑥 들어오다

A 왜 그렇게 갑자기 나가요?
B 프로젝트에 대해서 머리에 떠오른 게 있어요.

180
스치는 생각이 있어요.
I just had a stray thought.

 → 문득 스쳐가는 생각이 있을 때 써요.

A How can we afford a trip to Paris?
B I just had a stray thought. Why don't we use our credit cards?

afford ~할 여유가 있다   eg. Can we afford a new car?

A 파리 여행을 무슨 돈으로 가죠?
B 스치는 생각인데, 신용카드를 이용하면 어때요?

자신 있게 해결책 말하기

Solutions
- ☐ I've got just the ticket.   ☐ It's right before your eyes.   ☐ I figured it out.
- ☐ It's plain as day.   ☐ I know what to do.

081
좋은 수가 있어요.
I've got just the ticket.

→ ticket은 solution to a problem을 말해요.

A Daddy, I'm starving!
B I've got just the ticket. How about ordering a pizza?

starve 몹시 배 고프다

A 아빠, 배가 너무 고파요!
B 좋은 수가 있지. 피자 시켜 먹을까?

182
방법은 뻔해요.
It's right before your eyes.

→ The solution is obvious.

A How can we recruit more workers?
B It's right before your eyes. Put an ad on the Internet.

obvious 분명한, 뻔한   put an ad 광고를 내다

A 어떻게 해야 더 많이 팔 수 있을까?
B 방법은 뻔해요. 인터넷에 광고를 하세요.

183
알아냈어요.
I figured it out.

A Do you know why no one's smoking in here?
B I figured it out. This is a no-smoking restaurant.

figure~ out ~을 알아내다, 이해하게 되다

A 왜 담배 피우는 사람이 하나도 없죠?
B 전 알겠어요. 여긴 금연 식당이네요.

184
명명백백 해요.
It's plain as day.

 It's as obvious as daylight. 환한 대낮에는 모든 게 분명하죠?

A You're sure this is what we should do?
B Of course! It's plain as day!

what we should do 마땅히 할 일

A 이렇게 하면 되는 게 확실해요?
B 그럼요! 명명백백 합니다.

185
확실한 방안이 있어요.
I know what to do.

 I have a definite plan. You can trust me!

A How can we find a parking space downtown?
B Don't worry. I know what to do!

A 시내에서 주차할 곳을 어떻게 찾지?
B 걱정 말아요. 내게 확실한 방안이 있어요!

분석과 검토 할 때 쓰는 말

Analyses
- [ ] I'm going over it.
- [ ] I'm bouncing it around.
- [ ] I'm turning it over.
- [ ] I'll do a run-through.
- [ ] I'll give it a once-over.

186
검토 중입니다.
I'm going over it.

 → I'll review it. go over는 review, analyze와 같은 뜻.

A Have you formed an opinion about the research paper?
B I'm going over it right now.

A 연구논문에 대한 의견서를 작성했나요?
B 지금 검토 중입니다.

187
여러모로 따져 검토 중입니다.
I'm bouncing it around.

 → 여러 측면을 고려하면서 검토한다는 말.

A Going to Jamaica for your vacation?
B I'm bouncing it around, but I might go to Australia instead.

I might go to ~로 갈 수도 있다   instead 대신

A 휴가를 자메이카로 가기로 했어요?
B 여러모로 따져 보고 있는데, 호주로 갈지도 모르겠어요.

188
곰곰이 생각해보고 있어요.
I'm turning it over.

 → I'm considering it intensively.

A Are you really going to accept that offer?
B I'm turning it over. It's hard to decide.

intensively 집중해서, 골똘히   hard 어려운   accept 수락하다

A 그 제안을 수락할 건가요?
B 곰곰이 생각 중인데, 결정하기가 어렵네요.

189
면밀히 분석해보죠.
I'll do a run-through.

 → do a run-through는 analyze deeply와 같은 뜻.

A What did you think of their suggestion?
B I'll do a run-through first, and then I'll tell you.

A 그 쪽 제안에 대해 어떻게 생각해요?
B 면밀히 분석해본 뒤, 말씀드릴게요.

190
바로 검토해볼게요.
I'll give it a once-over.

 → I'll examine/look over it quickly.

A Is that information helpful?
B I'll give it a once-over. I'll let you know when I'm done.

be done 끝내다, 마치다

A 그 정보가 도움이 되나요?
B 바로 검토해 보고, 끝나는 대로 알려줄게요.

기분 좋게 맞장구 칠 때 쓰는 말

Breakthroughs
- [ ] Presto!
- [ ] That does the trick!
- [ ] That makes it clear.
- [ ] That irons it out.
- [ ] That solves it.

191

금방 해결됐죠!
Presto!

→ 이탈리아어에서 차용된 영어 표현이에요.

A How did you manage to get here on time?
B I offered the driver a tip and presto!

manage to do 그럭저럭 ~해내다

A 어떻게 정시에 도착할 수 있었나요?
B 운전기사에게 팁을 주었더니 금방 해결됐죠!

192

감쪽같이 됩니다!
That does the trick!

→ That works like magic! 속임수처럼 해결됐다는 말.

A Will my car run okay now?
B I'll just replace the spark plugs. That does the trick usually.

replace 교체하다, 대신하다

A 내 차가 제대로 달릴까요?
B 스파크 전원을 교체하죠. 그러면 대개 감쪽같이 되요.

Chapter 06

193
명쾌하군요. 잘 알겠어요.
That makes it clear.

A Turn left at the corner, and then you'll see the post office.
B That makes it clear!

clear 분명한, 명확한   eg. Is that clear?

A 모퉁이에서 왼쪽으로 돌면 우체국이 보여요.
B 잘 알겠습니다!

194
그러면 문제 없겠네요.
That irons it out.

 → 다림질로 주름을 펴듯 문제점이 제거된다는 말.

A We'll catch the express train to Montreal.
B That irons it out. We'll be able to avoid road traffic that way.

A 몬트리올까지 고속열차를 탈 겁니다.
B 그러면 문제 없겠네요. 교통체증을 피할 수 있겠어요.

195
그게 해답이군.
That solves it.

 → It's the answer/the right way to solve the problem.

A Just use e-cards instead for your wedding.
B That solves it. Thank you.

A 청첩장을 전자카드로 대신하세요.
B 그러면 되는군요. 고마워요.

제안할 때 쓰기 좋은 쉬운 말

Proposals

☐ What's the pitch?   ☐ Go at it this way   ☐ Consider this
☐ Let's try this.   ☐ Here's a game plan.

196

방안이 뭔데요?
What's the pitch?

→ 상대를 설득할 방안을 pitch라고 해요. 그래서 영업자가 소비자를 설득해서 물건을 사게 하는 것을 sales pitch라고 하죠.

A I think I have an idea for a promotion.
B Okay, what's the pitch? I hope it's useful!

idea for ~에 대한 아이디어   useful 유익한

A 홍보 아이디어가 있어요.
B 그래, 방안이 뭔데요? 유익한 거겠지!

197

이렇게 해봐.
Go at it this way

→ You may consider it from this angle.

A What's the best way to buy cosmetics?
B Go at it this way: check them online first!

A 화장품을 가장 잘 사는 방법이 뭐죠?
B 이렇게 해요. 우선 온라인에서 검색해 봐요.

검토 · 분석 · 해결할 때 입에 달게 되는 생생 표현

Chapter 06

198
이점을 고려해봐요.
Consider this

 여기서 this는 이어서 말할 내용을 가리켜요.

A How can I get a job soon?
B Consider this: apply to as many companies as possible.

apply to ~에 문의하다, 조회하다

A 어떻게 하면 빨리 취직이 될까?
B 이점을 고려해봐. 가능한 많은 회사를 알아 보는 거야.

199
이렇게 해보자.
Let's try this.

 try this는 정말 많이 쓰는 말. 음식을 먹어 보라고 권할 때도 쓰죠?

A I just can't get a signal with my cell phone!
B Let's try this: we'll move to another area.

get a signal 접속되다, 통신되다

A 휴대폰이 안 터지네!
B 이렇게 해봐. 장소를 옮겨보는 거야.

200
방법은 이거야.
Here's a game plan.

 게임에서 이기려면 전략이 필요하겠죠!

A I need to lose about 10kg!
B Here's a game plan: sign up for a boxing club!

A 체중을 10kg이나 빼야 해!
B 방법은 이거야. 복싱 클럽에 가입해!

견해를 피력할 때 흔히 쓰는 말

Paradigms & Understandings

☐ That's what my gut says. ☐ That's my take. ☐ That's my view.
☐ That's how I see it. ☐ Those are my thoughts.

201

그건 내 직감이야.
That's what my gut says.

→ **That's what I feel in my guts.** 바로 '필'이 올 때 써요. I have a gut feeling/a hunch that(~라는 직감이 들다)라는 표현도 알아 두세요.

A You think the stock market will rise today?
B No evidence, but that's what my gut says.

evidence 증거   eg. The police have found no evidence yet.

A 오늘 증시가 오를 것 같다는 거야?
B 증거는 없지만 내 직감에 그래.

202

내가 알기론 그래.
That's my take.

→ 여기서 take는 명사로 understanding, impression과 같은 뜻. 그의 연설이 어떤 것 같소? — What's your take on his speech?

A Do you really think Ken skipped work?
B That's my take. I haven't seen him all morning.

A 켄이 오늘 결근했다고요?
B 내가 알기론 그래. 오전 내내 안 보여요.

검토 · 분석 · 해결할 때 입에 달게 되는 생생 표현

Chapter 06

203
내 의견으론 그렇습니다.
That's my view.

 → That's my personal opinion. That's what I think.

  A You think Bob is the best man for the job?
　　　　 B That's my view. He has all the right qualifications.

the best person/man for ~의 적임자

  A 밥이 그 자리에 적임자라고요?
　　　　 B 내 의견으론 그렇습니다. 그는 자격이 있어요.

204
내 판단으론 그래.
That's how I see it.

 → That's just the way I see it. 내가 상황을 보는 방식이란 뜻.

  A You think Jerry won the lottery?
　　　　 B That's how I see it. That explains his sudden spending spree.

That explains 그게 ~한 이유다   spending spree 흥청망청 돈을 씀

  A 제리가 복권에 당첨됐다고요?
　　　　 B 내 판단으론 그래. 갑자기 돈을 펑펑 쓰잖아.

205
내 생각엔 그래요.
Those are my thoughts.

 → thoughts를 복수로 써야 해요!

  A Is Ronald really that selfish?
　　　　 B Those are my thoughts. He never helps anybody.

selfish 이기적인   cf. unselfish 이타적인

  A 로날드가 그렇게 이기적인가요?
　　　　 B 내 생각엔 그래요. 그는 아무도 돕지 않아요.

한쪽만 고려할 수 없을 때 하는 말

Paradoxes & Complexities

- [ ] There's another side.
- [ ] Look at it both ways.
- [ ] It's got pros and cons.
- [ ] Here's the rub/catch.
- [ ] It cuts both ways.

206
다른 측면도 있지요.
There's another side.

→ There are two angles to an issue. 또 다른 측면도 고려해야 한다는 말.

A Saving money in a bank is best.
B There's another side, though. Bank interest is very low.

A 은행 예금이 최고지요.
B 다른 측면도 있잖아요. 은행 이자는 아주 낮거든요.

207
양쪽 면을 봐야죠.
Look at it both ways.

A I want to live in the countryside, because it's cheaper.
B Look at it both ways: country life is also boring.

boring 따분한 eg. His gag is boring.

A 시골에서 살고 싶어요. 비용이 덜 드니까요.
B 양쪽 면을 봐야죠. 시골 생활은 따분하잖아요.

208
장단점이 있어요.
It's got pros and cons.

 It's got both good and bad sides.

  A What do you think about living alone?
B It's got pros and cons. Freedom but loneliness.
live alone 혼자 살다

  A 독신생활에 대해 어떻게 생각해요?
B 장단점이 있죠. 자유롭지만 외롭죠.

209
조건이 있어요.
Here's the rub/catch.

 구미가 당기는 제안에는 늘 조건이 붙기 마련이죠!

  A This apartment has a great view.
B Here's the catch: it's very expensive!
have a nice/great view 전망이 좋다

  A 이 아파트는 전망이 아주 좋네요.
B 조건도 있지요. 매우 비싸거든요!

210
양날의 칼인 셈이죠.
It cuts both ways.

 A double-edged sword can help or harm you.

  A Do you like working as a freelancer?
B Free but unstable. It cuts both ways.
unstable 불안정한 eg. Joan is emotionally unstable.

  A 프리랜서로 일하는 게 좋아요?
B 자유롭지만 불안정해요. 양날의 칼인 셈이죠.

CHAPTER 07

Starting and Stopping

Is this the company bowling team? It sure is. Want in? Isn't this the local parents' group? I'd like to join the school French Club here. You hopping on? How long have you... Why don't you join our research group? I'm a solo act, sorry. You're leaving our... Yeah, I'm jumping ship. I got a better offer. Is this the company bowling team? It sure is. Want in? Isn't this the local parents' group? It... You hopping on? How long have you studied French? Can I come to your party this Friday? Of course! The more, the merrier. Aren't yo... You're leaving our department? Yeah, from now on you're on your own. Why didn't you help carry our bags? Every man for himself; I've...

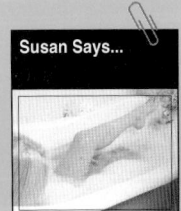

Susan Says...

Showers were made for men, but bathtubs were made for women!

Starting and Stopping

시작과 마무리를 위한 생생 표현

행동을 개시할 때 으레 쓰는 말

Beginning

- [ ] Let's get rolling. [ ] Let's hit it. [ ] Let's move.
- [ ] I'll get on it. [ ] I'll see to it.

211

시작해봅시다.
Let's get rolling.

→ 그냥 Let's roll.도 좋아요. 억양에서 '리듬' 이 느껴지죠?

A Are you ready to start the discussion?
B I sure am! Let's get rolling with it!

A 토론을 시작해도 될까요?
B 예! 시작해봅시다!

212

부딪혀보자.
Let's hit it.

물론 신체적으로 '부딪힌다' 는 뜻은 아니에요!

A Here, we've got a ton of work.
B So let's hit it now, before it gets too late.

a ton/tons of 많은(a lot of) eg. You made me waste a ton of time!

A 자, 일거리가 한 짐 있어요.
B 그럼, 부딪혀보자고. 너무 늦기 전에.

213
어서 움직입시다.
Let's move.

 → Be in a hurry! 어물 대지 말고 빨리 행동하자는 말.

A We need to get to the bus stop by 9:00.
B Okay, let's move, then.

A 9시까지 버스 정류장에 가야 돼요.
B 그래, 그럼 빨리 움직여야지.

214
바로 하겠습니다.
I'll get on it.

 → I'll do it right away. 원어민들은 do, start 대신 get on it을 즐겨 써요.

A Sue, you're supposed to set the table for our guests!
B I'll get on it, Mr. Grimm.

set the table 식탁을 차리다

A 수, 손님 식탁을 차려야지요!
B 바로 할게요, 그림 씨.

215
내가 처리할게요.
I'll see to it.

 → I'll take care of it. I'll resolve it. 'see to it'을 한 단어처럼 써요.

A Aren't you going to call Mr. Smith?
B Yes, I'll see to it in about five minutes.

A 스미스 씨에게 전화 안 해요?
B 예, 5분 내로 처리할게요.

긍정적으로 일하게 해주는 말

Continuing/Persevering
- Steady on!
- Stay in the game
- Stick to what you're doing
- Stay on target
- Keep it up

216
계속해봐요!
Steady on!

 → Steadily pursue/continue 포기하지 말라고 용기를 주는 말.

A   I'm about to give up on this.
B   Steady on! You can do it.

be about to 막 ~하려고 하다   eg. Wait! I'm about to leave.

A   난 그만 포기할래요.
B   계속해봐요! 당신은 할 수 있어요.

217
끝까지 해봐요.
Stay in the game

 → Who knows whether you'll win in the end? 9회말 만루 홈런! 게임을 끝까지 해봐야 알죠.

A   My research is going nowhere.
B   Just stay in the game and you'll finally figure it out.

go nowhere 성과가 없다

A   연구 성과가 전혀 없어요.
B   끝까지 해봐요. 그러면 성과가 나올 거예요.

218

지금처럼만 하세요.
Stick to what you're doing

 → Continue in your present position/activity 잘하고 있을 때 써요.

A Should I try to get a different job?
B Actually, I think you should stick to what you're doing.

A 다른 일을 찾아봐야 할까요?
B 아니오, 지금처럼만 계속 일 하세요.

219

목표에 집중하세요.
Stay on target

 → Continue to focus on current task/activity 목표를 잊지 말 것!

A Our deadline for the project is almost here.
B Just stay on target, and we're bound to meet it.
be bound to ~하게 되다 eg. We're bound to forget past pains.

A 프로젝트 마감일이 거의 됐어요.
B 목표에 집중해요, 그러면 맞출 수 있어요.

220

계속 수고해줘요.
Keep it up

 → Keep up the good work!

A I just convinced a client to re-sign with us.
B Keep it up. You're doing a great job.
convince+사람+to do ~이 …하도록 납득시키다, 수고해줘

A 고객과 재계약을 따냈습니다.
B 계속 수고해줘요. 잘 처리했어요.

막간 휴식이 목마를 때 나오는 말

Pausing

- [ ] Take five
- [ ] Step back for a minute
- [ ] Pick it up again later
- [ ] Leave it for now
- [ ] Let's take a breather.

221

5분만 쉬죠.
Take five

 → Let's take a 5-minute break.

　A I've been working for 8 straight hours.
　　　B Take five, then. You can come back to it later.

　A 8시간 내내 일했어요.
　　　B 그럼, 5분 쉬었다 다시 하세요.

222

잠시 멈췄다 해요.
Step back for a minute

 → Let's pause for a moment.

　A This work is really taking up a lot of my energy.
　　　B Step back for a minute then, and rest.
　　　take up (힘이) 들다, 소모하다

　A 이 일은 정말 에너지 소모가 엄청나요.
　B 그럼, 잠시 멈추고 쉬어요.

223

나중에 다시 할게요.
Pick it up again later

 I'll restart it later. pick up은 잠시 중단했다가 '다시 한다'는 뜻.

A Are you just going out without loading it?
B I'll pick it up again later in the day.
later in the day 이따가, 나중에

A 그거 전송하지 않고 외출할 거야?
B 이따가 다시 할게요.

224

일단 여기서 끝냅시다.
Leave it for now

 Let's stop it temporarily.

A Should we do another review of this?
B Let's leave it for now. Let's go grab a bite.
for now 우선은, 일단, 현재로는

A 이걸 또 검토해야 하나요?
B 일단 여기서 끝내고, 뭘 좀 먹으러 가죠.

225

쉬는 시간을 갖죠.
Let's take a breather.

 Let's take a pause to rest. 쉴 짬을 내자는 말.

A Let's practice one more time.
B We've been doing this all afternoon. Let's take a breather!

A 한 번 더 연습합시다.
B 오후 내내 했잖아요. 쉬는 시간을 갖죠!

행동 복귀를 알리는 말

Restarting

☐ Round 2!   ☐ Back to it!   ☐ Where did we leave off?
☐ Let's jump back in.   ☐ Back to the grind!

226

다시 시작합시다!
Round 2!

→ Let's do the second phase! 2라운드도 '계속 열심히' 뛰자고!

A Is our smoke break over now, Thelma?
B Yes, let's get back to work. Round 2!
get back to ~로 복귀하다, 다시 연락하다   eg. Check this file and get back to me.

A 흡연시간이 끝났나, 델마?
B 예, 일해야죠. 다시 시작합시다!

227

업무복귀!
Back to it!

→ Let's return to work/task/assignment!

A That's the boss signaling to us, isn't it?
B Yes, back to it, I guess!
signal 손짓하다

A 사장님이 손짓하시는데요, 그렇죠?
B 예, 업무복귀하란 말씀이죠!

228
어디까지 했었죠?
Where did we leave off?

 → Where did we stop working previously?

  A How should we finish this?
B Where did we leave off? Let's start from there.

  A 이걸 어떻게 마무리해야죠?
B 어디까지 했나요? 거기부터 다시 하죠.

229
속히 재개합시다.
Let's jump back in.

 → 다시 뛰어들자니? 속히 일로 복귀하자는 뜻.

  A Still a lot of products we haven't tested yet.
B Let's jump back in and finish them.

  A 아직도 테스트하지 않은 제품이 많네.
B 속히 재개해서 마치죠.

230
다시 일터로!
Back to the grind!

 → work 대신 grind를 썼죠. grind는 '단조롭고 지루한 일'을 말해요.

  A Looks like lunch is over.
B Okay guys, back to the grind! Plenty of work to do.

  A 점심시간이 끝난 것 같네.
B 여러분, 다시 일터로! 할 일이 많아요.

사고의 전환이 필요할 때 쓰면 좋은 말

Changing Plans

- [ ] Let's hit reverse.
- [ ] Let's change course.
- [ ] Let's switch gears.
- [ ] Let's start from scratch.
- [ ] Let's take a 180°.

231

반대로 해봅시다.
Let's hit reverse.

→ Let's change a plan entirely. 일이 잘 풀리지 않으면 역발상을!

A We can't fix the equipment this way.
B Let's hit reverse, then.

A 이렇게 해서는 이 장비를 고칠 수 없어요.
B 그럼 반대로 해보죠.

232

달리 해봅시다.
Let's change course.

→ Let's try another method.

A I think this meeting isn't productive at all.
B Let's change course, then.

productive 생산적인, 성과가 있는

A 이런 식의 회의는 전혀 성과가 없어요.
B 그럼 달리 해봅시다.

122

233
전략을 수정합시다.
Let's switch gears.

 → Let's change a plan/activity, as in a car switching gears.

A Our plan hasn't succeeded yet.
B Let's switch gears. Think of a different way.

A 우리의 계획이 먹히질 않아요.
B 전략을 수정합시다. 달리 생각해봐요.

234
처음부터 다시 해보죠.
Let's start from scratch.

 → scratch는 from the beginning이란 뜻.

A I can't figure out this design!
B Let's start from scratch. Who drew it up?

draw up (문서, 계획) 작성하다, 입안하다

A 이 디자인은 이해가 안 가요!
B 처음부터 다시 해보죠. 누가 작성한 건가요?

235
180도 돌려봅시다.
Let's take a 180°.

 → 한국말과 똑같죠!

A I think the opera might be too boring.
B Well, let's take a 180° and go to a musical instead.

A 오페라는 너무 따분할 것 같아.
B 그럼, 180도 돌려서 뮤지컬을 보러 가죠.

속도가 생명일 때 하는 말

Activity Speed Increases

☐ Pick up the pace　☐ Hop to it!　☐ Get the lead out!
☐ While we're still young!　☐ On the double!

236
속히 진행하세요.
Pick up the pace

→ Let's do it quickly.

A　Our inspection is in 45 minutes.
B　We need to pick up the pace if we want to be ready.

inspection 검사, 검열

A　45분 내로 검사를 해야 해요.
B　준비를 하려면 속히 진행하세요.

237
서둘러요!
Hop to it!

→ 깡충깡충 뛰듯이 서둘러 하라는 뜻.

A　Do you want me to carry these cartons outside?
B　Yes! Hop to it!

carton 판지 상자(cardboard box)

A　이 상자들을 다 내갈 건가요?
B　예! 서둘러요!

238
더 빨리 움직여요!
Get the lead out!

 신발에서 무거운 납덩이를 빼내면 가벼워서 빨리 뛸 수 있겠죠!

A I'm working as quickly as I can.
B Not fast enough for me: get the lead out!

not~ enough for me 내가 보기엔 ~이 아니다

A 최대한 빨리 일하고 있어요.
B 그 정도로는 멀었어. 더 빨리 해요.

239
세월 다 가겠다!
While we're still young!

 하도 느려서 그걸 보고 있는 우리가 '늙어버리겠다' 는 비유. 그러니 서둘러요!

A Here's page 3 of the project.
B While we're still young! 30 more pages to type!

A 여기 프로젝트 친 것, 3페이지 있어요.
B 세월 다 가겠네! 30 페이지는 더 쳐야죠!

240
(두 배) 빨리요!
On the double!

 You've got to work doubly fast! 평소의 배로 빨리 하란 뜻.

A When should I finish this ?
B On the double, that's when!

A 이걸 언제 끝내면 되죠?
B 평소보다 배는 빨리 해야죠!

종료를 알릴 때 툭 던지는 말

Terminating Activities/Plans

- End of the line
- It's all over.
- Finito!
- That's all she wrote!
- Over and done!

241

막판입니다.
End of the line

→ 다소 부정적인 뉘앙스가 들어 있어요.

A You're quitting the team?
B Yes, it's the end of the line for my sports career.

A 팀을 탈퇴할 건가요?
B 예, 제 운동 경력상 막판이에요.

242

모든 게 끝났어요.
It's all over.

→ Everything's done now. Just take the result.

A So our team can't go to the championship?
B It's all over: we lost in the playoffs.

championship 결승전

A 우리 팀은 결승전에 못 가죠?
B 모든 게 끝났어. 플레이오프에서 졌으니까.

시작과 마무리를 위한 생생 표현

Chapter 07

243
이젠 종쳤어요!
Finito!

 finished를 뜻하는 이탈리아어. 부정적인 어조로 미국인들이 자주 써요.

A You stopped eating at that restaurant?
B Finito! The prices there were too high.

stop -ing ~하는 것을 그만 두다

A 그 식당에서 식사 안 한다고요?
B 이젠 종쳤어요! 가격도 너무 비싸고.

244
그렇게 끝났어요!
That's all she wrote!

 she 대신 he를 쓰지는 않아요.

A The factory's closed down?
B That's all she wrote! No one works there anymore.

A 그 공장이 폐쇄됐다면서요?
B 그렇게 끝장났죠! 이제 아무도 일하지 않아요.

245
다 끝났어요!
Over and done!

 '완전히 끝났다'는 것을 강조할 때 써요.

A The boss is finished talking to us?
B Right, over and done.

A 사장님 말씀이 끝난 건가요?
B 예, 다 끝났습니다.

CHAPTER 08

Calls and Calling

Is this the company bowling team? It sure is. Want in? Isn't this the local parents' group? It I'd like to join the school French Club here. You hopping on? How long have you studied F Why don't you join our research group? I'm a solo act, sorry. You're leaving our departmen jumping ship. I got a better offer. Is this the company bowling team? It sure is. Want in? Isn't this the local parents' group? It is. You si You hopping on? How long have you studied French? Can I come to your party this Friday? Of course! The more, the merrier. Aren't y You're leaving our department? Yeah, from now on you're on your own. Why didn't you help carry our bags? Every man for himself; I'v

Susan Says...

Goodbye New York, hello Atlantic Ocean! A perfect weekend is a sailing weekend with friends!

Calls and Calling

전화 통화에서
가장 많이 쓰는
생생 표현

246 > 280

# 전화걸기

Making Calls

☐ Is Anna Kim in/there/available? ☐ May I speak to Mr. Watson? ☐ Please connect me to Dr Kim.
☐ Mr. Cozy, please. ☐ I'm calling for Mr. Waters.

246

안나 김 있나요?
Is Anna Kim in/there/available?

→ 말할 때는 in, there, available 중에서 입에 잘 붙는 걸 쓰세요. 물론, 들을 때는 다 알아야죠!

A Hello, City Telecom, Engineering Department.
B Is Mr. Carlson there?

A 여보세요? 시티텔레콤, 엔지니어링부입니다.
B 칼슨 씨 있나요?

247

왓슨 씨와 통화할 수 있나요?
May I speak to Mr. Watson?

→ May I 대신 Can I를 써도 되고, I'd like to speak to/with라고도 하죠.

A Thank you for calling Harper Real Estate.
B May I speak to Mr. Harold Foster?

thank you for calling 전화주셔서 감사합니다   real estate 부동산

A 하퍼 부동산에 전화주셔서 감사합니다.
B 해롤드 포스터 씨와 통화할 수 있나요?

248

김 박사님과 연결해주세요.
Please connect me to Dr. Kim.

 Put me through to Dr. Kim, please. 원어민에 따라 connect 대신 put me through to를 더 즐겨 쓰기도 해요.

A Hello, Chicago Investments.
B Please connect me to Dr. Kim. I have an urgent call for her.

an urgent call 급한 전화

A 안녕하세요? 시카고 인베스트먼트입니다.
B 김 박사님 연결 부탁해요. 급한 전화입니다.

249

코지 씨 부탁합니다.
Mr. Cozy, please.

 이 표현에서 please를 붙이는 것 잊지 마세요.

A This is Michigan Plastics, Gary Johnson speaking.
B Mr. Rubins, please.

사람+speaking (전화) ~입니다

A 미시건 플라스틱의 게리 존슨입니다.
B 루빈스 씨 부탁해요.

250

월터 씨 바꿔주세요.
I'm calling for Mr. Waters.

 한국에서는 잘 안 쓰지만 원어민들은 이 표현도 즐겨 써요.

A Can I help direct your call?
B I'm calling for Ms. Janis O'Doole.

direct one's call 전화를 돌려 주다, 연결해 주다

A 어디로 돌려 드릴까요?
B 제니스 오둘 씨 바꿔주세요.

 전화받기

Receiving Calls

☐ Hello, Susie Kim speaking. ☐ Personnel Department, how may I help you?
☐ Thank you for calling ☐ How may I direct your call? ☐ You've reached

251
여보세요? 수지 김입니다.
Hello, Susie Kim speaking.

→ This is Susie Kim. Speaking 대신 This is~를 써도 되죠.

A Hello, customer service, Amelia speaking.
B I'd like to speak to Ashton Crowley, please.
I'd like to speak to~ = May I speak to~

A 여보세요, 고객관리부, 아멜리아입니다.
B 애쉬톤 크롤리와 통화하고 싶은데요.

252
인사부입니다. 어떻게 도와드릴까요?
Personnel Department, how may I help you?

→ 부서로 직접 걸려 온 전화를 받을 때 쓰는 말이죠.

A General office, how may I help you?
B I'd like to know how to apply.
how+to do ~하는 방법 eg. Can you tell me how to use this machine?

A 총무부입니다. 어떻게 도와드릴까요?
B 지원방법을 알고 싶어요.

전화 통화에서 가장 많이 쓰는 생생 표현

Chapter 08

253
~에 전화주셔서 감사합니다.
Thank you for calling

Thank you for calling~으로 전화를 받은 뒤에 how may I help you?를 덧붙여요.

A Thank you for calling Star Travel. How may I help you?
B I'd like to confirm my reservation.

A 스타여행사로 전화주셔서 감사합니다. 어떻게 도와드릴까요?
B 예약을 확인하고 싶은데요.

254
어디로 연결해드릴까요?
How may I direct your call?

이 때 direct는 transfer, connect, put~ through와 같은 의미예요.

A JJ Cosmetics. How may I direct your call?
B I'd like someone in the Sales Department, please.
I'd like someone in ~에 근무하는 사람(이름을 모를 때)

A JJ 코즈메틱입니다. 어디로 연결해드릴까요?
B 영업부 직원과 연결해줘요.

255
~로 전화 주셨습니다.
You've reached

Thank you for calling~ 대신 쓸 수 있는 말.

A You've reached Kim's Hair Salon. How may I help you?
B I'd like to speak to Paula, my wife, please.

A 킴스 헤어살롱 입니다. 어떻게 도와드릴까요?
B 제 아내, 폴라와 통화하고 싶은데요.

통화 대기 요청

Holding a Line

☐ Could you please hold for a moment?   ☐ Would you mind holding the line?   ☐ Please stay on the line for a moment.   ☐ Please wait for a moment while I transfer you.   ☐ He's expecting your call.

256
잠시 기다려주시겠어요?
Could you please hold for a moment?

→ May I ask you to hold for a moment? Could you~ 로 시작되면 정중한 말.

A I'm calling for Allen. Is he in?
B I'll see. Could you please hold for a moment?

A 앨런 씨와 통화하고 싶은데, 있나요?
B 확인해 볼게요. 잠시 기다려주시겠어요?

257
기다려주시겠어요?
Would you mind holding the line?

→ Would you mind waiting on the line? 전화를 끊지 말고 기다리는 말.

A I'm trying to get in touch with Mr. Park. Is he in right now?
B I believe so. Would you mind holding the line for a moment?

get in touch with ~와 연락을 취하다

A 박 선생과 통화하고 싶은데요. 지금 계신가요?
B 그럴 겁니다. 잠시 기다려주시겠어요?

258
끊지 말고 잠시 기다리세요.
Please stay on the line for a moment.

 hold the line대신 stay on the line도 자주 써요. Please만 붙여도 정중한 느낌이 '확' 오죠.

A I'm calling for Akina, please, in Marketing.
B Please stay on the line for a moment, and I'll connect you to her.

A 마케팅 부의 아키나 바꿔주세요.
B 끊지 말고 잠시 기다리면, 연결해드릴게요.

259
연결하는 동안 기다리세요.
Please wait for a moment while I transfer you.

 transfer 대신 put you through도 좋죠. 좀 길지만, 자주 쓰는 말이니 입에 붙게 하세요!

A I'd like to speak with Colin Water. I'm a client of his.
B Please wait for a moment while I transfer you.

A 콜린 워터즈와 통화하고 싶어요. 그의 고객입니다.
B 연결하는 동안 잠시 기다리세요.

260
전화 오길 기다렸어요.
He's expecting your call.

 He's waiting for you to call back. 예상되는 전화를 받았을 때 하는 말.

A I'm phoning for Mr. Fisher. Jane Brown, here.
B He's expecting your call. Please wait for a moment while I put you through.

A 피셔 씨와 연결해주세요. 저는 제인 브라운입니다.
B 전화 오길 기다리셨죠. 연결하는 동안 잠시 기다리세요.

회답 전화걸기

Returning a Call

☐ I'm... returning Jim's call.　☐ I'm calling back Julie.　☐ Someone called me from this number.
☐ Let me speak to Mr. Fuller, please.　☐ I'm calling Tim's cell phone.

261

짐의 전화받고 걸었어요.
I'm... returning Jim's call.

→ 가장 흔히 쓰는 말. I'm 다음에 본인 이름을 넣어 말해요.

A BearTech Inc. May I help you?
B I'm Martha returning Mr. Jackson's call. Is he in?

A 베어텍 사입니다. 도와드릴까요?
B 마사라고 하는데, 잭슨 씨 전화받고 걸었어요. 계신가요?

262

쥴리에게 전화받고 겁니다.
I'm calling back Julie.

→ returning one's call 만큼 자주 쓰여요. 둘 중 하나 골라서 말해 보세요.

A Hello, my name's Fred, and I'm calling back Jason Lee.
B Fred! Jason, here. How are you doing?

A 여보세요, 난 프레드인데, 제이슨 리에게 전화받고 겁니다.
B 프레드! 나야, 제이슨. 어떻게 지내?

263

누군가 이 번호로 전화해서요.
Someone called me from this number.

 모르는 번호가 부재통화로 찍혔을 때 이렇게 말하세요.

A Sun Valley Shopping Complex.
B Someone called me from this number, but I'm not sure who.

A 선벨리 쇼핑센터입니다.
B 누군가 이 번호로 전화했는데, 누군지 모르겠네요.

264

풀러 씨와 연결 부탁해요.
Let me speak to Mr. Fuller, please.

 회답 전화를 하면서 먼저 연결 요청을 했다면, I'm returning his/her call.이라고 덧붙이세요.

A Smith&Carton. How may I help you?
B Let me speak to Bill Smith, please. I'm returning his call.

A 스미스앤카튼 사입니다. 어떻게 도와드릴까요?
B 빌 스미스와 연결 부탁해요. 그의 전화받고 걸었어요.

265

팀의 휴대폰이죠.
I'm calling Tim's cell phone.

 I'm calling for Tim on his cell phone. 휴대폰 주인이 전화를 받지 않은 경우 확인하는 말.

A Hello, May I ask who's calling, please?
B I'm Joy calling Ted's cell phone.

A 여보세요? 누구신가요?
B 조이라고 하는데, 테드의 휴대폰이죠.

전화 통화 불가

Declining a Call

☐ I'm sorry, but he can't speak right now. ☐ Would you like to hold? ☐ Sorry, but she's unavailable right now. ☐ I'm sorry, but he's out of town. ☐ Sorry, but she can't take calls now.

266
미안하지만, 지금은 통화가 안 돼요.
I'm sorry, but he can't speak right now.

→ He can't come to the phone right now. I'm sorry 또는 Sorry를 넣어서 말하세요.

A I'm calling for Mr. Short, please.
B I'm sorry, but he can't speak right now.

A 쇼트 씨와 통화하고 싶은데요.
B 미안하지만 지금은 통화가 안 돼요.

267
(통화 중인데) 기다리겠어요?
Would you like to hold?

→ If you'd like to hold, she'll talk to you. 통화가 짧다면 기다릴 수도 있겠죠.

A Could I speak to Sophie, please? It's somewhat urgent.
B I'm sorry, but she's on the phone right now. Would you like to hold?

be on the phone 통화 중이다   somewhat 약간, 다소

A 소피와 통화할 수 있나요? 좀 급한 일이에요.
B 미안하지만 지금 통화 중인데, 기다리겠어요?

268
미안해요, 그녀는 지금 통화할 수 없어요.
Sorry, but she's unavailable right now.

 → unavailable은 not available과 같죠. 만날 수 있는지, 통화가 가능한지 물어 볼 때 available 또는 unavailable을 써보세요.

A I'm sorry, but Mr. Hoffman's unavailable right now.
B I see. I'll call him back later.

A 미안합니다. 호프만 씨는 지금 통화할 수 없어요.
B 그럼, 나중에 다시 전화하죠.

269
죄송하지만, 그는 출장 중입니다.
I'm sorry, but he's out of town.

 → out of town일 때 말고도 자리에 없거나(away from his desk) 휴무(gone for the day)인 경우도 있겠죠. 뭐, 휴대폰으로 해야죠! Call his cell phone.

A May I speak with Mr. Imm, please
B I'm sorry, but he's out of town.

A 임 사장님과 통화할 수 있나요?
B 죄송하지만, 출장 중이에요.

270
미안하지만, 지금은 전화받을 수 없어요.
Sorry, but she can't take calls now.

 → She's in a meeting, so she can't speak with you. 여기서 take calls는 '전화를 받다'는 뜻. 전화를 걸다는? make a (phone) call이죠!

A May I speak to Anita, please?
B Sorry, but she can't take calls right now. May I take a message?

take a message 메모를 전하다/받다

A 아니타와 통화할 수 있나요?
B 미안하지만, 지금은 전화받을 수 없어요. 메모를 전할까요?

전화 건 사람 확인하기

Identifying Callers

- May I ask who's calling, please? □ Who may I say is calling, please? □ May I have your name, please?
- May I tell him who's calling, please? □ Could you please tell me who's calling?

271

누구신지 물어봐도 될까요?
May I ask who's calling, please?

→ 통성명을 하지 않고 전화 연결을 부탁할 때 써요.

A I'd like to be connected to Troy Baker.
B May I ask who's calling, please?

be connected to ~와 연결되다(be transferred to)

A 트로이 베이커 씨 부탁해요.
B 누구신지 물어봐도 될까요?

272

실례지만 누구신지요?
Who may I say is calling, please?

→ May I ask who's calling?과 맞바꾸어 써요. 이렇게 말하는 원어민들도 많답니다.

A Could I speak with Samuel Han?
B Who may I say is calling, please?

A 사뮤엘 한과 통화할 수 있나요?
B 실례지만 누구신지요?

273
성함이 어떻게 되세요?
May I have your name, please?

 이름을 바로 물어 보기도 하지요.

 A I'm calling for Ms. Robinson in Marketing.
B May I have your name, please?

사람+in+부서명 ~에 근무하는

 A 마케팅 부의 로빈슨 씨 바꿔주세요.
B 성함이 어떻게 되세요?

274
그에게 누구라고 전할까요?
May I tell him who's calling, please?

 tell 다음에 누가 왔는지 보세요. 전화 받을 사람(him)이죠? 아래 예문과 비교해서 연습해 보세요.

 A Please connect me to Jane Patterson.
B May I first tell her who's calling, please?

 A 제인 패터슨과 연결해주세요.
B 먼저 그녀에게 누구라고 전해드릴까요?

275
누구신지 말씀해주시겠어요?
Could you please tell me who's calling?

 이번엔 tell 다음에 me가 왔죠? Could you please~는 정중히 물어 볼 때 쓰는 상투어 예요.

 A I'd like to have a word with Nora Jeoung.
B Could you please tell me who's calling?

have a word with ~와 대화하다, 말하다

 A 노라 정과 통화하고 싶은데요.
B 누구신지 말씀해주시겠어요?

메모 전달하기

Taking Messages
- ☐ May I take a message? ☐ Would you like to leave a message? ☐ Would you like his voicemail?
- ☐ Would you like me to give him a message? ☐ Would you like me to pass her a message?

276
전할 말이 있나요?
May I take a message?

→ You may leave me a message. 가장 일반적인 말이죠.

A May I please speak with Joy Cole?
B He's out right now, and won't be back until 3:00. May I take a message?

won't be back until ~가 되어야 돌아 오다

A 조이 콜과 통화할 수 있나요?
B 지금 외출 중인데, 3시나 돼야 오세요. 전할 말이 있으세요?

277
메모를 남기실래요?
Would you like to leave a message?

→ take a message는 '메모를 받다'이고 leave a message는 '메모를 남기다'죠!

A May I speak to Ms. Gentry, please?
B She's unavailable right now. Would you like to leave a message?

A 젠트리 씨와 통화할 수 있나요?
B 지금은 통화가 안 돼요. 메모를 남기실래요?

278
음성 메시지를 남기실래요?
Would you like his voicemail?

 voicemail을 이용해도 좋겠네요.

A I'd like to speak with Jake, please.
B He's out to lunch right now. Would you like his voicemail?

A 제이크하 통화하고 싶은데요.
B 점심 식사하러 나갔어요. 음성 메시지를 남기실래요?

279
그에게 메모 전해드릴까요?
Would you like me to give him a message?

 Would you like me to~는 '내가 ~해 드릴까요' 란 뜻. 한번에 입에 붙도록 연습하세요.

A Please transfer me to Ms. Kim So-ri.
B She's stepped out for a moment. Would you like me to give her a message?

give ~ a message ~에게 메모를 전하다   step out (잠깐) 외출하다

A 김소리 씨에게 연결해주세요.
B 잠깐 밖에 나갔는데, 메모 전해드릴까요?

280
그녀에게 메모 전해드려요?
Would you like me to pass her a message?

 give 대신 pass를 써도 아주 좋아요!

A May I speak to Ms. Klein, please?
B She's on the phone. Would you like me to pass her a message?

A 클라인 씨와 통화할 수 있나요?
B 통화 중인데, 메모 전해드려요?

CHAPTER 09

Health

Is this the company bowling team? It sure is. Want in? Isn't this the local parents' group? It is. You signing up? We'd like to join the school French Club here. You hopping on? How long have you studied French? Can I come to your party this Friday? Of course! The more, the merrier. Aren't you Why don't you join our research group? I'm a solo act, sorry. You're leaving our department? Yeah, from now on offer. Is this the company bowling team? It sure is. Want in? Isn't this the local parents' group? It is. You signing up? We need more p You hopping on? How long have you studied French? Can I come to your party this Friday? Of course! The more, the merrier. Aren't y You're leaving our department? Yeah, from now on you're on your own. Why didn't you help carry our bags? Every man for himself; I'

Susan Says...

Now this is the best way to greet the morning: yoga on the beach!

Health

쉬운 말로
건강을 챙기는
생생 표현

281 > 315

복통·요통·근육통 등의 통증 말하기

Aches & Pains

- [ ] I've got a stomachache.
- [ ] I've got a pain in my foot.
- [ ] My shoulder is hurting.
- [ ] My back has been killing me.
- [ ] Except that my neck feels painful

281

배가 아파요.
I've got a stomachache.

 stomachache, toothache, earache 등 신체 부위 단어에 ache만 붙이면 '아프다' 는 의미가 되니 쉽죠!

A How are you feeling today, Barney?
B I've got a terrible stomachache.

A 오늘은 몸 상태가 어때요, 바니?
B 배가 몹시 아파요.

282

발에 통증이 있어요.
I've got a pain in my foot.

 ache 대신 pain을 썼죠. I've got a pain(통증이 있어요)-어디에?-in my foot.

A You've been limping all day.
B That's because I've got a pain in my foot.

limp 절뚝거리다 That's because ~해서 그렇습니다

A 하루종일 절뚝거리고 있군요.
B 발에 통증이 있어서 그래요.

283

어깨가 아파요.
My shoulder is hurting.

 → I've got a pain in my shoulder. '고통을 갖고 있다'는 표현 대신에 hurting을 써서 '~이 아프다'고 말해도 좋아요!

A You're supposed to drive this time?
B Actually, my shoulder is hurting, so I don't want to drive.

be supposed to ~하기로 되어 있다

A 이번엔 당신이 운전하기로 했죠?
B 그런데, 어깨가 아파서 못하겠어.

284

허리가 계속 아파요.
My back has been killing me.

 → I've been suffering from backache. 아픈 증세가 한동안 지속된 경우에 써요. kill을 쓴 것은 '죽일 정도로' 아프다는 뜻.

A What's the matter, Mrs. White?
B My back has been killing me.

A 뭐가 문제인가요, 화이트 부인?
B 허리가 계속 아파요.

285

목이 뻐근한 것 빼고요.
Except that my neck feels painful

 → I'm all right except that I've got a pain in my neck. Except that 주어+동사 구문은 '~란 사실만 빼고'란 뜻.

A Do you feel okay today?
B Yes, except that my neck feels painful.

feel painful 고통스럽다, 아프다

A 오늘은 괜찮으세요?
B 예, 목이 뻐근한 것 말고는요.

머리가 맑지 못하면 나타나는 증세

Head & Mental

- [ ] I'm dizzy.
- [ ] I'm seeing double.
- [ ] Everything's blurry.
- [ ] I can't see straight.
- [ ] I need to rest my eyes.

286
현기증이 나요.
I'm dizzy.

 → '어지럽다, 현기증이 나다'는 dizzy라고 해요. 발음도 좀 '디-지' 하죠? 느낌상 현기증이 있다 싶으면 I'm feeling a little dizzy.라고 말하세요!

A Hey, Ward, how was that amusement ride?
B It was fun, but now I think I'm dizzy.

amusement (park) 놀이(공원)

A 이봐, 워드, 놀이공원 탈것은 어땠어요?
B 재밌었죠, 생각하면 좀 현기증이 나지만요.

287
두 개로 보여요.
I'm seeing double.

 → I'm seeing two images where there is only one. 말 그대로죠.

A You look really tired.
B I am. So much so that I'm seeing double.

so much so that 매우/몹시 그러하여 ~하다

A 아주 피곤해 보여요.
B 그래요. 그래서 사물이 두 개로 보일 정도죠.

288

모든 게 뿌옇게 보여요.
Everything's blurry.

 → My vision is not clear. 마치 안개가 낀듯 뿌연 상태를 blurry하다고 해요.

A Didn't you see me? I was waving at you!
B Sorry, everything's a little blurry right now.

wave at ~를 향해 손을 흔들다

A 날 못 봤어요? 당신에게 손을 흔들었는데요!
B 미안해요, 모든 게 좀 뿌옇게 보여서요.

289

초점이 잘 안 맞아요.
I can't see straight.

 → 여기서 straight는 clearly focused란 뜻입니다.

A You've been driving for over 10 hours.
B Yeah, I can't even see straight right now.

I can't even ~조차 할 수 없다

A 당신, 10시간 넘게 운전했어요.
B 그래선지 눈에 초점도 잘 안 맞는 것 같네.

290

눈에 휴식이 필요해.
I need to rest my eyes.

 → 서류 검토나 모니터를 너무 오래 보면 눈이 아프죠? 그럴 때 써요.

A Want to keep reading through the rest of these papers?
B Not now. I need to rest my eyes.

keep+-ing 계속해서 ~하다   the rest of ~의 나머지

A 이 논문들 나머지도 검토하시겠어요?
B 지금은 말고요. 눈을 좀 쉬어야겠어요.

술마신 뒤에 오는 증상들

Alcohol-related Illnesses

☐ I'm drunk/blasted/wasted. ☐ I'm hung over. ☐ I blacked out.
☐ I passed out. ☐ I threw up.

291
만취했어!
I'm drunk/blasted/wasted.

 → drunk 말고 blasted나 wasted도 자주 쓰는 말이에요. 한번 말해 보세요.

A You drank too much Soju!
B I know. I'm blasted, but I don't care!

I don't care! 상관없어!

A 소주를 너무 많이 마셨어!
B 알아. 난 만취했어! 그래도 상관없어!

292
술이 덜 깼어.
I'm hung over.

 → Morning sickness after heavy drinking the night before 여러분도 겪어 보셨죠? hangover는 명사로 '숙취', be hung over는 '숙취 상태에 있다'란 뜻.

A You drank a lot last night.
B That's why I'm hung over now!

A 어젯밤 과음했어요.
B 그래서 아직도 술이 덜 깼죠.

293
필름이 끊겼어요.
I blacked out.

 → Drink so much that you lose memory or control 소위 '필름이 끊긴' (film is cut) 상태를 말해요.

A What happened last night?
B To be honest, I blacked out and can't remember a thing.

A 어젯밤 어떻게 된 거에요?
B 실은, 필름이 끊겼어요. 하나도 기억이 않나요.

294
만취해서 뻗었어요.
I passed out.

 → 시트콤에서 자주 들을 수 있는 말. 어른들 앞에선 쓰지 마세요!

A Don't drink so much this time, Jill!
B I won't. Last time I had 3 bottles of wine and then passed out.
a bottle of ~한 병   eg. I drank 2 bottles of Soju.

A 질, 이번엔 너무 많이 마시지 말아요!
B 안 그럴게요. 지난번에 와인 3병 먹고 뻗었잖아요.

295
토했어요.
I threw up.

 → I vomited. 원어민들은 threw up을 즐겨 써요.

A I told you not to mix beer and whiskey!
B Sorry, that's what made me throw up, I think.
tell+사람+not to do ~에게 …하지 말라고 하다

A 맥주와 위스키를 섞지 말라고 했죠!
B 미안, 그것 때문에 토한 것 같아.

피곤하면 툭 내뱉게 되는 말

Fatigue

☐ I'm worn out.   ☐ I can't go another step.   ☐ I'm bone-tired.
☐ I'm out of energy.   ☐ I've lost my drive.

296
녹초가 됐어요.
I'm worn out.

 → I'm tired to death. 너무 피곤해서 몸이 닳아 빠진(worn out) 물건 같다는 말.

A How would you like to go bowling with us?
B I'd love to, but I'm worn out.

go+-ing ~하러 가다   eg. go shopping

A 우리와 볼링 치러 갈래요?
B 그러고 싶지만, 너무 피곤해서요.

297
한 발짝도 더 못 가겠어요.
I can't go another step.

 → I'm so tired that I cannot walk anymore 말 그 대로예요.

A You did pretty well to run the marathon so fast!
B Maybe, but I can't go another step now!

run the marathon 마라톤을 뛰다

A 마라톤에서 아주 빨리 잘 달리던데요!
B 하지만 지금은 한 발짝도 더 못 가겠어요.

298

뼈마디까지 쑤셔요.
I'm bone-tired.

 → I'm so tired that I "feel it in my bones". 한국말로도 이렇게 표현하죠?

A How's your life been since you had your second son?
B I'm bone-tired between housework and caring for kids.

How's(has) your life been since~ ? ~이래로 어떻게 지내요?   care for 돌보다

A 둘째 아들까지 얻고 어떻게 지내세요?
B 집안일에 애들 돌보느라, 뼈마디까지 쑤셔요.

299

기력이 없어요.
I'm out of energy.

 → I'm not strong enough to act. 쉽고 재밌는 표현이죠? 써 보세요.

A Aren't you coming rollerblading with us?
B I'm out of energy. You guys have a good time, though.

You guys 너희들(친한 사이에 씀)

A 우리와 인라인 타러 안 갈래요?
B 기력이 없어요. 재밌게 타세요.

300

의욕이 없어요.
I've lost my drive.

 → drive는 뭔가 하고자 하는 '의욕, 추진력'을 뜻하는 말.

A Won't you review the rest of these client emails?
B I've lost my drive. I guess I need some rest.

review 검토하다   eg. Won't you review my essay?

A 고객이 보낸 이메일들을 검토 안 할 건가요?
B 의욕이 없어요. 좀 쉬어야 할까봐요.

유행성 질병에 관해 자주 쓰는 말

Airborne Sicknesses

- [ ] I've caught a cold/the flu.
- [ ] I'm coming down with something.
- [ ] I picked up a case of poison ivy.
- [ ] There's a flu going around.
- [ ] I caught measles from him.

301
감기/독감에 걸렸어요.
I've caught a cold/the flu.

 감기에 '막 걸렸다'는 뜻. 이미 '걸린 상태'라면 I have a cold.라고 해요. catch는 외부적인 요인으로 질병이 생겼을 때 써요.

A Alicia, you've been coughing all day!
B I think I've caught the flu.

cough 기침하다 all day 하루종일

A 종일토록 기침을 하네요, 앨리샤!
B 독감에 걸린 것 같아요.

302
어딘가 몸이 안 좋아요.
I'm coming down with something.

 coming down with는 원어민들이 아주 잘 쓰는 말. '병에 걸리다'는 뜻.

A You've been resting in bed all day!
B I'm coming down with something. I feel too weak to rise.

rest in bed 누워있다 too~ to 너무 ~해서 …할 수 없다

A 온종일 침대에 누워 있는 거예요!
B 어딘가 몸이 안 좋아. 못 일어나겠어.

303

옻이 옮았어요.
I picked up a case of poison ivy.

 pick up a case는 receive an illness와 같은 뜻.

A What happened to your skin?
B I picked up a case of poison ivy!

poison ivy 덩굴옻나무

A 피부가 어떻게 된 거예요?
B 옻이 옮았어요.

304

독감이 유행이래요.
There's a flu going around.

 going around는 사람들 사이에 질병이 번지는 것을 말해요(spreading among people).

A Why are you wearing that surgical mask?
B There's a flu going around, and I don't want to catch it.

wear (얼굴·몸에) 쓰다, 입다

A 왜 위생 마스크를 하고 있어요?
B 독감이 유행이래요, 걸리고 싶지 않거든요.

305

그한테 홍역이 옮았어요.
I caught measles from him.

 I got sick from somebody. 옮긴 상대를 밝힐 때는 from을 써요.

A What was your worst childhood disease?
B I caught the measles from my younger brother.

measles 홍역

A 어린시절 걸렸던 최악의 질병은 뭐죠?
B 동생에게서 홍역이 옮았었죠.

내장기관에 탈이 났을 때 쓰는 말

Stomach/Intestinal Problems
- ☐ I've got an upset stomach. ☐ I'm backed up. ☐ I can't keep anything down.
- ☐ I'm irregular. ☐ I've lost my appetite.

306
배탈이 났어요.
I've got an upset stomach.

→ **My stomach is out of order.** 배탈은 a stomach disorder/trouble/upset으로 말해도 좋습니다!

A Try this apple pie. It's delicious!
B Not now. I've got an upset stomach.

try+음식 한번 먹어 보다, 시식(음)하다

A 이 사과파이 좀 들어봐요. 맛있어요!
B 지금은 못 먹어요. 배탈이 났어요.

307
변비가 생겼어요.
I'm backed up.

→ constipated [kάnstəpèitid] 라는 전문 용어를 쓰기 보다는 이렇게 말하면 쉽죠.

A You sure are drinking a lot of tea!
B I'm backed up, so I'm hoping this will help.

I'm hoping (that) ~하길 바라다

A 차를 엄청 마시는군요!
B 변비가 생겼어요. 좀 도움이 될까 해서요.

308
음식을 넘길 수가 없어요.
I can't keep anything down.

 → I can't eat food without throwing it up. 이런 경험 있으시죠?

A You can't seem to eat anything! Some chicken soup?
B Right now I can't keep anything down.

A 도통 못 드시는 것 같네요! 닭고기 수프는요?
B 지금은 음식을 넘길 수가 없어요.

309
설사가 나요.
I'm irregular.

 → I've got diarrhea. diarrhea[daiərí:ə]란 말이 어려우면 이렇게 말하세요.

A Why are you taking that medicine?
B I'm irregular today, so I'm hoping this will help.

take a medicine 약을 복용하다   irregular 불규칙적인, 설사가 나는

A 그 약은 왜 드세요?
B 오늘 설사가 나서요. 좀 나아질까 해서요.

310
식욕이 없어요.
I've lost my appetite.

 → I have no hunger for anything. 영어는 '입맛이 없다'가 아니라 '식욕을 잃었다'고 해요.

A Hey, Dennis! Come over and have a piece of pizza!
B Sorry, but I've got a fever, so I've lost my appetite.

get/have a fever 열이 있다

A 이봐, 데니스! 이리 와서 피자 좀 먹어요.
B 미안해요, 열도 나고, 식욕이 없어요.

목과 코가 아플 때 하는 말

Nose & Throat Ailments

- ☐ I've got a sore throat.
- ☐ I've got a stuffy nose.
- ☐ I've got a runny nose.
- ☐ I've got a nosebleed.
- ☐ I've got sinus trouble.

311
목이 따끔거려요.
I've got a sore throat.

→ 영어로 '목이 아프다'는 99% 이렇게 말해요. 정도가 심하다면 bad나 terrible을 넣어서 I've got a bad sore throat.라고 하세요.

A You wanted some cold medicine, right?
B Yeah, I've got a sore throat.

A 감기약 달라고 했죠?
B 그래요, 목이 따끔거려서요.

312
코가 막혔어요.
I've got a stuffy nose.

→ I'm stuffed-up. 코가 막히면 정말 답답하죠!

A Why are you speaking so strangely?
B I've got a stuffy nose. It interferes with my talking.

stuffy 꽉 찬, 막힌   interfere with 방해하다

A 말하는 게 왜 그래요?
B 코가 막혀서요. 말하기 힘드네요.

313
콧물이 나요.
I've got a runny nose.

 콧물이 줄줄… 보기도 좋지 않고, 괴롭습니다. runny nose를 기억하세요!

A Is your cold almost gone?
B Yes, but I've still got a runny nose.

be gone 사라지다, 없어지다   still 여전히, 아직도

A 감기는 다 나았어요?
B 예, 콧물은 아직 나지만요.

314
코피가 나요.
I've got a nosebleed.

 한국말과 똑같죠? '코-피'=nose-bleed. 잠깐, blood가 아니라 bleed예요.

A What's wrong with you? You've got blood on your face!
B Sorry, I've got a nosebleed from this high altitude.

on one's face ~의 얼굴에   altitude 고도

A 무슨 일이에요? 얼굴에 피가 묻었네요.
B 미안, 고도가 높아지니 코피가 나서요.

315
비강이 약해요.
I've got sinus trouble.

 비강이 약한 분들 많죠? 비강은 sinus예요. trouble은 ache/pain/problem과 같은 뜻.

A Why do you keep sneezing?
B Sorry, I've got sinus trouble.

A 왜 계속 재채기를 하세요?
B 미안해요, 비강이 좀 약해요.

CHAPTER 10

Time

Is this the company bowling team? It sure is. Want in? Isn't this the local parents' group? It is. You signing up? We nee I'd like to join the school French Club here. You hopping on? How long have you studied French? Can I come to your Why don't you join our research group? I'm a solo act, sorry. You're leaving our department? Yeah, from now on you Is this the company bowling team? It sure is. Want in? Isn't this the local parents' group? It is. You signing up? We need more parents. You hopping on? How long have you studied French? Can I come to your party this Friday? Of course! The more, the merrier. Aren't y You're leaving our department? Yeah, from now on you're on your own. Why didn't you help carry our bags? Every man for himself; I'v

Susan Says...

For businesswomen, respect is never given; it has to be earned. And earning respect comes only through success.

Time

하루에도 수십 번 쓰는 시간 관련
생생 표현

316›350

입에 바로 붙는 기간과 빈도 표현

Periods of Time/Frequency

- [ ] Anytime!
- [ ] Not in a million years!
- [ ] The sooner the better
- [ ] No rush!
- [ ] Later!

316
언제라도!
Anytime!

→ At any time, whenever seems convenient or appropriate 때와 장소를 불문하고 아무때나 괜찮다는 뜻.

A Thanks for the ride home.
B Anytime! I'm happy to help.

I'm happy to 기꺼이(즐겁게) ~하다

A 집까지 바래다줘서 고마워요.
B 언제라도! 기꺼이 도와드리죠.

317
죽었다 깨나도 아닙니다!
Not in a million years!

→ It could never happen even if 1 million years passed. 백만 년이 흘러도 아닌 것은 아니라는 강한 의지를 나타내요.

A Are you gonna vote for Mr. Smith in the election?
B Not in a million years! I disagree with everything he stands for!

vote for/against 찬성/반대 투표하다   disagree with ~에 반대하다

A 선거에서 스미스 씨에게 투표할 건가요?
B 죽었다 깨나도 아닙니다! 그의 모든 공약에 반대해요.

하루에도 수십 번 쓰는 시간 관련 생생 표현

318

빠를수록 좋아요.
The sooner the better

 잘 알고 있는 표현이죠! 언제 만날까요? — The sooner, the better!

A When should I arrive at the party?
B The sooner the better, so you don't miss any of the fun!

don't miss ~을 놓치지 마라   eg. Don't miss the soccer game tonight!

A 파티에 언제 도착하면 되나요?
B 빠를수록 좋아요. 그래야 재미있는 것을 모두 즐길 수 있죠.

319

급할 것 없어요!
No rush!

 Please take your time. 급할 것 없이 천천히 하라는 뜻. 원래 문장은 There's no rush.예요.

A I'll bring those files for you in just a second.
B No rush! I have plenty to do already.

bring 갖다 주다   have plenty to do 할 일이 많다

A 그 파일들을 바로 갖다 드릴게요.
B 급할 것 없어요. 지금 할 일이 많으니까요.

320

나중에요!
Later!

 Let's do it later. 지금 말고 '더 늦게' 하자는 말. See you later!(나중에 보자!)

A Can I ask you to help me with this program?
B Later! I'm just about to go into a conference.

be about to 막 ~하려고 하다

A 이 프로그램 좀 도와줄래요?
B 나중에요! 지금 회의에 들어가야 해요.

촌각을 표현하는 말

Brief Periods of Time

- [ ] In a minute
- [ ] I'll be right there.
- [ ] Just give me a second
- [ ] Just hold on
- [ ] Before you know it

321

잠시만요.
In a minute

 **Just wait for a minute/second.** 친한 사이에 써요. in 없이 Just a minute/moment/second라고 해도 좋아요.

A Can you come over here for a second?
B In a minute. I'm on the phone right now.

A 잠깐 이리 좀 와줄래요?
B 잠시만요. 지금 통화 중이에요.

322

곧 갈게요.
I'll be right there.

 상대방이 있는 곳으로 가겠다는 의미. I'll go~가 아니라 be동사를 써요! 같은 뜻으로 I'm on my way.도 알아 두세요.

A Aren't you going to join us for lunch?
B I'll be right there, Mom.

A 점심 같이 안 할 거니?
B 곧 갈게요, 엄마.

하루에도 수십 번 쓰는 시간 관련 생생 표현

323

조금만 기다려줘요.
Just give me a second

 → Please wait a little bit longer. 초나 분이나 짧기는 매한가지겠죠. second 대신 minute를 써도 OK!

A Aren't you finished uploading that database?
B Just give me a second, and I'll be through.
upload 전송하다   be through 끝나다(finish)

A 데이터 전송을 다 안 했어요?
B 조금만 더 기다리면 끝납니다.

324

잠시 기다리세요.
Just hold on

 → Hang on a moment/second. 전화 통화에도 자주 쓰죠. Hold on, please.

A I need you in my office right away.
B I'm coming. Just hold on.
I'm coming. (상대방이 있는 곳으로) 갑니다.

A 당장 내 사무실로 오세요.
B 갑니다. 잠시만 기다리세요.

325

어느새
Before you know it

 → It'll be done before you're even aware of it. 문득 시간이 '휙' 지나갔다고 느낄 때 쓰세요.

A The weather sure is getting cooler.
B Right. Before you know it, summer will be over.
get cooler/warmer 더 선선해/따뜻해지다

A 날씨기 정말 선선해지네요.
B 그래요. 어느새 여름이 가버리겠죠.

시간이 좀 걸릴 때 하는 말

Long Periods of Time

- I'm going to be a while.
- Check back later
- Not anytime soon
- Who can tell?
- It'll take some time.

326
시간이 좀 걸려요.
I'm going to be a while.

 → If you're in a hurry, don't wait for me. 상대방이 급한듯 물어 볼 때 기다리지 말라고 암시를 주는 말.

A Are you going to be long in the shower?
B I'm going to be a while. Sorry.

be long/ be a while 오래/한동안 걸리다

A 샤워하는 데 오래 걸려요?
B 좀 걸릴 겁니다. 미안해요.

327
나중에 오세요.
Check back later

 → You need to contact me later. 옷을 찾으러 갔는데 아직 세탁이 안 되었다면 주인은 이렇게 말합니다. 이와 비슷한 상황에서 다 써요.

A When will my car be repaired?
B We're still going over it right now. Check back later.

be repaired/fixed 수리가 되다   go over 검사하다

A 언제 내 차가 수리되나요?
B 아직 검사 중이니, 나중에 오세요.

328
당장은 안 돼요.
Not anytime soon

 → You've got to wait for a while. 언제가 될지는 모르지만 지금 당장은 곤란하다는 뜻.

A When are you going on your next vacation?
B Not anytime soon, though I could certainly use one!

though 비록 ~이지만

A 다음 휴가는 언제 갈 건가요?
B 당장은 안 돼요. 가긴 가야 하는데!

329
누가 알겠어요?
Who can tell?

 → Nobody knows! 예측하기 힘든 상황에 대해 냉소적으로 한마디 툭 던질 때 써요.

A How long do you think this traffic jam will last?
B Who can tell? Rush hour in Seoul is always like this.

How long~ last? ~이 얼마나 지속될까요?

A 이 교통체증이 언제쯤 풀릴까요?
B 누가 알겠어요? 서울의 출퇴근 시간대는 항상 이래요.

330
한참 걸립니다.
It'll take some time.

 → Allow us enough time for it. 급히 할 수 있는 일이 아니라고 말할 때 써요.

A When will I know my test results?
B It'll take some time. I'd estimate 4 weeks, minimum.

estimate 어림잡다, 짐작하다

A 테스트 결과를 언제 알 수 있나요?
B 한참 걸립니다. 최소한 4주는 잡아야죠.

시도 때도 없이 일어나는 일들

Frequently/Continuously

☐ Night and day ☐ 24/7 ☐ Day in, day out
☐ Around the clock ☐ Every minute!

331

밤낮이 따로 없죠.
Night and day

→ It happens 24 hours a day, continuously. 끊임없이 지속되는 상황에 써요.

A Is your baby really that noisy?
B You bet! Night and day he seems to cry!

noisy 시끄러운, 소란한   **that** (부사) 그렇게도

A 아기가 그렇게 보채요?
B 말 마세요! 밤낮으로 운답니다!

332

하루 24시간, 일주일 내내
24/7

→ Twenty four hours a day, seven days a week. 한국말로는 '일년 열두 달' 이라고 하던가요?

A What's your biggest concern nowadays?
B Getting a job! I seem to worry about that 24/7.

one's biggest concern 최대 관심사

A 요즘 최대 관심사는 뭔가요?
B 취직이죠! 하루 24시간, 일주일 내내, 그 걱정 뿐입니다.

하루에도 수십 번 쓰는 시간 관련 생생 표현

333
날이 새나 지나
Day in, day out

 → **All day, every day** 눈만 뜨면 하는 일(daily routine)이 똑같아 권태감을 느낄 때 툭 던지는 말.

- A Why do you say your life's so boring?
- B Because I do the same thing day in, day out.

- A 왜 인생이 지루하다고 말하는 거죠?
- B 매일같이 똑같은 일을 하니까요.

334
24시간 내내
Around the clock

 → **Continuously, each hour** 시침이 한 바퀴 돌듯이 끊어짐없이 지속된다는 뜻.

- A Do you have staff here for the night shift?
- B We sure do. We keep workers here around the clock.

night shift 야간 근무

- A 야간 근무 직원도 있나요?
- B 그럼요, 이곳은 24시간 근무하게 되어 있지요.

335
1분도 눈을 못 떼요!
Every minute!

 → **I keep doing it all the time.** 분, 초까지도 지속된다는 것을 강조한 말. 매순간 그대 생각 뿐이라오! — I think about you every minute, darling!

- A Are you watching the stock market again?
- B Every minute! It's always changing.

- A 또 증권 시황을 보고 있군요?
- B 1분도 눈을 못 떼요! 항상 변하거든요.

어쩌다 있는 일들

Infrequently

- [ ] Off and on
- [ ] Once in a blue moon
- [ ] Not in ages
- [ ] Every once in a while
- [ ] Once in a lifetime

336

하다 말다 해요.
Off and on

→ **It sometimes occurs, sometimes does not.** 불규칙하게 일어나는 상황에 써요. on and off로 바꿔 말해도 좋아요.

A Do you exercise sometimes?
B Off and on, though I know I should do it a lot more.

a lot more 훨씬 더 많이/자주

A 가끔 운동을 하세요?
B 하다 말다 해요. 더 자주 해야 할 텐데.

337

가뭄에 콩 나듯 하죠.
Once in a blue moon

→ **Very rarely, "as often as one sees a blue moon"** '푸른 달'을 볼 확률이 얼마나 될까요? 그렇게 드물다는 뜻.

A Do you and your husband still go out to movies?
B Once in a blue moon. I wish we did it more often.

go out to movies/ go to the movies 영화 보러 가다

A 남편과 여전히 영화관람하세요?
B 가뭄에 콩 나듯이요. 좀 자주 갔으면 좋겠어요.

338

한동안 못했죠.
Not in ages

 오랫동안 하지 못했던 일이나 행동을 꼬집어 말할 때 써요.

A Haven't you been to a bowling alley?
B Not in ages. After I got married, I gave stuff like that up!

stuff like that 그런 것 eg. Do you carry stuff like this?(이런 것도 파나요?)

A 볼링장에 가 본 적 없어요?
B 한동안 못 갔죠. 결혼 후엔 그런 건 포기했어요.

339

어쩌다가 한 번이요.
Every once in a while

 Sometimes but not too often 아주 가끔씩 일어나는 일에 써요. every는 생략가능 합니다.

A Do you visit your in-laws a lot?
B Every once in a while. I'm just too busy to do that.

A 처가엔 자주 가세요?
B 어쩌다가 한 번이요. 바빠서 갈 시간이 없어요.

340

일생에 단 한 번
Once in a lifetime

 It's only likely to happen once in your lifetime. 놓치기 아까운 절호의 기회를 표현할 때 써요.

A Take it! It's a once in a lifetime opportunity!
B Maybe, but I'm still not convinced.

still not convinced 확신이 가지 않다

A 수락해! 일생에 단 한 번 오는 기회야!
B 글쎄, 아직 확신이 서지 않아요.

시작을 알리는 쉬운 말

Starting Times
- [ ] It's time.   - [ ] We're on.   - [ ] Time to get going
- [ ] Just about now   - [ ] Just this instant

341
시간 됐어요.
It's time.

→ This is the proper time to start something. 한국말과 거의 같죠! '~할 시간이다' 라고 덧붙이려면 'to+동사' 를 끼워 넣으세요. It's time to say goodbye.

A It's about 2:35, Mrs. Durden.
B It's time, then. Let's start the meeting.

A 더든 여사님, 2시 35분입니다.
B 시간 됐군요. 회의를 시작합시다.

342
곧 시작됩니다.
We're on.

→ "on" means "the start of an activity or performance" 행동 개시가 곧 이루어질 때 써요.

A I'd like to get a few more things for this.
B There's no time. We're on now.

A 여기에 몇 가지를 더 넣고 싶은데.
B 시간이 없어요. 곧 시작됩니다.

하루에도 수십 번 쓰는 시간 관련 생생 표현

343

출발할 시간입니다.
Time to get going

 구어체에서는 start의 의미로 get going을 자주 사용해요.

 A The concert starts at 8:30.
B It's 7:15 now. That means it's time to get going.

That means~ 그렇다면 ~하다 eg. That means he's innocent.

 A 음악회는 8시 반에 시작합니다.
B 지금 7시 15분이니까, 출발해야 할 시간이군.

344

지금쯤이요.
Just about now

 대략 '지금쯤 되겠다' 싶을 때 써요. 음식이 언제 나올까요? — Just about now.

 A When should we call Mr. Johnson in New York?
B Just about now. It's 11:30 p.m. in Tokyo, which means it's about 9:30 a.m.

 A 뉴욕의 존슨 씨에게 언제 전화할까요?
B 지금쯤. 도쿄가 오후 11시 30분이니까 거긴 오전 9시 30분 되겠네.

345

지금 막
Just this instant

 this instant는 '지금, 이 순간'이란 뜻. just this instant도 자주 사용해 보세요.

 A Is Dr. Kim in from Los Angeles?
B Yes, he arrived just this instant. He's waiting for you.

 A LA에서 김 박사님이 오셨나요?
B 예, 방금 도착하셔서, 기다리고 계세요.

종료 · 마감을 알리는 쉬운 말

Ending Times

- [ ] Time's up.   [ ] We're out of time.   [ ] That's a wrap.
- [ ] Let's call it a day.   [ ] Beat the clock

346
시간이 다 됐습니다.
Time's up.

→ "Time Over"라고 하지 않도록 주의하세요!

A Can't I have a few more minutes, professor?
B No, time's up! Hand in your paper.

hand in 제출하다(submit)

A 교수님, 몇 분 더 주실 수 없나요?
B 안 돼, 시간 다 됐으니 답안지를 제출해요.

347
시간이 없습니다.
We're out of time.

→ We're running out of time, 또는 Time's running out.도 자주 쓰죠. 부족한 시간이 안타까울 때 이렇게 한마디!

A Do you want to continue the negotiations?
B No, we're out of time. We'd better purchase now.

continue 계속하다   **purchase** 구입하다

A 협상을 계속 할 건가요?
B 아뇨, 시간이 없어요. 지금 구입하는 게 낫겠어요.

348
그걸로 마쳐요.
That's a wrap.

 → Let's wrap things up now. wrap은 명사와 동사로 모두 쓰여요. 깔끔히 포장하듯 마무리하자는 뜻.

A I think we all agree with the plan.
B Okay, that's a wrap, then. Let's put it into effect.
put~ into effect 실시하다, 실행하다(carry out)

A 모두가 계획에 찬성하는 것 같아요.
B 좋아요, 이만 마치고, 실행에 옮깁시다.

349
오늘은 이만 합시다.
Let's call it a day.

 → "call it a day" means "end work activities for the day" 하루 마감을 알리는 말이죠.

A We've been working here since 6:00 a.m. and it's almost midnight!
B Right, let's call it a day.

A 오전 6시부터 일했는데, 벌써 자정이네!
B 자, 그럼 오늘은 그만하죠.

350
제한 시간에 끝내요.
Beat the clock

 → Work against the clock. 시간과 한판 붙어 이기려면 엄청난 집중력이 필요하겠죠!

A Remember that you have a time limit!
B Sure! I can beat the clock.
remember that ~를 명심하다   beat 물리치다, 이기다

A 시간 제한이 있다는 것을 명심해요!
B 예! 제한 시간에 끝낼 수 있어요.

CHAPTER 11

Possibilities and Impossibilities

Is this the company bowling team? It sure is. Want in? I'd like to join the school French Club here. You hopping me out. Why don't you join our research group? I'm a solo act, sorry. You're leaving our department? Yeah, from now on you're on your own. company bowling team? It sure is. Want in? Isn't this the local parents' group? It is. You signing up? We need more parents. This is th You hopping on? How long have you studied French? Can I come to your party this Friday? Of course! The more, the merrier. Aren't You're leaving our department? Yeah, from now on you're on your own. Why didn't you help carry our bags? Every man for himself; I

Coffee: the secret fuel of every high-performance woman on the American East Coast.

Possibilities and Impossibilities

가능한 일·
불가능한 일에 쓰는
생생 표현

351 > 385

부탁을 쉽게 들어줄 때 하는 말

Ease

- [ ] No problem!
- [ ] Simple!
- [ ] Consider it done
- [ ] Be my guest
- [ ] Easy as pie

351

문제 없어요! 별것도 아닌데요!
No problem!

→ No trouble at all! I'm happy to help you anytime.

A Thanks for the ride.
B No problem! Let me know if you need me.

A 태워줘서 고마워요.
B 별것도 아닌데요! 필요하면 말해요.

352

간단해요!
Simple!

→ It's easy to do or understand. 반대로 보기보다 쉽지 않을 때는 It's not that simple. 또는 Not as simple as that으로 말해요.

A How did you graduate from college in only 3 years?
B I took more classes per semester. Simple!

A 대학은 어떻게 3년 만에 졸업했어요?
B 학기마다 더 많은 수업을 들었어요. 간단하죠!

353
바로 해줄게요.
Consider it done

 → I'll do it immediately. 이미 한 것이나 진배없다는 말.

A Would you bring me a carton of milk from the store?
B Okay, consider it done!

A 가게에서 우유 한 팩 사다줄래요?
B 예, 바로 사다줄게요!

354
그러세요.
Be my guest

 → Please, go right ahead. You can do as you please.

A Could I try out your new motorbike?
B Be my guest.

A 새로 산 당신 오토바이를 탈 수 있나요?
B 그러세요.

355
식은 죽 먹기죠.
Easy as pie

 → It's as simple as eating a pie. Piece of cake도 많이 쓰죠.

A Wasn't it hard to learn Chinese?
B At first, but after a while it was easy as pie.

at first 처음에는(at the beginning)

A 중국어는 배우기 어렵지 않나요?
B 처음엔 그렇지만 좀 지나면 아주 쉬워요.

일을 감당하기 어려울 때 하는 말

Difficulty

- [ ] That'll take some doing. [ ] No small matter. [ ] Not without some work.
- [ ] That's a tall order. [ ] That's/That'd be pushing it.

356

좀 힘들 것 같아요.
That'll take some doing.

→ I need a hard effort to do that. 노력은 해보겠지만, 장담하기 어렵다는 말.

A Can you get the job done by tomorrow?
B That'll take some doing. I'm short of my staff.

be short of ~이 부족하다

A 내일까지 일을 끝낼 수 있어요?
B 좀 힘들 것 같아요. 일손이 부족해요.

357

그리 간단치 않아요.
No small matter

→ The issue is not that easy. It's rather complicated.

A I need you to get all the contracts reviewed before lunch.
B I'll try, but that's no small matter.

need~ to do ~에게 …하도록 당부하다

A 점심 전까지 모든 계약서를 검토하세요.
B 해보겠지만, 그리 간단치 않아요.

358

엄청 어렵습니다.
Not without some work

 → It's a very tough job. some은 a lot of의 뜻.

A You'll be able to bring us the case?
B Well, not without some work.

A 우리가 사건을 맡게 해줄 수 있겠죠?
B 글쎄요, 엄청 어렵겠는데요.

359

그건 힘들어요.
That's a tall order.

 → It's a difficult order to carry out. 여기서 tall은 '감당하기 힘든(demanding), 어려운(difficult)' 이란 뜻이에요.

A Get everything ready for the party by noon.
B That's a tall order. It's already 11:30.

A 정오까지 파티 준비를 끝내요.
B 그건 힘듭니다. 벌써 11시 30분인데요.

360

턱도 없어요.
That's/That'd be pushing it.

 → 감당하기 너무 힘든 일에 대해 푸념처럼 내뱉는 말.

A We have enough chairs for 120 guests, don't we?
B That's pushing it. We have enough for 80 or so.

or so 정도, 대략 eg. We raised 2 million dollars or so for charity.

A 120명이 앉을 좌석이 충분하죠?
B 턱도 없어요. 80석 정도 있는걸요.

절대로 있을 수 없는 일이 생기면

Impossibility

☐ When pigs fly!   ☐ Can't be done   ☐ No way Jose!
☐ Not on your life!   ☐ Not a chance!

361

천지가 개벽하면 모를까!
When pigs fly!

→ **No way!** 돼지가 날다니… '말도 안 된다'는 뜻.

A You're going to win the lottery this time!
B When pigs fly! I never buy a lottery ticket.

A 이번엔 당신이 복권에 당첨될 거야!
B 말도 안 돼! 복권 같은 것은 절대 안 사.

362

불가능해요.
Can't be done

→ **It's not possible.** 상대에게 바로 'NO' 할 때 써요.

A We need to buy a bigger house in a year.
B Can't be done, honey. We can't afford that.

can't afford (경제적으로) 여유가 없다

A 1년 안에 더 큰 집을 사야겠어.
B 불가능해요, 여보. 돈이 없잖아요.

가능한 일 · 불가능한 일에 쓰는 생생 표현

Chapter 11

363
안 돼!
No way Jose!

 Jose는 No Way와 운을 맞춰 Ho-say라고 발음해요.

A I'll pay for the taxi.
B No way Jose! I'll pay this time.

A 택시비는 내가 내지.
B 안 돼! 이번엔 내가 낼게.

364
그런 일은 결코 없을 거야!
Not on your life!

 일생을 걸어도 안 된다니… '똥고집'에 박수를!

A Are you going to the ballet tonight?
B Not on your life! Such a boring thing!

A 오늘밤 발레 보러 갈 건가요?
B 그런 일은 결코 없지! 그렇게 따분한 걸!

365
가능성 제로야!
Not a chance!

A Will Japan win the soccer game this time?
B Not a chance! We're gonna give them a real beating!

give~ a real/thorough beating ~를 대패/완패시키다

A 이번 축구에서 일본이 이길까?
B 가능성 제로야! 우리가 화끈하게 이길 거야!

가능성을 딱히 장담하지 못할 때

Uncertain Possibility
- [ ] Could be
- [ ] Difficult to say
- [ ] It's a toss-up.
- [ ] I give it 50-50.
- [ ] No way to tell

366

아마도 그럴 겁니다.
Could be

→ I'm not so sure, but it's likely to happen.

A Is Sally going to quit after her marriage?
B Could be. I heard her fiance is very rich.

A 샐리가 결혼하면 일을 그만둘까요?
B 아마도 그렇겠죠. 약혼자가 아주 부자래요.

367

확실치 않아요.
Difficult to say

→ It's not easy to know about that now.

A Do you think he's still alive?
B Difficult to say. They're still searching for him.

search for 찾다, 수색하다   eg. The police is searching for her body.

A 그가 아직 살아 있을까요?
B 확실치 않아요. 아직 수색 중이니까요.

368

확률은 절반이야.
It's a toss-up.

 동전을 던져 앞면(head)과 뒷면(tail)이 나올 확률은 절반이죠.

A Is it going to snow today?
B It's a toss-up. Pretty cold, but no clouds.

A 오늘 눈이 올까요?
B 확률이 반반이야. 춥긴 한데 구름이 없으니.

369

50대 50이야. 반반이야.
I give it 50-50.

 그냥 Fifty-fifty, 라고도 해요.

A Is Warren going to show up for cocktails tonight?
B I give it 50-50.

show up (모습을) 드러내다, 나타나다

A 워렌이 오늘밤 칵테일 파티에 올까?
B 난 50대 50이라고 봐.

370

가늠하기 힘들어요.
No way to tell

 There's no way to know right now.

A Can't we hire a secretary anytime soon?
B No way to tell. No one seems suitable.

anytime soon 곧, 언제라도   suitable 적당한

A 비서가 곧 뽑히지 않겠어요?
B 예측이 쉽지 않아요. 적격자가 아직 없으니.

일의 성사를 고무시키는 말

Making it Possible

- [ ] I'll find a way.
- [ ] One way or another
- [ ] Make it happen
- [ ] Bring it to life
- [ ] Make it a reality

371

방법을 찾아 볼게요.
I'll find a way.

→ I can manage to do that one way or another.

A Can you get all these loaded on the truck?
B Don't worry. I'll find a way.

get (things) loaded (물건을) 싣다

A 이걸 모두 트럭에 실을 수 있어요?
B 걱정 마요. 방법을 찾아볼게요.

372

어떻게 해서든
One way or another

→ 뭔가 가능한 방안을 백방으로 찾아서 일이 되도록 하겠다는 뜻.

A You really plan on buying that piece of land?
B That's right: one way or another!

plan on ~를 계획하다

A 그 땅을 사겠다는 건가요?
B 그럼요. 어떻게 해서든!

373
해내겠습니다.
Make it happen

 → I'll succeed no matter what. 꼭 성공시키겠다는 의지 표명!

A I need you to increase our sales this year.
B We'll make it happen.

A 올해 매출 증대를 이루어야 하네.
B 해내겠습니다.

374
생생히 살려내게.
Bring it to life

 → 아무리 좋은 기획도 실행에 옮기지 못하면 '죽은' 것. 생생히 '실현한다'는 의미예요.

A This is an excellent plan!
B We'll need to bring it to life now.

A 훌륭한 기획이야!
B 이제 그걸 생생히 살려내야죠.

375
실현 시키도록 해요.
Make it a reality

 → Let's make a plan or goal into a reality. 현실로 만들어보란 뜻.

A This is an almost impossible goal!
B Regardless, we have to make it a reality.
regardless 그럼에도 불구하고

A 이건 거의 불가능한 목표예요!
B 그럼에도 불구하고, 실현 가능하게 해야지.

방안을 모색할 때 흔히 쓰는 말

Finding Solutions

☐ Is that doable? / Can that be done? ☐ I'll look into it. ☐ See if it can be done
☐ Let's put something together. ☐ Come up with something

376
그게 가능하겠어요?
Is that doable? / Can that be done?

 → Is that possible to do? 현실적으로 가능한지 묻는 말.

  A We'll kick off the marketing campaign soon.
  B Is that doable? We haven't decided a theme yet.

  A 곧 홍보 마케팅이 시작될겁니다.
  B 그게 가능하겠어요? 1주일밖에 안 남았는데요.

377
(방안을) 찾아볼게요.
I'll look into it.

 → I'll investigate/search/review it.

  A Would it be possible to change the color of it?
  B I'll look into it, and let you know.
  Would it be possible to do ~이 가능하겠습니까?

  A 그 색깔을 바꿀 수 있습니까?
  B 방안을 찾아보고, 알려드릴게요.

188

378

가능한지 알아보죠.
See if it can be done

 I'll see if it can be done. 여기서 see는 check의 뜻.

A Would it be possible to move in next week?
B I'll see if it can be done.

A 다음주에 이사할 수 있을까요?
B 가능한지 알아보죠.

379

함께 머리를 짜봅시다.
Let's put something together.

 여럿이 생각을 모아 베스트 방안을 마련하자는 말이죠.

A We've got to do something to rescue her!
B Let's put something together.

rescue 구하다 eg. Please tell me who rescued me from the fire.

A 그녀를 구하기 위해 뭔가를 해야죠!
B 함께 머리를 짜봅시다.

380

뭔가 안을 내봐요.
Come up with something

 come up with는 think of와 같은 뜻.

A How can we fit all of these into the car?
B Come up with something. There must be a way.

fit~ into ~을 …에 맞추다(넣다)

A 어떻게 이걸 다 차에 넣죠?
B 뭔가 방안을 내봐요. 방법이 있을 테니까요.

장애물에 걸려 푸념하고 싶다면

Obstacles

- [ ] It's standing in the way.
- [ ] We've hit a wall.
- [ ] We can't get around
- [ ] It's blocking the way.
- [ ] It won't let us.

381

그게 방해 요인이죠.
It's standing in the way.

→ 주어 자리(It)에 '방해 요인'을 넣어 말해요.

A Shouldn't we be investing more in R&D?
B But our small budget is standing in the way.

invest 투자하다 stand in the way 방해(저지)하다

A 연구개발에 더 투자해야 하지 않나요?
B 그렇긴 하지만, 저 예산이 문제인거죠.

382

벽에 부딪혔어요.
We've hit a wall.

→ We can move no further. 더 이상 진전이 없다는 말.

A How're things going on your team project?
B I think we've hit a wall.

A 팀 프로젝트는 어떻게 돼가요?
B 벽에 부딪혔어요.

383

~을 피할 수 없습니다.
We can't get around

 → We can't avoid that. We can't deal with it successfully. get around 는 장애요인을 잘 '해결하다'는 뜻. 여기선 can't가 있으니 반대 의미죠.

A What's the worst thing about winter here?
B We can't get around snow during that season.
the worst thing about ~에 대한 최대 단점

A 이곳 겨울의 최대 단점은 뭐예요?
B 그 동안 눈을 피할 수 없다는거죠.

384

그게 길을 막고 있어요.
It's blocking the way.

A Why haven't you closed the deal yet?
B Our disagreement on price is blocking the way.
close the deal 협상/계약을 끝내다 block 막다

A 왜 아직도 계약 마무리가 안 됐어요?
B 가격 견해차가 길을 막고 있어요.

385

그것 때문에 못해요.
(It) won't let us.

 → 여기서 let은 allow의 뜻.

A Don't you and your wife go out for dinner sometimes?
B Rarely! Children won't let us.
go out for 외식하다(dine out) rarely 좀처럼 ~않다 eg. I rarely see my ex-boyfriend.

A 아내와 가끔 외식을 하세요?
B 거의 못해요! 애들 때문에 못해요.

CHAPTER 12

Trust and Reliance

Is this the company bowling team? It sure is. Want in? Isn't this the local parents' group? I'd like to join the school French Club here. You hopping on? How long have you studied Why don't you join our research group? I'm a solo act, sorry. You're leaving our depa jumping ship. I got a better offer. Is this the company bowling team? It sure is. Want in? Isn't this the local parents' group? It is. You si You hopping on? How long have you studied French? Can I come to your party this Friday? Of course! The more, the merrier. Aren't y You're leaving our department? Yeah, from now on you're on your own. Why didn't you help carry our bags? Every man for himself; I've

Susan Says...

If something goes badly, forget about it; something better will come along later.

Trust and Reliance

믿고 의지하는 사회 생활을 위한
생생 표현

386 › 420

믿음을 주는 쉽고 좋은 말

Trust

- [ ] Take me at my word
- [ ] Count on me
- [ ] I'm your man.
- [ ] Without fail
- [ ] I won't let you down.

386

내 말을 믿어줘요.
Take me at my word

→ Take my words to be true. 라고 해도 되죠.

A Are you sure you got in before midnight last night?
B Yes, mom. Please take me at my word.

Are you sure~? ~이 확실해요?

A 어젯밤 자정 전에 들어 온 게 맞니?
B 예, 엄마. 내 말을 믿어줘요.

387

날 믿어.
Count on me

→ You can trust me. 기댈 수 있고(rely on) 믿을 만한(count on) 사람이 필요해요!

A You can give a speech at the wedding?
B Count on me! I'll be sure to do a good job.

be sure to do 틀림없이 ~하다

A 결혼식 사회를 볼 수 있죠?
B 날 믿어요! 잘 해낼 테니.

388
(당신은) 나만 믿어요.
I'm your man.

 → I'm the one that you can rely on completely.

A Have these files sorted by noon, please.
B I'm your man. It'll be done by that time.

sort 분류하다 by ~까지

A 이 파일들을 정오까지 분류해 놓으세요.
B 저만 믿으세요. 그때까지 해놓겠습니다.

389
실수 없이
Without fail

 → 실수 없이 '반드시' 해야 할 것, 또는 규칙적인 운동처럼 '늘' 하는 일에 써요.

A Is the last bus to Philadelphia at 11:15?
B Yes, so be at the terminal by 11:00, without fail.

A LA행 막차 시간이 11시 15분인가요?
B 예, 11시까지는 꼭 터미널에 도착하세요.

390
실망시키지 않을게요.
I won't let you down.

 → I won't disappoint you. So don't worry and be happy!

A I want you to make a good impression on him.
B I won't let you down, mom.

make a good impression on ~에게 좋은 인상을 주다

A 그에게 좋은 인상을 주도록 해라.
B 실망시키지 않을게요, 엄마.

충성심을 보여주는 든든한 말

Loyalty

☐ I'm with you all the way.   ☐ I'll back you up.   ☐ I'm behind you 100%.
☐ Your wish is my command!   ☐ Whatever you need

391

끝까지 함께 남겠습니다.
I'm with you all the way.

 → I'm with you to the very end of a task/assignment/goal.

A Are you going to support me?
B Naturally! I'm with you all the way.

naturally 당연히   all the way 항상, 늘

A 나를 지지해 줄거죠?
B 그럼요! 끝까지 함께 남겠습니다.

392

도와드릴게요.
I'll back you up.

 → I'll support/help you. 입장을 지지하거나 도와줄 때 써요.

A Can anyone operate the slides for me?
B I'll back you up, Ms. Porter.

A 누가 슬라이드 작동 좀 해줄래요?
B 제가 도와드리죠, 포터 씨.

393

100% 지지합니다.
I'm behind you 100%.

 → I'm supporting you completely.

A Have you seen my proposals, Ms. West?
B I reviewed them, and I'm behind you 100%.

A 웨스트 씨, 제 제안서 보셨나요?
B 검토했어요, 100% 지지해줄게요.

394

받들어 모시죠!
Your wish is my command!

 → 상관의 명령을 '받들듯' 잘 따르겠다는 위트가 담긴 표현!

A Can you bring me a bottle of beer?
B Yepp! Your wish is my command.

A 맥주 한 병 갖다줄래요?
B 옙! 받들어 모시죠.

395

필요하시면 뭐든지요.
Whatever you need

 → I'm happy to do whatever you need/want.

A I may have a lot of demands on you.
B Whatever you need, sir. I'm here to serve.

demand on ~에 대한 요구[청] 사항

A 내가 요구하는 일이 많을 겁니다.
B 필요하시면 뭐든지요, 사장님. 절 부르세요.

자신 있을 때 툭 던지는 말

Confidence
☐ Count on it ☐ No doubt ☐ It's a sure bet.
☐ I'd bet my life. ☐ Sure as anything!

396

확실합니다.
Count on it

 → It's a certainty. I'm sure about that completely.

A Lisa's going to get promoted this time?
B Count on it. Everybody knows that.
get promoted 승진하다

A 리사는 이번에 승진하겠죠?
B 확실해요. 다들 아는데요.

397

분명해요.
No doubt

 → 의심의 여지없이 말 그대로 '사실'임을 강조할 때 써요.

A Are you sure everyone's read the memo?
B No doubt! I put them on all the desks myself.
myself 내가 직접 eg. I'll read it myself.

A 확실히 모두가 메모를 읽었나요?
B 분명해요! 내가 직접 모든 책상 위에 올려놓았어요.

398
장담합니다.
It's a sure bet.

 → I'm absolutely sure about that. You won't fail!

　A There'll be a place to park downtown today?
　　　　B It's a sure bet. It's a holiday.

a place to park 주차공간(parking space)

　A 오늘은 시내에 주차공간이 있겠지?
　　　　B 장담해요. 휴일인데요.

399
맹세코 그래요.
I'd bet my life.

 → 하나뿐인 생명을 걸 정도로 '확실한' 일에 써요.

　A You think Jack's surfing the Internet again?
　　　　B I'd bet my life. He's always doing that at the office instead of working.

surf the Internet 인터넷 검색을 하다

　A 잭이 또 인터넷 검색 중이란 말이지?
　　　　B 맹세코 그렇다니까요. 사무실에서 일은 않고 항상 그것만 해요.

400
그렇고 말고요!
Sure as anything!

 → Absolutely!와 같은 뜻. 강조할 때 써요.

　A Is Mr. Bobson going to retire today?
　　　　B Sure as anything! I've just heard from his secretary.

retire 은퇴하다, 물러나다

　A 봅슨 씨가 오늘 물러난다고?
　　　　B 그렇고 말고요! 그의 비서한테 방금 들었어요.

오랜 우정을 전하는 친근한 말

Established Relationships

- [ ] We're old buddies.
- [ ] We've gone the distance.
- [ ] We go back a long way.
- [ ] We met way back.
- [ ] We're like brothers/sisters.

401

죽마고우예요.
We're old buddies.

 → Old pal/friend/bosom buddy 원어민들이 가장 자주 쓰는 말.

A How do you know Mr. Meister? You two seem very familiar.
B We're old buddies. We met in college.

A 마이스터 씨는 어떻게 알아요? 두 분이 잘 아는 사이 같아요.
B 죽마고우예요. 대학에서 만났죠.

402

함께 겪은 일이 많죠.
We've gone the distance.

 → 함께 먼 길을 가면서 이런 저런 일을 겪다 보면 자연히 친해지겠죠!

A You and Alvin served together in the army?
B Yeah, we've gone the distance.

serve in the army 군 복무하다

A 앨빈과 군 복무 같이 했죠?
B 예, 함께 겪은 일이 많죠.

403

왕년부터 아는 사이죠.
We go back a long way.

 → We've known each other for a long time. a long way는 for a long time 의 뜻.

A You and Blair grew up in the same town?
B That's right. We go back a long way.

grow up 자라다

A 블레어와 같은 고향에서 자랐어요?
B 그래요. 왕년부터 아는 사이죠.

404

예전에 만났어요.
We met way back.

 → We met a long time ago.

A Tim seems to know almost everything about you!
B We met way back. He lived on my block.

know everything about ~에 대해 속속들이 알다

A 팀은 너에 대해 모르는 게 거의 없어!
B 예전에 만났으니까. 우린 같은 동네에 살았어.

405

친형제/자매 같죠.
We're like brothers/sisters.

 → 가족처럼 허물없이 지내는 사이란 말이에요.

A You're always hanging out with Jim. Why's that?
B We're like brothers.

hang out with ~와 어울리다

A 늘 짐과 붙어 다니죠. 왜 그래요?
B 친형제 같은 사이니까요.

믿을 수 있는 사람과 정보가 필요해!

Reliance

- [ ] You can lean on me.
- [ ] It's a reliable source.
- [ ] Only you can!
- [ ] I'll come through.
- [ ] Trust no one but myself

406

날 의지하세요.
You can lean on me.

힘들고 지칠 때 기댈 수 있고 도움을 주는 사람! Depend/Relay on me.도 좋아요.

A I'm too busy with housework nowadays.
B I'll help you out, honey. You can lean on me.

help out (시간을 따로 내서) 도와주다

A 난 요즘 집안일로 너무 바빠요.
B 여보, 내가 도와줄게. 날 의지해요.

407

믿을 만한 자료예요.
It's a reliable source.

권위있는 곳에서 나온 정보로 믿을 수 있다(trustworthy)는 말.

A Do you think we can rely on this information?
B It's a reliable source written by a top official.

source 근거 자료   top official 고위관리

A 이 정보를 믿어도 될까요?
B 고위관리가 작성한 믿을 만한 자료예요.

믿고 의지하는 사회생활을 위한 생생 표현

Chapter 12

408
당신만이 할 수 있어요!
Only you can!

 참여를 촉구할 때 자주 써요.

A Only you can! A dollar help saves hundreds of animals.
B Here you go. Keep up with a good job.

hundreds of 수백만의, 수많은

A 당신만이 할 수 있어요! 1달러로 수많은 동물을 구할 수 있어요.
B 여기요. 수고하세요.

409
내가 해낼 겁니다.
I'll come through.

 You can rely on me. I'll succeed no matter what!

A This is a very risky job. Can you handle it?
B Of course! I'll come through.

A 아주 위험한 일인데, 해낼 수 있겠소?
B 그럼요! 해낼 겁니다.

410
의지할 건 자신 뿐이죠.
Trust no one but myself

 험한 세상에 '청산천하 유아독존' 하겠다고요? 여기서 but은 except(~을 제외하고)의 뜻

A You don't seem to trust anybody, Harry.
B Why should I? Trust no one but myself!

A 해리, 넌 아무도 믿지 않지?
B 왜 믿어야 해? 의지할 건 나 뿐이야!

팀워크를 고취시키는 쉽고 좋은 말

Team Spirit

- [ ] We're in this together.
- [ ] Everyone's onboard.
- [ ] Everyone pitched in.
- [ ] We're in the same boat.
- [ ] Let's put our heads together.

411

동참합니다.
We're in this together.

 → We're sharing the same difficulties.

A I'm sorry I'm not contributing much.
B That's OK. We're in this together.

contribute 기여하다, 도움이 되다

A 난 별로 도움이 못 돼요.
B 괜찮아요. 우리가 동참할 거니까.

412

모두 동의합니다.
Everyone's onboard.

 → Everyone agrees. '배에 승선했다(onboard)'는 것은 항해 중에 닥칠지도 모를 재난까지도 암묵적으로 동의한다는 뜻!

A No one's disagreed with the policy change?
B No, everyone's onboard.

A 바뀐 규정에 반대하는 사람 없죠?
B 없어요. 모두가 동의합니다.

413
모두가 십시일반했죠.
Everyone pitched in.

 → Everyone contributes/assists. pitch in은 조금씩 '보태어 돕다'는 뜻.

A Did you buy that gift for Jim?
B No, everyone pitched in money from around the office.

A 당신이 짐 선물을 샀나요?
B 아뇨, 사무실 직원 모두가 십시일반했어요.

414
한 배를 탄 거야.
We're in the same boat.

 → We share the same risk.

A This is my first time giving a talk in front of people.
B We'll be with you, so we're in the same boat.

This is my first time ~는 처음이다

A 사람들 앞에서 연설은 처음이에요.
B 우리가 함께 할 거야. 우리도 한 배를 탄 거라고.

415
머리를 모아봅시다.
Let's put our heads together.

 → Let's combine our thoughts. Two heads are better than one.

A I just can't make much sense out of this.
B Okay, let's put our heads together and see if we can't figure it out.

make sense out of ~을 이해하다(understand)

A 도무지 이게 무슨 말인지 모르겠어요.
B 그럼, 함께 머리를 모아서 풀 수 있나 봅시다.

한결같은 마음과 행보를 전하는 말

Steadfastness

- [ ] Like a rock
- [ ] Through thick and thin
- [ ] Come Rain or shine
- [ ] No matter what
- [ ] I'm true-blue.

416

버팀목 같은 사람
Like a rock

→ Strong and enduring, like a rock 버팀목이 되는 사람.

A How would you describe your mother?
B She's been like a rock in my family.

A 어머님은 어떤 분이세요?
B 우리 가족의 버팀목이시죠.

417

좋을 때나 어려울 때나
Through thick and thin

→ thick은 good times를 thin은 bad times를 말해요.

A How long have you known Esther?
B Since middle school. We've gone through thick and thin together.

A 이스터를 안 지 얼마나 돼요?
B 중학교부터요. 좋을 때나 어려울 때나 함께 했죠.

418
비가 오나 개나
Come Rain or shine

 → 한국말과 똑같죠!

A You're going to keep saving for a house?
B Come rain or shine! I'll never give up my dream.
save for ~를 위해 저축하다

A 내집 마련을 위해 저축을 계속하세요?
B 비가 오나 개나! 절대로 꿈을 포기하지 않아요.

419
어떤 일이 있어도
No matter what

 → I don't care what happens.

A You're going to continue holding your stocks?
B No matter what, I'll never sell. I believe they'll rise later on.
hold one's stocks 주식을 계속 보유하다

A 주식을 계속 보유할 건가요?
B 어떤 일이 생겨도, 팔지 않아요. 나중엔 반등할 겁니다.

420
난 골수 팬이죠.
I'm true-blue.

 → I'm loyal to a person/place/organization.

A You still support your hometown team?
B Of course! I'm true-blue to the team.

A 여전히 고향팀을 응원하세요?
B 암요! 고향팀 골수 팬인 걸요.

CHAPTER 13

Requests, Invitations & Denials

Is this the company bowling team? It sure is. Want in? All employees should join. I'd like to join the school Fre[nch club]. Aren't you going to stay with our group? Sorry, you hav[e to]. Why don't you join our research group? I'm a solo act, sorry. You're leaving our department? Yeah, from now on you're on your own. [...] company bowling team? It sure is. Want in? Isn't this the local parents' group? It is. You signing up? We need more parents. This is th[e ...] You hopping on? How long have you studied French? Can I come to your party this Friday? Of course! The more, the merrier. Aren't [...] You're leaving our department? Yeah, from now on you're on your own. Why didn't you help carry our bags? Every man for himself; [...]

Susan Says...

For better or worse, I'm in command of my own life—in every way.

Requests, Invitations & Denials

생활의 기본, 요청·초대·거절을 위한 생생 표현

421 > 455

순간적으로 요청할 게 있다면

Requests for Attention/Help

- [ ] Could you give me a sec?   - [ ] Could you spare a minute?   - [ ] With you in ten
- [ ] I just need five.   - [ ] Just hear me a second

421
잠시만요?
Could you give me a sec?

 → Wait for a second/minute, please.

A I'm on my way out for the day.
B Could you give me a sec? Just a couple of questions.

A 난 퇴근합니다.
B 잠시만요? 몇 가지 질문이 있어요.

422
잠시 기다려주시겠어요?
Could you spare a minute?

 → 원어민들은 wait 대신 spare도 자주 써요.

A Everybody's here? We'll leave right now.
B Could you spare a minute? Joy hasn't been here yet.

A 모두 왔죠? 바로 출발합니다.
B 잠시 기다려주시겠어요? 조이가 아직 안 왔어요.

생활의 기본, 요청·초대·거절을 위한 생생 표현

Chapter
•• 13

423
10분이면 돼요.
With you in ten

 → I'll be with you in ten. I'll be there in 10 minutes.

A Aren't you coming?
B Just need to straighten up my desk. With you in ten.

straighten up 바르게 하다, 정리하다

A 안 오는 거야?
B 책상 정리만 하고요. 10분이면 돼.

424
5분만 더 주세요.
I just need five.

 → I just need 5 minutes more. Another five minutes, please.

A Aren't you done repairing that fax machine?
B I just need five and then I'll be through.

do repairing 수리하다

A 그 팩스 아직도 안 고쳤어요?
B 5분만 더 주면 다 끝나요.

425
잠시만 내 말 들어봐요.
Just hear me a second

 → Please listen to me for just one second.

A My final answer is no.
B Just hear me a second. You might change your mind.

change one's mind 마음이 바뀌다

A 내 대답은 '노' 입니다.
B 잠시만 내 말 들어봐요. 마음이 바뀔지도 몰라요.

엄포를 놓아 지시해야 한다면

Demands/Orders

- [ ] It's not a request.   - [ ] Do as I say.   - [ ] Straight from the top
- [ ] Don't make me repeat it.   - [ ] Is something wrong with your ears?

426

부탁이 아니라 명령이오.
It's not a request.

 → This is an order, not a request.

A Do I really have to get it done by tonight?
B Yes, and it's not a request.

A 정말로 오늘밤에 끝내야 한단 말입니까?
B 그래, 이건 명령이네.

427

내 말대로 하시오.
Do as I say.

 → 가타부타 토를 달지 말고 바로 실행하라는 엄명!

A It doesn't seem fair, sir.
B Do as I say, Jane. I don't have time to argue.
argue 언쟁하다   eg.I don't want to argure with you.

A 사장님, 이건 불공평합니다.
B 내 말대로 해요, 제인. 언쟁할 시간이 없어요.

생활의 기본, 요청 · 초대 · 거절을 위한 생생 표현

Chapter 13

428
상부에서 바로 내려 온
Straight from the top

 → the top은 최고위층(senior managers/executives)을 말해요.

A We have to increase output by 9% this month?
B Yes, that comes straight from the top.

have to do ~해야 한다   increase 증가시키다

A 이달에 생산량을 9%로 증가시키라뇨?
B 그래요, 상부의 지시요.

429
두 번 말하지 않겠소.
Don't make me repeat it.

 → Do as I've just told you.

A So I have to bring him from the airport?
B That's right, by 5:00. Don't make me repeat it.

A 내가 그를 공항에서 데려와야 합니까?
B 그렇소, 5시까지요. 두 번 말하지 않겠소.

430
귀가 먹었소?
Is something wrong with your ears?

 → Didn't you hear my orders clearly?

A Why do we have to work so late tonight?
B Is something wrong with your ears, Mike? I already told you why!

A 왜 오늘 야근을 해야만 하죠?
B 귀가 먹었소, 마이크? 이미 이유를 말했잖소!

단호하게 거절할 때 툭 던지는 말

Refusals (Informal)
- [ ] No can do.
- [ ] Not in this lifetime
- [ ] You're wasting your breath.
- [ ] Read my lips: N-O.
- [ ] N-O spells "no!"

431
안 돼요.
No can do.

→ It's impossible. We cannot do it.

A Can I buy a ticket for the next movie showing?
B No can do. We're all sold out.

A 다음 상연 영화표를 살 수 있나요?
B 안 돼요. 매진됐습니다.

432
죽어도 안 돼! 절대로 없을거요!
Not in this lifetime

 → 내 눈에 흙이 들어와도 할 수 없다! 엄청난 과장이죠?

A How about having dinner with me tonight?
B With a loser like you? Not in this lifetime!

loser 패배자, 별 볼일 없는 자

A 오늘 저녁 같이 할래요?
B 당신 같은 멍청이와? 그런 일은 절대로 없어요!

433

헛수고하지 마요.
You're wasting your breath.

 → I've made up my mind, so you cannot convince me.

A I want to explain a couple of things about this product.
B You're wasting your breath. I'm not interested.

waste one's words/breath 헛수고하다

A 이 제품에 대해 몇가지 설명드리겠습니다.
B 괜히 헛수고하지 마요. 관심 없어요.

434

안 된다고 했습니다.
Read my lips: N-O.

A Isn't there any chance that I can get into this taxi?
B Read my lips: N-O. Catch a different one!

Isn't there any chance~? ~할 수 없겠습니까?

A 이 택시에 탈 수 없겠어요?
B 안 된다고 했죠. 다른 차로 타세요.

435

똑똑히 들어요, '안 돼요!'
N-O spells "no!"

 → 아예 NO의 철자와 의미를 말해주죠. 몹시 귀찮게 할 때 써요.

A Can't I get just one more piece of pie?
B N-O spells "no"! You've already had too much, Tim.

A 파이 한 조각만 더 먹으면 안 돼요?
B 똑똑히 들어, '안 돼!' 너무 많이 먹었잖니, 팀.

공손하게 요청할 때 쓰면 좋은 말

Honorific Requests

- ☐ Sir/Ma'am, could you please
- ☐ I'm sorry, but could you please
- ☐ Forgive me for asking, but could you (please)
- ☐ Could I trouble you to
- ☐ Is there any way you could

436

~ 해주시겠어요?
Sir/Ma'am, could you please

 모르는 사람에게 공손하게 요청할 때 가장 흔히 써요.

A Is there something wrong?
B Sir, could you please move? This seat is already taken.

The/This seat is taken. 정해진 좌석이다.

A 뭐 잘못된 게 있나요?
B 선생님, 자리를 옮겨주시겠어요? 여긴 주인이 있어요.

437

죄송하지만, ~해주시겠어요?
I'm sorry, but could you please

A Did I do anything wrong?
B I'm sorry, but could you please leave your bags at the front desk?

leave 남기다, 맡기다

A 내가 뭘 실수했나요?
B 죄송하지만, 짐을 프론트에 맡겨주시겠어요?

438

말씀드리기 죄송하지만
Forgive me for asking, but could you (please)

A Did you say something to me?
B Forgive me for asking, but could you please turn off your cell phone?

turn off ~을 끄다   eg. Could you turn off the light?

A 뭐라고 하셨나요?
B 말씀드리기 죄송하지만, 휴대폰을 꺼주시겠어요?

439

폐를 끼쳐도 될까요?
Could I trouble you to

 상대방이 귀찮아 할지도 모를 일을 부탁할 때 써요.

A Are you going this way, Lorra?
B Yes. Could I trouble you to give me a ride?

give~ a ride   ~를 차로 태워주다

A 이쪽 방향으로 가요, 로라?
B 예, 폐가 되겠지만 태워주겠어요?

440

혹시 ~해주실 수 있나요?
Is there any way you could

A Do you need anything?
B Is there any way you could loan me $20?

loan 빌려주다, 대출해주다

A 뭐 필요한 것 있어요?
B 혹시 20달러 빌려주실 수 있나요?

# 기분 상하지 않게 거절하기

Polite Refusals

☐ I'd love to, but   ☐ Can I take a rain check?   ☐ Catch you next time
☐ Some other time   ☐ Sorry, but I can't.

441
그러고 싶지만
I'd love to, but

→ I'm afraid to tell you, but I can't do that.

A Aren't you going to come to my wedding?
B I'd love to, but I'll be out of town that weekend.

be out of town 출장 가다

A 내 결혼식에 올 거죠?
B 그러고 싶지만, 그 주에 출장을 가야 해요.

442
다음 기회에 할까요?
Can I take a rain check?

→ rain check(우천시 교환권)은 알고 계신 표현이죠. 지금은 안 되지만 다음엔 꼭 하겠다는 약속!

A What about coming over for dinner this evening?
B Sorry. But can I take a rain check?

A 오늘 저녁 먹으러 우리 집에 올래요?
B 미안해요. 대신 다음 기회를 주겠어요?

443
나중에 봐.
Catch you next time

 I can't join you this time. Let's meet later.

A. Aren't you going to join us?
B. Catch you next time. I have to stay here and work.

A. 우리와 같이 안 갈 거야?
B. 나중에 봐. 난 여기서 일해야 돼.

444
언제 기회가 되면
Some other time

 rain check처럼 '꼭 하겠다'는 약속은 아니에요.

A. Can't you come to our company picnic?
B. Some other time. I'll have to visit my parents.

A. 우리 회사 야유회에 올 수 없어요?
B. 언제 기회가 되면요. 부모님 뵈러 가야 해요.

445
안 되겠어요.
Sorry, but I can't.

A. What about coming hiking with us this Saturday?
B. Sorry, but I can't. I have to babysit that day.
come/go + -ing ~하러 가다

A. 이번 토요일에 우리와 하이킹 갈래요?
B. 안 되겠어요. 그 날 아기 봐야 해요.

최후통첩할 때 으레 쓰는 말

Ultimatums
- [ ] My way or the highway
- [ ] Take it or leave it
- [ ] Like it or not
- [ ] It's this or nothing.
- [ ] That's my final offer.

446
그렇게 하든지, 그만두든지
My way or the highway

→ You may either do it my way or leave. 날 따르든지 아니면 딴 길로 가란 말이죠.

A This doesn't seem like the best way.
B Just do it, my way or the highway.

seem like ~인 것처럼 여겨지다

A 이게 최선의 방법은 아닌 것 같아요.
B 잠자코 그렇게 하든지, 아니면 그만두든지요.

447
수락하든지 말든지
Take it or leave it

→ This is my final offer. Either accept it or go away.

A I'm not going to pay such a high price!
B That's the only price we're offering. Take it or leave it.

A 그렇게 비싸게 줄 수는 없어요.
B 그 가격 이하는 안 되요. 사든지 말든지 하세요.

448

원하든 말든
Like it or not

 본인 의지와는 상관없이 따를 수밖에 없는 일에 써요.

A I have to leave this place? That's awful!
B Well, you've got to go, like it or not.

A 이 곳을 떠나야 해요. 너무 싫은데!
B 당신이 원하든 말든 떠나야겠지요.

449

이거 말고 대안은 없어요.
It's this or nothing.

 더 이상의 대안은 없으니 현재의 제안을 수락하라는 말!

A Don't you have any better cars I could rent?
B I'm sorry, but it's this or nothing.

A 좀 더 좋은 차로 임대할 수 없나요?
B 죄송하지만, 이 차 아니면 없습니다.

450

마지막 제안입니다.
That's my final offer.

A I won't sell for only $22!
B That's my final offer. I won't go any higher.

I won't (거부) ~하지는 않겠다   eg. I won't allow you to stay here!

A 22달러에는 안 팝니다!
B 마지막 제안이요. 더 비싸게는 안 사요.

부담 없이 초대할 때 쓰는 말

Invitations

☐ Make yourself at home ☐ Come on over ☐ Don't be a stranger.
☐ Come (on) in ☐ Join in/Join us

451
편히 하세요.
Make yourself at home

→ Make yourself comfortable. 자신의 집처럼 편히 하란 뜻.

A I've come for your conference.
B Thanks for coming by, Mr. Brown. Please make yourself at home.

come by 들르다, 방문하다(drop by)

A 컨퍼런스에 참석차 왔습니다.
B 와주셔서 감사합니다, 브라운 씨. 자, 편히 하세요.

452
놀러 와요.
Come on over

→ If you're not busy, come to my place and enjoy yourself.

A Are you busy tonight?
B No, come on over and have a drink.

A 오늘밤, 바빠요, 해리?
B 아뇨, 놀러 와요. 한 잔 하게.

453

친하게 지내요.
Don't be a stranger.

 → Let's get to know each other better. 낯선 사람으로 지내지 말고 서로 친해보자는 뜻.

A Thanks for the dinner.
B It was nothing. Don't be a stranger. Come back again soon!

A 저녁 잘 먹었어요.
B 별 것도 아닌데요. 친하게 지내요. 또 오세요!

454

들어와요.
Come (on) in

 → Come in, please. 습관적으로 come과 in사이에 on을 넣어 말하는 원어민들이 많아요.

A Hello, is Mr. Brown in?
B Yes he is. Why don't you come on in?

A 브라운 씨 계신가요?
B 예, 계세요. 들어오시죠?

455

함께 해요.
Join in/Join us

A That looks like a really tasty pizza you guys are having.
B It sure is. Join in and have a slice!

slice 조각(piece)   eg. a slice of bread/cake

A 먹고 있는 피자, 정말 맛있어 보이는데.
B 그래요. 와서 한 조각 먹어봐요.

CHAPTER 14

Warnings and Danger

Is this the company bowling team? It sure is. Want in? Isn't this the local parent I'd like to join the school French Club here. You hopping on? How long have y Why don't you join our research group? I'm a solo act, sorry. You're leaving o Yeah, I'm jumping ship. I got a better offer. Is this the company bowling team? It sure is. Want in? Isn't this the local parents' group? It You hopping on? How long have you studied French? Can I come to your party this Friday? Of course! The more, the merrier. Aren't y You're leaving our department? Yeah, from now on you're on your own. Why didn't you help carry our bags? Every man for himself; I'v

Susan Says...

You never really appreciate all the fun you have in college until it's over!

you signing up? We need more parents. This is the company union desk, right? Right! In or out? All employees should join. h? Can I come to your party this Friday? Of course! The more, the merrier. Aren't you going to stay with our group? Sorry, you have to count me out. eah, from now on you're on your own. Why didn't you help carry our bags? Every man for himself; I've got no time to help you guys. You're leaving the company? p? We need more parents. This is the company union desk, right? Right! In or out? All employees should join. I'd like to join the school French Club here. with our group? Sorry, you have to count me out. Why don't you join our research group? I'm a solo act, sorry. help you guys. You're leaving the company? Yeah, I'm jumping ship. I got a better offer.

Warnings and Danger

경고 · 위험을 알리는 생생 표현

456>490

상대에게 경고할 때 쓰는 말

Warning

☐ You'd better think twice. ☐ Not if I were you. ☐ You're asking for trouble.
☐ I wouldn't. ☐ You're playing with fire.

456

한 번 더 생각해봐요.
You'd better think twice.

 → Think it over again before you answer/make a decision. 단 한 번에 올바른 판단을 내릴 수는 없겠죠.

A I'm thinking of starting up my own business.
B You'd better think twice. That's not easy at all.
start up one's own business 창업하다

A 창업을 해볼 생각이야.
B 한 번 더 생각해봐요. 쉬운 일이 아니에요.

457

나라면 안 해요.
Not if I were you

 → I wouldn't do it if I were you.

A I'll drive. I've only had a few drinks.
B Not if I were you. You might crash!
crash 충돌하다

A 내가 운전할게. 몇 잔밖에 안 마셨으니까.
B 나라면 안 해요. 차를 박을지도 몰라요!

경고 · 위험을 알리는 생생 표현

Chapter 14

458

화를 자청하는 겁니다.
You're asking for trouble.

 → You may provoke big trouble/problems.

A I'll put more salt on this steak.
B That'll ruin your stomach! You're asking for trouble, Ted.

ruin 망치다

A 스테이크에 소금을 더 쳐야겠군.
B 그러면 위장에 나빠요! 테드, 화를 자청하는군요.

459

나라면 안 그럴 텐데
I wouldn't

 → I wouldn't do that if I were you.

A I think I'll leave work a little earlier today.
B I wouldn't. The boss might see you.

A 오늘 좀 일찍 퇴근할까봐.
B 나라면 안 그럴 텐데. 사장님이 보실지 모르죠.

460

불장난 하는 거예요.
You're playing with fire.

 → 한국말과 같죠. 불장난처럼 위험한 일에 써요.

A I want to buy a dress with the company credit card.
B You're playing with fire. You know that's not allowed!

be allowed 허가되다, 허용되다

A 회사 카드로 옷을 살까봐.
B 불장난 하는 거예요. 그건 안 되는 일이죠!

위기 상황이 예감될 때 쓰는 말

Risks

- [ ] It's a long shot.
- [ ] It's dicey.
- [ ] Bad odds. / I don't like the odds.
- [ ] It's a minefield.
- [ ] There's no safe angle.

461

아주 힘들 겁니다.
It's a long shot.

→ 먼 거리에서 치는 '샷'이 적중할 확률은 낮겠죠. 성공하기 힘들 때 쓰는 말.

A Do you think I'll get the job?
B Well, there are a lot of people applying, so it's a long shot.

A 내가 취직할 수 있을까요?
B 글쎄, 구직자가 워낙 많아서, 힘들 거야.

462

위험 부담이 있어요.
It's dicey.

→ It's very risky. 주사위 게임에서 나온 말.

A Should we drive all the way to Busan in this rain?
B Maybe it's too dicey to go.

all the way 내내, 계속

A 이렇게 비가 내리는데 부산까지 운전해서 가야 할까요?
B 글쎄, 너무 위험해서 갈 수 없겠는데.

463

확률이 낮아요.
Bad odds. / I don't like the odds.

 → There's a low possibility/percentage/chance of success.

A Isn't the metro bus going to arrive on time?
B They have fewer of them, so I don't like the odds.

A 지역 버스가 정시에 올까요?
B 차가 몇 대 줄어서, 그럴 확률이 낮아요.

464

지뢰밭 같아요.
It's a minefield.

 → It's a very risky situation, like walking through a minefield.

A How's your office atmosphere?
B Everyone's always so sensitive. It's a minefield!

atmosphere 분위기   sensitive 예민한, 날카로운

A 사무실 분위기가 어때요?
B 모두가 늘 예민한 상태죠. 지뢰밭 같아요.

465

언제 어떻게 될지 모르죠.
There's no safe angle.

 → 어느 쪽 각도에서도 안전하지 않다면? 심각한 위기상황에 써요.

A Can't we continue to use this old machine?
B Of course, but there's no safe angle.

A 이 구닥다리 기계를 계속 쓸 수는 없겠죠?
B 쓰죠, 언제 고장날지는 모르지만요.

경솔함을 꾸짖는 한마디!

Recklessness

- [ ] That's a fool's game.
- [ ] If I were an idiot
- [ ] That's against common sense.
- [ ] No good can come of it.
- [ ] It'll blow up in your face.

466
그건 바보 짓이야.
That's a fool's game.

→ That's very foolish. You know better than that.

A Do you ever gamble at the horse track?
B That's a fool's game. I don't want to waste my money like that.

A 경마 내기 해본 적 있어요?
B 그건 바보 짓이야. 그런 곳에 돈을 낭비하고 싶지 않아.

467
바보 멍청이라면요.
If I were an idiot

→ It's ridiculous. Only if I were a fool, I might do it.

A Wouldn't you ever drive without a license?
B If I were an idiot, I might do something like that.

A 무면허 운전해 본 적 없죠?
B 바보 멍청이라면 그럴지도 모르죠.

468
상식적으로 납득이 안 돼.
That's against common sense.

 I don't get it. It's not reasonable at all. against는 '~에 어긋나는, 반대되는'이란 뜻이죠.

A I'm thinking of refusing the promotion.
B What? That's against common sense, Karen.

A 승진을 거절할 생각이야.
B 뭐? 상식적으로 납득이 안 돼, 카렌.

469
그래봐야 좋을 것 없지.
No good can come of it.

 No good result can arise from an action.

A I'm going to give Mann a beating!
B No good can come of it. Just forget about him.

give~ a beating ~를 패주다

A 만 녀석을 한방 먹여줄 거야.
B 그래봐야 좋을 것 없지. 그에 대해 잊게.

470
체면만 구길 거야.
It'll blow up in your face.

 자신의 얼굴에 폭탄 터뜨리는 꼴이니, 이득 될 게 없다는 말.

A I'm gonna challenge the boss! He's a stupid guy! Don't! It'll blow up in your face.

challenge 도전하다, 대들다 eg. Did you challenge the professor?

A 상사에게 대들어야겠어. 멍청한 놈이거든!
B 관둬! 체면만 구길 거야.

협박이 필요할 때 흔히 하는 말

Threats

- [ ] See what happens
- [ ] Don't push me.
- [ ] I'll make you sorry.
- [ ] Keep talking!
- [ ] Leave me alone!

471
어디 두고 보자.
See what happens

→ **You may regret it!** 계속 그러면 후회할 걸!

A You're a foolish guy!
B Oh yeah? Stop your insults or see what happens.

insult 모욕, 욕설

A 멍청한 녀석 같으니!
B 어, 그래? 그만 하지 않으면, 어떻게 되나 봐라.

472
건드리지 마.
Don't push me.

→ **Don't provoke me.** 성질 돋우지 말라는 경고!

A You idiot! Are you still working here?
B Don't push me, or I'll show you what I'm made of.

A 멍청이! 너 아직도 여기서 일하냐?
B 건드리지 마, 안 그러면 내가 쓴 맛을 보여줄 테니.

경고 · 위험을 알리는 생생 표현

Chapter 14

`473`

후회하게 해주지.
I'll make you sorry.

 → I'll make you regret it. You'll be sorry.

A You'd better give up while you can!
B No way! I'll make you sorry for what you've said.

what you've said 네가 말한 것을

A 할 수 있을 때 포기하시지!
B 그럴 수 없지! 네 말을 후회하게 해줄 테다.

`474`

계속 말해봐라! 떠들어 보시지!
Keep talking!

 → Continue talking, and I may harm you.

A You're not even worth challenging.
B Oh yeah? Keep talking!

worth +-ing ~할 만하다, 가치가 있다

A 넌 대들지도 못하지.
B 어, 그래? 계속 말해봐라!

`475`

날 내버려 둬!
Leave me alone!

A I'll introduce you to Cozy. You need to see someone else.
B I can deal with things by myself, Mom. Just leave me alone!

deal with 처리하다, 다루다

A 코지를 소개해 줄게. 넌 새로운 사람을 만나야 해.
B 내 일은 알아서 해요, 엄마. 그냥 내버려둬요!

주의를 요할 때 쓰면 좋은 말

Caution

☐ Consider all sides   ☐ Don't rush in.   ☐ Look before you leap
☐ Better safe than sorry   ☐ Check and double-check

476
모든 면을 고려해야죠.
Consider all sides

→ 분석 가능한 면(sides)을 모두 따져 보란 뜻.

A What do you think of this budget plan?
B We need to consider all sides before we use it.

budget plan 예산안   consider 고려하다

A 본 예산안이 어떻습니까?
B 사용 전에 모든 면을 고려해야죠.

477
급하게 결정하지 마세요.
Don't rush in.

 → Don't hurry to make a decision.

A Isn't it a good idea to send my kids to a private school?
B Don't rush in. They aren't cheap.

it's a good idea to do ~하는 것은 좋다

A 자녀를 사립학교에 보내는 게 좋겠죠?
B 급하게 결정하지 마세요. 거긴 비싸죠.

478

심사숙고하세요.
Look before you leap

 높이 도약하려면 미리 철저한 준비가 필요하지요.

- A I'm going to accept this job.
- B Look before you leap! You may have to work long hours!

work long hours 장시간 근무하다

- A 이 직장에 들어갈거야.
- B 심사숙고하세요. 장시간 근무해야 할지도 몰라요.

479

나중에 후회하는 것보다 낫죠.
Better safe than sorry

- A Do we really need this test again?
- B Just once more. Better safe than sorry.

- A 이 테스트를 또 해야 할까요?
- B 한 번만 더요. 나중에 후회하는 것보다 낫죠.

480

몇 번이고 점검하세요.
Check and double-check

 실수하기 쉬운 일을 미리 점검할 때 써요.

- A Are you sure you've got the tickets for our trip?
- B Yes, I checked and double checked.

- A 여행 티켓을 확실히 갖고 있죠?
- B 예, 몇 번이나 점검했어요.

고통과 위험은 성공의 또 다른 얼굴

Risks & Benefits

- [ ] No pain, no gain.
- [ ] Who dares, wins.
- [ ] Deeds, not words!
- [ ] I'll beat the odds.
- [ ] Nothing's too big for me.

481

고생 끝에 낙이 오죠.
No pain, no gain.

 잘 알고 있는 표현이죠! Use it more often!

A Your stocks are down 12% this month! You don't mind?
B No pain, no gain. They'll rise later.

mind 신경쓰이다, 염려되다

A 보유 주식이 이달에 12%나 떨어졌는데, 괜찮아요?
B 고생 끝에 낙이 오는 법. 나중에 오르겠죠.

482

성공하려면 위험도 감수해야죠.
Who dares, wins.

 호랑이 굴에 들어가야 호랑이를 잡는 법!

A Do you have any advice for me as a new salesman?
B Yes, who dares, wins.

A 신참 영업자인 제게 해줄 충고가 있나요?
B 그래, 성공하려면 위험도 감수해야 한다는 것이지.

경고·위험을 알리는 생생 표현

Chapter 14

483

말이 아니라 행동을!
Deeds, not words!

 → Action speaks louder than words.

A I'm thinking of trying to lose weight.
B Deeds, not words! Why don't you go on a diet?

A 체중을 줄여야겠어요.
B 말이 아니라 행동을! 다이어트를 시작하지 그래?

484

예상을 깨고 해낼 거야.
I'll beat the odds.

 → I'll succeed despite low odds of success.

A No one thinks that you can win the marathon.
B Don't worry. I'll beat the odds.

A 아무도 당신이 마라톤에서 승리할 거로 안 봐요.
B 걱정 마요. 예상을 깨고 해낼 테니.

485

못할 게 없죠.
Nothing's too big for me.

 → 한다고 맘만 먹으면 해내고 만다는 의지!

A You sure you can handle this?
B Don't worry. Nothing's too big for me.

A 확실히 이 걸 처리할 수 있겠나?
B 걱정 말아요. 못할 게 없습니다.

큰 실수를 따끔히 지적할 때

Catastrophes

- You really dropped the ball.
- See what you did!
- Now you've done it!
- Can't you do anything right?
- What were you thinking?

486
큰 실수를 했어요.
You really dropped the ball.

→ You made a big and obvious mistake. 운동 경기의 중요한 순간에 공을 놓친 것에 비유.

A: I'm sorry I failed to bring meat to the picnic.
B: Well, you really dropped the ball, honey.

failed to do ~하지 못하다

A: 야유회에 고기 가져 오는 걸 잊어서 미안해요.
B: 당신, 정말 큰 실수를 했어요.

487
사태를 똑똑히 봐요!
See what you did!

→ Look at the huge mistake you made!

A: I'm sorry I spilled coffee on your dress.
B: See what you did! The whole outfit is ruined!

spill 쏟다 outfit 의상, 옷

A: 옷에 커피를 쏟아서 미안해요.
B: 어떻게 됐나 봐요! 옷이 전부 망가졌어요!

경고 · 위험을 알리는 생생 표현

Chapter 14

488
이번에 대형사고 쳤어!
Now you've done it!

 → You really did it this time! 라고도 해요.

A   Why's everyone looking at me so strangely?
B   Now you've done it! You forgot to show up for the 8:00 meeting!

show up for ~에 참석하다, 나타나다

A   왜 모두가 그런 눈으로 보세요?
B   이번에 대형사고 쳤어요! 8시 회의에 불참했잖아요!

489
좀 제대로 할 수 없어요?
Can't you do anything right?

A   I'm not sure why I overlooked those figures.
B   Can't you do anything right? It wrecked the annual report!

overlook 간과하다   wreck 망치다(ruin), 오점을 남기다

A   그 숫자들을 왜 못 보았는지 모르겠어요.
B   좀 제대로 할 수 없나? 연말보고서를 망쳤어!

490
넋 놓고 있었어요?
What were you thinking?

 → Are you insane or something?

A   I'm not sure why I didn't see that streetlight.
B   What were you thinking? You could've killed us!

A   신호등을 왜 못 보았는지 모르겠어요.
B   넋 놓고 있었어요? 우리를 죽일뻔 했어요!

CHAPTER 15

Skepticism and Doubt

Is this the company bowling team? It sure is. Want in? Isn't this the local parents' group? I'd like to join the school French Club here. You hopping on? How long have you studied French? Why don't you join our research group? I'm a solo act, sorry. You're leaving... Yeah, I'm jumping ship. I got a better offer. Is this the company bowling team? It sure is. Want in? Isn't this the local parents' group? You hopping on? How long have you studied French? Can I come to your party this Friday? Of course! The more, the merrier. Aren't you leaving our department? Yeah, from now on you're on your own. Why didn't you help carry our bags? Every man for himself; I'

Susan Says...

There are two essential things every woman needs: great taste in wine and great taste in men.

Skepticism and Doubt

회의와 의심이 생기면 쓰게 되는 생생 표현

491 › 525

회의적인 생각이 들 때면

Skepticism

- [ ] Not likely
- [ ] Don't hold your breath.
- [ ] Get real
- [ ] I doubt it.
- [ ] Come off it!

491

아닐 걸요.
Not likely

→ It's not probable. 모든 상황에 다 써요.

A The new boss will be better than the old one?
B Not likely. Most bosses are the same, in my opinion.

in one's opinion ~의 견해로

A 새 상사가 예전 상사보다 나을까요?
B 아닐 걸요. 상사들은 대개 비슷하니까.

492

기대하지 마세요.
Don't hold your breath.

→ Don't expect something. 괜히 숨 안 쉬고 있다가 당신만 죽어요!

A We're supposed to get a big bonus this year, aren't we?
B Don't hold your breath.

A 올해는 보너스가 두둑하겠죠?
B 기대하지 마세요.

242

회의와 의심이 생기면 쓰게 되는 생생 표현

Chapter 15

493
현실적으로 생각해.
Get real

 → Be realistic! 앞에 You'd better을 넣어 말하기도 해요.

A I'm thinking of buying a farm.
B You'd better get real. What do you know about farming?

You'd(had) better ~하는 게 좋다/더 낫다

A 농장을 살 생각이야.
B 현실적으로 생각해요. 당신이 농장에 대해 뭘 아는데요?

494
글쎄요. 회의적이에요.
I doubt it.

 → It's not likely to happen. I'm not confident about it.

A Isn't Mr. Joo ready to sign the agreement?
B He's been delaying for weeks, so I doubt it.

A 주 씨가 합의서에 서명하지 않겠어요?
B 몇주 동안 미뤘는데, 회의적이에요.

495
집어치워요!
Come off it!

 → Stop trying to deceive yourself. Don't be delusional.

A I'm thinking of going to night school to get a degree.
B Come off it! With your schedule, you'd never find time to study!

get a degree 학위를 얻다/받다

A 야간학교에 들어가서 학위를 따야겠어
B 그만둬요! 당신 일정에 공부할 시간이 어딨어요!

의견이 다를 때 툭 던지는 말

Incredulity/Disagreement

- [ ] Can't be
- [ ] Not in my book
- [ ] No way in the world
- [ ] Not a hope
- [ ] Won't happen

496

그럴 리가 없어요.
Can't be

→ It can't be true. There must be some mistakes.

A Our revenue went up 7% for the month!
B Can't be! The trend was down in the report I read.

revenue 총 수입　go up 증가하다

A 이달 수입이 7% 증가했대요!
B 그럴 리가 없어요. 내가 본 보고서에는 떨어졌어요.

497

난 그리 생각하지 않아요.
Not in my book

→ in my book은 in my opinion과 같은 뜻이에요.

A Look outside! Isn't the weather great?
B I hate rainy days, so not in my book.

A 밖을 봐요! 멋진 날씨잖아요?
B 나는 비오는 날을 싫어해요. 그러니 내겐 아니죠.

498

절대로 불가능해요.
No way in the world

 → There is no possible way in the entire world.

A Do you think our rival will get this deal?
B No way in the world. We're sure to win it.

A 우리 경쟁사가 이번 건을 딸까요?
B 절대로 그렇게는 안 돼. 분명코 우리가 이길 테니까.

499

가망성이 없어요.
Not a hope

A Are you still going to Bali this summer?
B There's not a hope.

A 올 여름 여전히 발리에 갈 건가요?
B 가망성이 없어요.

500

그런 일은 없을 거야.
Won't happen

 → There's no possibility of it happening.

A Annie said we're going to get a puppy.
B Won't happen. Mom hates dogs.

A 애니 말이 우리에게 강아지가 생긴대!
B 그런 일은 없을 거야. 엄마가 개를 싫어하시잖아.

의구심이 들면 툭 던지는 말

Doubt
- [ ] I'll believe it when I see it.
- [ ] Sell it someplace else
- [ ] That's hard to swallow.
- [ ] I wasn't born yesterday.
- [ ] I wouldn't bet on it.

501
눈으로 봐야 믿겠어요.
I'll believe it when I see it.

→ I won't believe it until it appears right before my eyes.

A Bill says that he's going to buy a bike.
B I'll believe it when I see it. He can't afford that.

A 빌이 오토바이를 산대요.
B 눈으로 봐야 믿지. 그럴 돈이 없을 테니까.

502
다른 사람에게나 말씀하시지.
Sell it someplace else

→ 신뢰할 수 없는 사람의 말에 대해 냉소적으로 대꾸할 때 써요.

A Miles is going to be our new manager.
B Sell it someplace else! He's not qualified for that.

be qualified for ~할 자격을 갖추다

A 마일즈가 새 지배인이 된대요.
B 다른 사람에게나 말씀하시지. 그는 자격이 안 돼요.

503

믿기 힘들어요.
That's hard to swallow.

 → What you said is not believable. 믿을 수 없는 물건을 덥석 '삼키지'는 않지요!

A Our team won last night, 5-2.
B What? That's hard to swallow.

A 어젯밤에 우리팀이 5대2로 이겼대!
B 뭐라구? 믿기지 않는데.

504

난 어린애가 아니에요.
I wasn't born yesterday.

 → I'm not foolish enough to be tricked.

A This is the cheapest price.
B I wasn't born yesterday. I know that you can offer me a lower one.

A 이게 최하 가격입니다.
B 난 어린애가 아니에요. 더 싸게 주실 수 있잖소.

505

그건 아닐 거야.
I wouldn't bet on it.

A Do you think we'll find a seat on the subway?
B I wouldn't bet on it. The trains are all very crowded at this time of day.

bet on ~에 걸다, 내기하다   at this time of day/month/year 하루/월/연 중 이맘때

A 지하철에 좌석이 있을까?
B 없을 거야. 하루 중 이때가 가장 붐비니까.

냉소적인 말대꾸를 즐기려면

Cynicism

- [ ] I've heard/seen it before.
- [ ] So what?
- [ ] That's it?
- [ ] Don't make a fuss.
- [ ] Nothing special

506

들어 본 건데. 본 적이 있어.
I've heard/seen it before.

 It's nothing new to me. 전혀 새로울 게 없다는 반응!

A Isn't that an amazing trick?
B I don't think so. I've seen it before.

A 저건 기막힌 마술 아니니?
B 난 별로야. 저런 것을 본 적이 있어.

507

그게 어쨌다고?
So what?

A I think Mr. Waters is upset at your attitude.
B So what? He's nothing to do with us.

be nothing to do with ~와 무관하다

A 워터스 씨가 당신 태도에 언짢아해요.
B 그게 어쨌다고요? 우리와 상관없는 사람인데요.

508
그게 전부인가요?
That's it?

 → Is that the end? Isn't there any more?

A Here's our selection of men's ties for you.
B Only 4 styles? That's it?

A 여기, 남성 타이 종류입니다.
B 겨우 4개요? 그게 전부인가요?

509
소란 떨지 마요.
Don't make a fuss.

 → It's no big deal. Stop fussing!

A Did you see Winston's new car?
B No big deal. Don't make a fuss. There are sports cars all over LA.

A 윈스톤 씨의 새 차 봤어요?
B 별일 아니니, 소란 떨지 마요. LA에는 흔한 게 스포츠카예요.

510
별것도 아니네.
Nothing special

 → It's not excellent or beautiful. You may feel disappointed.

A How was the opera last night?
B Nothing special. Just a lot of fat people singing.

A 지난 밤 오페라 어땠어요?
B 별것도 아니던데. 뚱보들이 많이 나와 노래하더군.

반대 의견을 전하는 쉬운 말

Opposition

- [ ] Not if I have any say
- [ ] Over my dead body
- [ ] Don't even think (about) it!
- [ ] No-go. / That's a no-go.
- [ ] I won't have it.

511
내 의견은 반대입니다.
Not if I have any say

→ 여기서 say는 영향력(influence)을 말해요.

A So your daughter's going to study in Germany?
B Not if I have any say. She's too young for that.

too young for ~하기에 너무 어린

A 따님이 독일로 유학간다고요?
B 내 의견으론 안 보내죠. 그러기엔 아직 어려요.

512
내 생전엔 안 돼.
Over my dead body

→ As long as I live, I will never allow it. 죽어 시체가 되면 모를까…

A You'll be sent to the local branch?
B Over my dead body! That would be insulting.

insulting 모욕적인, 굴욕을 주는

A 지방 지사로 전근 가신다고요?
B 내 생전엔 안 돼! 그건 내게 모욕적이야.

513
꿈도 꾸지 말게!
Don't even think (about) it!

 생각조차 하지 말라니! '불가하다'는 엄포 놓기!

A Shouldn't we rewrite the entire plan?
B Don't even think it! It would take too much time!

A 기획안을 전부 재작성해야 하지 않나요?
B 꿈도 꾸지 말게! 그건 시간이 너무 걸려!

514
불가능해요.
No-go. / That's a no-go.

 It's simply impossible.

A Aren't we going to be able to board this flight?
B No-go. The plane's already full.

full (좌석) 다 찬, 빈자리가 없는

A 이 비행기를 탈 수 없을까요?
B 불가능해요. 좌석이 다 찼어요.

515
허락 못해요.
I won't have it.

 I won't allow it. have는 allow의 뜻.

A The staff want to break for lunch now.
B I won't have it. Don't they see how busy we are?

A 직원들이 점심 시간을 갖자는데요.
B 허락 못해요. 얼마나 바쁜지 안 보여요?

불신이 가득하면 튀어 나오는 말

Disbelief
- I don't buy it.
- (Right!) And I'm the king of England!
- I don't believe a word of it.
- Stop pulling my leg.
- In your dreams!

516
전혀 안 믿어.
I don't buy it.

→ I don't believe it is true or genuine. 영화에서 자주 듣는 말이죠. buy는 believe의 뜻.

A   All staff will be offered stock options.
B   Options are only for directors, so I don't buy it.

A   모든 직원에게 스톡옵션을 준대요.
B   그건 임원들이나 받는 거죠. 난 안 믿어요.

517
(그게 사실이면) 난 영국 왕이게!
(Right!) And I'm the king of England!

→ If what you say is true, then "I'm the king of England".

A   I was once mistaken for a movie star. Did you know that?
B   Right—and I'm the king of England!

be mistaken for ~로 오인되다

A   한번은 날 영화배우로 오인하더라니까.
B   그게 사실이면, 난 영국 왕이게!

518

한마디도 안 믿어요.
I don't believe a word of it.

- A The CEO says that he's retiring next month.
- B I don't believe a word of it. This is the third time.

- A CEO께서 내달에 물러나신대요?
- B 한마디도 안 믿어요. 이번이 세 번째인 걸요.

519

농담 그만해요.
Stop pulling my leg.

 Don't try to trick or deceive me.

- A Your face was in the newspaper today.
- B Stop pulling my leg. There's no way that could happen.

There's no way ~할 방도가 없다

- A 당신이 오늘 신문에 나왔어요.
- B 농담 그만해요. 그럴 리가 없지.

520

꿈에서 그랬겠지!
In your dreams!

 It's possible only in your dreams.

- A Did you know that I used to be a model?
- B In your dreams. You don't seem anything like a model.

used to (과거 상태) ~였다   eg. I used to like him, but not anymore.

- A 내가 모델 했었다는 것 알아요?
- B 꿈에서 그랬겠지! 전혀 모델 같지 않은데.

확실한 증거를 요구할 때 쓰는 말

Verification

- [ ] Says who?
- [ ] Got it in writing?
- [ ] Prove it to me. / Got proof?
- [ ] Show me!
- [ ] Back it up!

521
누가 그래요?
Says who?

→ Who can prove this? What is this based on?

A The school's going to be closed next week!
B Says who? I don't buy that.

A 학교가 다음주에 폐교된대요!
B 누가 그래? 말도 안 돼.

522
서면으로 받았어요?
Got it in writing?

→ Do you have formal/written documents?

A Mr. Dake promised to pay us next week.
B That's great news, but have you got it in writing?

promise to do ~하기로 약속하다

A 다께 씨가 다음주에 지불하겠답니다.
B 좋은 소식이군, 한데 그걸 서면으로 받았어요?

523

증명해봐요.
Prove it to me. / Got proof?

A I lived in Brazil for over 6 years.
B Prove it to me. Speak a few lines of Portuguese.

A 난 6년이나 브라질에서 살았어요.
B 증명해 봐요. 포루투칼어 몇 마디 해봐요.

524

보여줘요!
Show me!

→ I don't believe your words. 말이 아니라 구체적인 자료를 요구할 때 툭 던지는 말.

A This investment will earn you a lot of money.
B Oh yeah? Show me! I want to see a spreadsheet.

A 이번 투자로 엄청 돈을 벌겁니다.
B 그래요? 어디 봅시다! 스프레드시트를 보여주세요.

525

물증을 봅시다!
Back it up!

→ 물증(physical evidence)을 요구할 때 써요.

A This MP3 player will last for a long time.
B Back it up! Give me a warranty.

last 지속되다, 유지되다   warranty 보증서

A 이 MP3플레이어는 오래 씁니다.
B 물증을 봅시다! 보증서를 보여줘요.

CHAPTER 16

Personal Enquiries

Is this the company bowling team? It sure is. Want in? Isn't this the local parents' gro[up] I'd like to join the school French Club here. You hopping on? How long have you stu[died] Why don't you join our research group? I'm a solo act, sorry. You're leaving our dep[artment?] jumping ship. I got a better offer. Is this the company bowling team? It sure is. Want in? Isn't this the local parents' group? It is. You si[gn] You hopping on? How long have you studied French? Can I come to your party this Friday? Of course! The more, the merrier. Aren't y[ou] You're leaving our department? Yeah, from now on you're on your own. Why didn't you help carry our bags? Every man for himself; I'v[e]

Susan Says...

You'll never get lucky unless you take the chance of rolling the dice.

Personal Enquiries

일상 안부
대화에 쓰는
생생 표현

매일 하는 안부 인사, 생기발랄하게!

General Greeting

- How are you today? / How're you doing?
- Feeling okay?
- How's everything?
- Everything A-OK?
- Anything on your mind?

526
안녕하세요? 어떻게 지내요?
How are you today? / How're you doing?

A How're you doing, Ryan?
B I'm okay, William. And yourself?

And yourself? = And you?/ And how are you?

A 라이언, 어떻게 지내요?
B 잘 지내요, 윌리엄. 당신은요?

527
(건강은) 괜찮아요?
Feeling okay?

→ Are you feeling okay/fine?의 줄임말. 감정이나 건강 상태를 묻는 말.

A Phillip, hey! Feeling okay today?
B I think so, though I may be catching a cold.

though 비록 ~이지만   catch a cold 감기 걸리다

A 이봐, 필립! 오늘 건강은 괜찮아요?
B 예, 감기가 들 것 같긴 하지만요.

일상 안부 대화에 쓰는 생생 표현

Chapter 16

528
두루두루 어때요?
How's everything?

 → How's everything (going) with you?의 줄임말.

A How's everything, Corrine?
B Great! Thanks for asking!

Thanks for asking! 안부 물어줘서 감사하다는 뜻.

A 코린, 두루두루 어때요?
B 아주 좋아요! 신경 써줘서 고마워요!

529
별일 없죠?
Everything A-OK?

 → A-OK는 best/top/great와 같은 의미예요.

A You look a little down, today. Everything A-OK?
B I'm fine. I just didn't sleep well last night, that's all.

A 좀 가라앉아 보여요. 별일 없죠?
B 없어요. 그냥 어제 잠을 좀 설쳤을 뿐이에요.

530
뭐 신경 쓰이는 일 있어요?
Anything on your mind?

 → 늘 보던 표정이 아니라면, What's new? How's it going? 같은 의례적인 인사말 뒤에 건네볼 수 있는 표현.

A You look so thoughtful today. Anything on your mind?
B No, I'm okay.

thoughtful 사색에 잠긴

A 오늘 생각이 많아 보이는데, 뭐 신경 쓰이는 일 있어요?
B 아뇨, 별일 없어요.

신경이 예민해져 있다면

Annoyance

- [ ] What's eating/bugging you? [ ] You on edge? [ ] Monkey on your back?
- [ ] Trouble? [ ] Worries?

531

성가신 일이라도 있어요?
What's eating/bugging you?

→ Is something bothering you seriously? 뭔가 마음을 갉아 먹거나 벌레처럼 성가시게 하는 일이 있는지 묻는 말.

- A What's bugging you, Sue? You look really annoyed.
- B I can't find my cell phone. I left it somewhere in the office, though!

- A 성가신 일이라도 있어요, 수? 불안해 보여요.
- B 휴대폰이 없어졌어요. 사무실 어딘가에 뒀는데!

532

불안하세요?
You on edge?

→ 절벽 난간에 서 있는 것처럼 안절부절한 상태를 말해요.

- A Jack, you on edge about something?
- B Today's my first job interview. I haven't prepared much.

- A 잭, 뭐 불안한 일 있니?
- B 오늘이 첫 면접이야. 준비를 많이 못했거든.

일상 안부 대화에 쓰는 생생 표현

Chapter 16

533
안절부절, 왜 그래요?
Monkey on your back?

 → Are you very nervous? 야생 원숭이가 등에 올라탔을 때 심정에 비유한 것.

　A Monkey on your back, Shannon?
　　　　B I'm wondering if I left my door unlocked at home!
　　　　I'm wondering if ~인지 궁금하다, 의문이다

　A 안절부절, 왜 그래요, 샤논?
　　　　B 집 문을 잠그지 않은 것 같아서요.

534
문제 있어요?
Trouble?

 → Do you have any problem/trouble?

　A You've been on the phone all day. Trouble?
　　　　B Yes, one of our customers has a lot of problems.

　A 종일 전화를 붙잡고 있네요. 문제 있어요?
　　　　B 예, 고객 한 분이 문제가 심각해요.

535
걱정 있어요?
Worries?

　A Worries? You look as if something's really on your mind.
　　　　B Yes, I'm concerned about a medical test I had.
　　　　be concerned about ~에 대해 염려하다, 걱정하다

　A 걱정 있어요? 신경 쓰이는 게 있어 보여요.
　　　　B 예, 건강검진 결과가 걱정돼요.

의기소침해진 친구에게 한마디!

Depression
- [ ] What's got you down? [ ] Why so blue? [ ] Why the long face?
- [ ] Down? [ ] No smile today?

536
왜 기운이 없어요?
What's got you down?

→ What's making you depressed?

A What's got you down? You've been looking gloomy all day.
B I had a big fight with my husband.

gloomy 우울한, 기분이 가라앉는

A 왜 기운이 없어요? 종일 우울해 보여요.
B 남편과 심하게 다퉜거든요.

537
왜 생기가 없어요?
Why so blue?

→ 우울하면 얼굴에 발그레한 생기가 없어지죠. 여기서 blue는 sad와 같은 뜻.

A Why so blue? You're usually so happy!
B Our family dog died last night.

A 왜 생기가 없어요? 당신은 발랄하잖아요!
B 우리 개가 지난 밤에 죽었어요.

Chapter 16

538
왜 풀 죽은 얼굴이죠?
Why the long face?

 → What made you so sad? You look so unhappy. long face는 sad face 란 뜻.

A Why the long face, Vera? You're usually so positive!
B My proposal was rejected by the supervisor.

reject 거절하다, 거부하다

A 왜 풀 죽은 얼굴이죠, 베라? 늘 긍정적이잖아요.
B 내 제안서가 상사에게 퇴짜 맞았어요.

539
우울해요?
Down?

 → Are you feeling down? Are you unhappy?

A Down? You've been staring at the floor all day.
B The boss just blamed me for a big mistake.

blame~ for ~를 …에 대해 책망하다

A 우울해요? 종일 바닥만 보고 있잖아요.
B 사장님한테 큰 실수했다고 혼났어요.

540
웃음을 잃었군요?
No smile today?

A No smile today? You've been frowning all the time.
B Sorry, I'm just in a bad mood about a lot of things.

frown 찡그리다   in a bad mood 기분이 언짢은

A 웃음을 잃었군요? 내내 찡그리고 있어요.
B 미안, 여러 가지로 마음이 언짢아요.

뭔가 불안해 보이는 상대에게 한마디!

Unsettledness

☐ You're not yourself. ☐ You seem out of sorts. ☐ You somewhere else?
☐ Something on your mind? ☐ Penny for your thoughts

541

다른 사람 같아요.
You're not yourself.

→ You aren't acting in your usual manner.

A You're not yourself today. Trouble?
B It's my son's first day at the daycare center. I'm worried.

A 오늘, 다른 사람 같아요. 문제 있어요?
B 아들을 보육원에 처음 맡기는 날이라, 걱정되요.

542

불안해 보여요.
You seem out of sorts.

→ out of sorts는 unsettled/uneasy와 같은 뜻.

A You seem out of sorts. Something bothering you?
B I just need to have a cigarette.

A 불편해 보이는데, 안 좋은 일이라도 있나요?
B 담배가 당겨서요.

543
멍청히 무슨 생각해요?
You somewhere else?

 마치 마음이 엉뚱한 곳에 가 있는 것 같다는 비유.

A Hey, Ted, you somewhere else? Are you worried?
B I'm just thinking about Mary. She's expecting soon.

expect (a baby) 아기를 낳다

A 이봐, 테드, 멍청히 무슨 생각해요?
B 메리 생각을 했어요. 곧 출산을 하거든요.

544
마음 쓰이는 게 있나요?
Something on your mind?

 What's your concern? You're worrying about something, aren't you? 아! 계획이나 의도를 뜻하는 (have) something in mind와 헷갈리지 마세요!

A Something on your mind? You look tense.
B I'm worried about this month's sales totals.

tense 긴장된, 몹시 예민한

A 마음 쓰이는 게 있나요? 긴장돼 보여요.
B 이달 총매출이 걱정되요.

545
뭔지 말해봐요.
Penny for your thoughts

 생각하는 비를 말하면 '돈'을 주겠다니? 그정도로 상대의 고민에 대해 알고싶다는 뜻.

A Penny for your thoughts. You look worried.
B Nothing serious. I just need to find a new place.

A 뭔지 말해봐요. 근심 있어 보이는데.
B 별것 아니에요. 이사 갈 곳을 찾아야 해요.

화를 삭이지 못할 때 한마디!

Anger
- [ ] What's got you steamed?   - [ ] Why so hot and bothered?   - [ ] Someone pushed your button?
- [ ] What set you off?   - [ ] You look ready to blow.

546

뭐 때문에 열 받았어요?
What's got you steamed?

→ 한국말과 같죠! 화나면 뜨거운 증기가 모락모락…

A Your whole face looks red. What's got you steamed?
B Mr. Han was shouting at me for over an hour.

A 얼굴이 벌개요. 뭐 때문에 열받았어요?
B 한 부장이 한 시간 넘게 고함을 치잖아요.

547

왜 그렇게 화났어?
Why so hot and bothered?

→ hot은 angry, bothered는 annoyed와 같은 뜻.

A I saw you kick over a chair! Why so hot and bothered?
B I'm just frustrated about a lot of things!

be frustrated about ~에 낙담하다, 좌절하다

A 의자를 차고 있네! 왜 그렇게 화가 났어?
B 그냥 여러 가지로 되는 게 없어요!

일상 안부 대화에 쓰는 생생 표현

Chapter •• 16

548

누구 때문에 화난 거죠?
Someone pushed your button?

 → Someone made you angry? 멱살 잡고 싸우는 장면이 떠오르네요…

A Someone pushed your button, Tim?
B Sorry, I'm just still angry over what Drew said.

A 누구 때문에 화난 거야, 팀?
B 미안, 드루가 한 말 때문에 아직 분이 안 풀려.

549

뭐 때문에 폭발한 거야?
What set you off?

A You look really angry. What set you off?
B That saleswoman was very rude to me.

rude 무례한

A 화가 단단히 났네. 뭐 때문에 폭발한 거야?
B 저 판매 사원이 아주 무례하게 굴잖아요.

550

폭발 직전이군.
You look ready to blow.

 → You seem to explode with anger.

A You look ready to blow! Something bad happened?
B Yes, some fool hit my car while it was parked!

while ~하는 동안 eg. Enjoy yourself while you can.

A 폭발 직전이군요! 뭐 안 좋은 일 있어요?
B 예, 어떤 멍청이가 주차된 내 차를 받았어요!

267

호기심이 생길 때 하게 되는 말

Curiosity

- [ ] Looking for something?
- [ ] Something you want to ask me?
- [ ] Out with it
- [ ] Questions?
- [ ] Let's hear it.

551

뭘 찾고 있어요?
Looking for something?

→ 한국말과 다르지 않죠? 궁금하니까, 주어(You)도 생략하고 바로 말해요! You're looking for something? You need something?

A Looking for something?
B I want the brown suitcase you bought for me. Do you know where I can find it?

A 뭘 찾고 있어요?
B 당신이 사준 갈색을 가방 찾는데, 어디 있는지 알아?

552

내게 말할 게 있나요?
Something you want to ask me?

→ You want to ask me something? Something이 더 궁금해서 문장 앞으로 이동했죠!

A Something you want to ask me? You seem to be curious.
B I just wanted to get your advice on this research.

curious 궁금한 get one's advice on …에 대해 ~의 조언을 구하다

A 내게 말할 게 있나요? 궁금한 게 있는 듯한데.
B 이 연구에 대해 조언 좀 해주세요.

553

어서 말해봐요.
Out with it

 → Speak your question. Don't hesitate. 생각만 하지 말고 '발설'을 하란 뜻.

A Out with it, Marvin. I can read your face.
B I was wondering if I could keep this book.

keep (물건) 보관하다, 소유하다

A 어서 말해봐, 마빈. 네 얼굴에 쓰여 있어.
B 이 책을 가져도 되는지 몰라서요.

554

질문 있나요?
Questions?

 → Do you have questions?

A Questions? Now's the time to ask them.
B Could you please go over slide #4 again?

A 질문 있나요? 질문 시간입니다.
B 4번 슬라이드 다시 설명해주시겠어요?

555

자, 들어보자.
Let's hear it.

 → I want to hear your question/what's on your mind.

A Let's hear it, Amy. I know you've got a question.
B Can I go out and play right now?

A 에미, 자 들어보자. 네가 무슨 질문이 있는지.
B 지금 나가서 놀아도 돼요?

가족의 안부를 묻고 싶다면

Family

- [ ] Everything okay at home?
- [ ] How're the wife and kids?
- [ ] How're things at home?
- [ ] How's the home front?
- [ ] How're the little ones?

556

댁 내 평안하시죠?
Everything okay at home?

 → Is everything fine among your family members?

　A　Everything okay at home, George?
　　　B　My son was very ill for a while. But he's OK now.

　A　댁 내 평안하시죠, 조지?
　　　B　한동안 아들이 아팠는데, 이젠 괜찮아요.

557

아내와 애들은 잘 있죠?
How're the wife and kids?

 여자에겐 이렇게 — How're the husband and kids?

　A　How're the husband and kids? They keeping you busy?
　　　B　Yes! I hardly have any time left over for myself weekends.

　　keep~ busy ~를 바쁘게 하다　hardly 거의 없다

　A　아내와 애들은 잘 있죠? 바쁘시겠군요?
　　　B　예! 주말엔 내 시간이 전혀 없어요.

일상 안부 대화에 쓰는 생생 표현

Chapter 16

558
가정생활은 어때요?
How're things at home?

 → How's your family?와 같은 말이에요.

  A How're things at home, Al?
B Fine, thanks, though being a married man's not easy!

  A 앨, 가정생활은 어때요?
B 좋아요, 결혼한 남자로 사는 게 쉽지는 않지만요!

559
별일 없죠?
How's the home front?

 → 전쟁중에 국내에 남겨진 가족의 안부를 묻는 말에서 비롯된 표현.

  A How's the home front? Is Tom still having problems in School?
B Yes, but he's slowly improving.

home front 국내 전선, 후방의 국민 have problems in ~에 문제점이 있다

  A 별일 없죠? 톰은 아직도 학교적응을 잘 못하나요?
B 예, 그래도 조금씩 나아지고 있어요.

560
자녀들은 잘 있어요?
How're the little ones?

 → little ones는 children을 말해요.

  A How're the little ones? Staying healthy?
B Yeah, they're great, thanks.

  A 자녀들은 잘 있어요? 건강하죠?
B 예, 잘 있어요.

CHAPTER 17

Customer Service

Is this the company bowling team? It sure is. Want in? Isn't this the local parents' group? I'd like to join the school French Club here. You hopping on? How long have you studied Why don't you join our research group? I'm a solo act, sorry. You're leaving our depart jumping ship. I got a better offer. Is this the company bowling team? It sure is. Want in? Isn't this the local parents' group? It is. You s You hopping on? How long have you studied French? Can I come to your party this Friday? Of course! The more, the merrier. Aren't y You're leaving our department? Yeah, from now on you're on your own. Why didn't you help carry our bags? Every man for himself; I'

Susan Says...

A lot of men enjoy talking, but I prefer ones that can listen.

Customer Service

생활 속 서비스
현장에서 쓰는
생생 표현

561 ▸ 595

고객에게 도움을 제안하는 말

Assistance

☐ How may I help you (sir/ma'am)?   ☐ Is there anything you need?   ☐ Could I show you something?
☐ Are you interested in anything special?   ☐ Could I recommend something to you?

561

어떻게 도와드릴까요?
How may I help you (sir/ma'am)?

→ What can I do for you (sir/ma'am)?

A How may I help you, ma'am?
B I'm looking for a size 8 dress, preferably in white.
preferably 선호하기는, 가급적이면

A 어떻게 도와드릴까요, 부인?
B 8호 치수를 찾고 있는데, 흰색이면 더 좋겠군요.

562

필요하신 게 있나요?
Is there anything you need?

→ Are you looking for anything in particular?

A Is there anything you need?
B No, I'm just browsing right now.
browse 둘러보다, 훑어보다   eg. She was browsing through fashion magazines.

A 필요하신 게 있나요?
B 아뇨, 지금 둘러보는 중이에요.

563

뭘 좀 보여드릴까요?
Could I show you something?

A Could I show you something?
B I'd like to look around first, if you don't mind.
if you don't mind 괜찮다면

A 뭘 좀 보여드릴까요?
B 괜찮다면, 우선 둘러보고요.

564

특별히 마음에 둔 게 있나요?
Are you interested in anything special?

 물건 구경을 한참 하고 있다면 십중팔구 이렇게 묻곤 하죠.

A Are you interested in anything special?
B I'm just looking at what you have. I might ask for your help later.
ask for one's help (~의) 도움을 요청하다

A 특별히 마음에 둔 게 있나요?
B 여기 물건을 구경하고 있어요. 필요하면 나중에 부르죠.

565

맞는 물건을 추천해드릴까요?
Could I recommend something to you?

A Could I recommend something to you?
B Yes, I'm looking for something in black, please.
in black 색깔 앞에는 in을 씀.

A 맞는 물건을 추천해드릴까요?
B 예, 검정색으로 된 걸로요.

고객을 마중할 때 쓰는 말

Seeing Off

- ☐ Thank you for coming.
- ☐ Have a nice day/good evening.
- ☐ Please come again.
- ☐ Thanks for your visit!
- ☐ See you again soon!

566
들러주셔서 감사합니다.
Thank you for coming.

 → 가장 일반적으로 쓰는 말이에요.

A Thank you for coming!
B You're welcome. I had a great time.

A 들러 주셔서 감사합니다.
B 천만에요. 잘 놀다 갑니다.

567
안녕히 가세요. 안녕히 계세요.
Have a nice day/good evening.

 → 손님과 직원 모두 서로에게 쓰면 좋은 말.

A Have a nice day!
B Thank you, miss.

A 안녕히 계세요!
B 감사합니다, 아가씨.

568

또 오세요.
Please come again.

 한국말과 똑같아요! 답변은 I will! 또는 Thanks.로 말해요.

A Finished shopping? Please come again soon!
B Thanks a lot.

A 쇼핑 다하셨어요? 또 오세요.
B 감사합니다.

569

방문해주셔서 감사합니다!
Thanks for your visit!

A Did you enjoy your tour of Mickey Land? Thanks for your visit!
B Thanks, I had a great time.

A 미키랜드 구경이 재미있으셨나요? 방문해주셔서 감사합니다.
B 고마워요, 재밌었어요.

570

조만간 또 오세요!
See you again soon!

A Thanks for coming to Aspen! See you again soon!
B Thanks! This was the best ski trip ever!

the best trip ever 이제껏 한 여행 중 최고

A 아스펜 방문에 감사드립니다! 조만간 또 오세요!
B 고마워요! 최고의 스키여행이었어요!

고객의 불편사항을 점검하는 말

Customer Comfort Enquiries

- ☐ Everything okay? ☐ Problems? ☐ Anything wrong?
- ☐ Comfy? / Comfortable? ☐ Full?

571

불편한 점 없으세요?
Everything okay?

→ 고객의 안위를 점검할 때 가장 자주 쓰는 말.

A Everything okay? Perhaps you'd like a menu brought to your room?
B Maybe later, thanks.

Perhaps you'd like~? 혹시 ~을 원하세요?

A 불편한 점 없으세요? 메뉴를 방으로 갖다드릴까요?
B 나중에요, 고마워요.

572

문제가 있나요?
Problems?

→ Were there any problems with your drinks/meals?

A I noticed you didn't finish your drinks. Problems?
B Everything's fine. We'd just like to pay our bill.

notice 알아차리다, 눈치채다

A 술을 남기셨네요. 문제가 있나요?
B 없습니다. 그만 계산을 하려고요.

573

불편하신 데라도 있나요?
Anything wrong?

A You called for me, sir. Anything wrong?
B Could I have a pillow for my seat, please?

call for (큰소리로) ~를 부르다/요청하다   eg. Who called for a cup of coffee?

A 부르셨죠, 손님. 불편하신 데라도 있나요?
B 좌석에 쿠션 좀 갖다주겠어요?

574

편안하세요?
Comfy? / Comfortable?

 comfy는 comfortable과 같은 말. 줄임말이 유행이죠?

A Here are the cushions you asked for. Comfy?
B Yes, thanks very much.

A 요청하신 쿠션입니다. 편안하세요?
B 예, 감사합니다.

575

많이 드셨나요?
Full?

 Are you full? I hope you had enough to eat. Full? 한 단어로도 통해요!

A Full? I hope you enjoyed our Texas buffet.
B Yes, everything was very tasty, thanks.

tasty 맛있는(delicious)

A 많이 드셨나요? 텍사스 뷔페가 입에 맞으셨길 바래요.
B 예, 모든 게 아주 맛있었어요.

고객을 대기시킬 때 하는 말

Waiting

☐ Please wait. ☐ I'll get her. ☐ Sorry you had to wait.
☐ Thanks for your patience. ☐ Sorry I couldn't talk to you earlier.

576
기다리세요.
Please wait.

A I'm Janice Roth. I've got an appointment with Mr. Berman.
B Please wait. I'll check to see if he's in.

have/get an appointment with ~와 약속이 있다

A 제니스 로스예요. 버먼 씨와 약속이 되어 있어요.
B 기다리세요. 계신지 볼게요.

577
불러다 드릴게요.
I'll get her.

 → I'll tell him/her that you're here to see.

A Is Mrs. Woods in? I'm Barbara Carter from Dynaco Inc.
B Just a moment, please. I'll get her.

사람이름+from ~에 근무하는, ~에서 온

A 우즈 여사 계세요? 다이나코 사에서 온 바바라 카터예요.
B 잠시 기다리세요. 불러다 드릴게요.

578
기다리게 해서 죄송해요.
Sorry you had to wait.

A Sorry you had to wait, Ms. Levy. Would you like to step into my office?
B Thanks a lot, Mr. Epstein.

step into 들어 오다(get/come in)

A 기다리게 해서 죄송해요, 레비 씨. 들어오시겠어요?
B 감사합니다, 엡스타인 씨.

579
오래 기다리셨지요.
Thanks for your patience.

 → Thanks for waiting for a long time.

A Thanks for your patience, Mr. Wang. So how was your trip?
B Fine, thanks. I'm very pleased to see you again.

patience 인내, 참을성

A 오래 기다리셨지요, 왕 사장님. 여행은 어떠셨나요?
B 좋았어요. 다시 뵙게 되어 기쁩니다.

580
더 일찍 응대하지 못해 죄송해요.
Sorry I couldn't talk to you earlier.

 → 먼저 고객이 있거나 지체 시간이 길어졌을 때 이렇게 말문을 열어요.

A Sorry I couldn't talk to you earlier. Thanks for waiting.
B No problem at all, Mr. O'Rourke.

A 더 일찍 응대하지 못해 죄송해요. 기다려줘서 감사합니다.
B 괜찮습니다, 오로케 씨.

물건을 건네면서 하는 말

Handing over Items

- [ ] Here you are.
- [ ] Here's what you ordered.
- [ ] Would you like a bag?
- [ ] Would you like that gift-wrapped?
- [ ] For here or to go?

581

여기 있습니다.
Here you are.

가장 일반적으로 쓰는 말이죠.

A Here you are. Enjoy your purchase!
B Thanks a lot. I will.

purchase 구입물품

A 여기 있습니다. 잘 쓰세요!
B 감사합니다. 그럴 거예요.

582

주문하신 것 나왔어요.
Here's what you ordered.

A Here's what you ordered: two beers and one gin and tonic.
B Thanks a lot.

A 주문하신 것 나왔어요. 맥주 두 잔, 진토닉 한 잔이요.
B 감사합니다.

583

쇼핑백 드릴까요?
Would you like a bag?

 Do you need a bag? 또는 그냥 Bag?도 좋아요!

A Your total comes to $47.70. Would you like a bag?
B Yes, please. That would help a lot.

come to (계산) ~에 이르다

A 합계가 47달러 70센트네요. 쇼핑백 필요하세요?
B 예, 주세요. 그러면 아주 좋겠군요.

584

선물용으로 포장해드릴까요?
Would you like that gift-wrapped?

 일반적인 포장은 Shall I wrap this?라고 말해요.

A You'll really enjoy this jacket. Would you like that gift-wrapped?
B Yes, please. It's a gift for my daughter.

A 재킷이 아주 맘에 들 겁니다. 선물용으로 포장해드릴까요?
B 아, 예. 딸에게 줄 선물이죠.

585

여기서 드실 건가요, 포장인가요?
For here or to go?

 패스트푸드점에서 늘 듣는 말이죠.

A Two cheese burgers. Will that be for here or to go?
B For here, please.

A 치즈버거 두 개요. 여기서 드실 건가요, 포장인가요?
B 여기서 먹을 겁니다.

고객만족을 확인해보는 말

Confirmations

- Did you enjoy your time here?
- Did you get that ...?
- How was your time here?
- Was anything uncomfortable?
- Something wrong?

586

즐겁게 지내셨나요?
Did you enjoy your time here?

→ Did you have a good time here?

A Did you enjoy your time here at the hotel?
B Yes, it was great. I loved everything about Melbourne.

A 이곳 호텔에서 즐겁게 지내셨나요?
B 예, 만족합니다. 멜버른이 아주 맘에 들었어요.

587

~하셨나요?
Did you get that ...?

→ 고객이 요구한 것이 이루어졌는지 확인할 때 써요.

A Hello, sir, did you get that room upgrade that you wanted?
B Yes, I did. The new room is much better.

A 원하시는 더 나은 방으로 옮기셨나요?
B 네. 새 방이 훨씬 좋아요.

588

여기서 지내시기 어땠어요?
How was your time here?

A Mr. Joo, how was your time here in Dublin?
B Great! I got a lot of business done and also some sightseeing, too.

A 주 사장님, 이곳 더블린에서 지내시기 어땠어요?
B 좋았어요! 성사된 사업도 많았고 관광도 좀 했죠.

589

불편하신 점은 없었나요?
Was anything uncomfortable?

→ Was everything okay?라고 해도 좋아요.

A Was anything uncomfortable?
B No, everything here was really nice, thanks.

A 불편하신 점은 없었나요?
B 아뇨, 모든 게 아주 좋았어요.

590

맘에 안 드는 게 있으세요?
Something wrong?

→ 고객의 불만이 예상될 때 써요.

A Something wrong? You didn't finish your fish.
B It was delicious, but I've had enough, thanks.
I've had enough.=I'm full.

A 맘에 안 드는 게 있으세요? 생선을 남기셨네요.
B 맛있었는데, 배가 불러서요.

고객의 요구를 들어 주지 못할 때

Giving Customers Negative Information

- [ ] Not right now, sorry.
- [ ] Sorry, it's against the rules.
- [ ] Sorry, it's store/company policy.
- [ ] I'd like to help you, but
- [ ] I'm afraid not.

591
당장은 못합니다.
Not right now, sorry.

→ I'm afraid, but I can't take your request now.

A Isn't the restaurant open yet?
B Not right now, sorry. We don't open until 2:00.

not open until ~가 돼야 열다

A 식당 문을 아직 열지 않나요?
B 당장 열지는 못해요. 2시가 돼야 엽니다.

592
죄송하지만 규정상 안 됩니다.
Sorry, it's against the rules.

→ **It is not allowed.** against는 '~에 거슬리는, 반대되는'이란 뜻.

A My kids can't swim in the hotel pool alone?
B Sorry, it's against the rules.

alone 홀로, 단독으로 (by oneself)

A 아이들끼리 호텔 수영장을 이용할 수 없다고요?
B 죄송하지만 규정상 안됩니다.

593
죄송하지만 규정이 그렇습니다.
Sorry, it's store/company policy.

 policy는 '규정, 정책, 규칙'이란 뜻. 모든 조직에 다 써요!

A Can't I pay for this item by installments?
B Sorry, it's store policy to have customers pay all at once.

by installments 할부로   all at once 한꺼번에 모두

A 이걸 할부로 살 수 없나요?
B 죄송하지만 규정상, 일시불로 하셔야 합니다.

594
도와드리고 싶지만
I'd like to help you, but

 but 다음에 안 되는 이유를 넣어 말해요.

A Why can't we get a ticket to Phoenix?
B I'd like to help you, but they're all sold out right now.

A 어째서 피닉스행 표를 살 수 없나요?
B 도와드리고 싶지만, 지금 매진되었어요.

595
죄송하지만 없어요.
I'm afraid not.

A Don't these shoes come in any other color?
B I'm afraid not, ma'am. Black's the only color we have.

any other (이것 말고) 다른 것

A 이 구두 다른 색깔은 없어요?
B 죄송하지만 없어요. 검정색으로만 나와요.

CHAPTER 18

Enthusiasm and Encouragement

Is this the company bowling team? It sure is. Want in? I'd like to join the school French Club here. You hopping on? Aren't you going to stay with our group? Sorry, you have to. Why don't you join our research group? I'm a solo act, sorry. You're leaving our department? Yeah, from now on you're on your own. We're the company bowling team? It sure is. Want in? Isn't this the local parents' group? It is. You signing up? We need more parents. This is the... You hopping on? How long have you studied French? Can I come to your party this Friday? Of course! The more, the merrier. Aren't you... You're leaving our department? Yeah, from now on you're on your own. Why didn't you help carry our bags? Every man for himself; I've...

Susan Says...

Young, successful and handsome: keep looking until you meet a man who meets that exact description.

Enthusiasm and Encouragement

용기와 열정을
북돋아 주는
생생 표현

596 › 630

열광적으로 동조할 때 어울리는 말

Enthusiasm
- ☐ I'm all for it. ☐ I like the idea! ☐ Perfect!
- ☐ Sounds like a plan! ☐ Right on!

596

전적으로 동의합니다.
I'm all for it.

 → I strongly agree with it. For에 '찬성'의 뜻이 있다는 것 아시죠? all은 부사로 '전적으로, 완전히'란 뜻. 이젠 완전히 끝났어! – It's all over now!

 A What do you think about moving into the suburb?
B I'm all for it. We can have a bigger house there.
move into the suburb 교외로 이사 가다

 A 교외로 이사하는 것 어때요?
B 난 전적으로 동의해요. 더 큰 집을 구할 수 있잖아요.

597

괜찮은 생각이야!
I like the idea!

 → 쉽지만 자주 쓰는 말이에요!

 A What do you think of running an Internet cafe near the school?
B I like the idea! I can help after the school.
run 운영하다 eg. I may run a hobby shop.

 A 학교 근처에 인터넷 카페를 운영하는 게 어때?
B 괜찮은 생각이야! 학교 끝나면 나도 도울게.

용기와 열정을 북돋아 주는 생생 표현

Chapter •• 18

598
완벽해요! 좋아요!
Perfect!

 마음에 꼭 드는 제안에 대해 톡 튀어나오는 말!

A What about going into that karaoke? It looks great!
B Perfect! I'm in the mood to sing since I've had a few drinks.

be in the mood to do ~할 기분이다, ~이 내키다

A 저 노래방에 가는 것 어때요? 근사해 보이는데!
B 좋아요! 몇 잔 했더니 노래하고 싶네.

599
그래요! 짱이다!
Sounds like a plan!

 What a great idea! 미리 짜놓은 일처럼 동의한다는 말.

A Why don't we set up a blind date for Sam?
B Sounds like a plan!

set up a blind date for ~에게 미팅 주선을 하다

A 샘에게 '소개팅' 시켜주는 게 어때?
B 그래요!

600
좋아요! 예!
Right on!

 Yes! 열광적으로 동의를 표현할 때 씨요.

A I'm going to persuade dad to buy a new car.
B Right on, Roy! I'm sure you'll convince him!

persuade 설득하다   convince 납득시키다

A 아빠께서 새 차를 사도록 설득할 거야.
B 좋아, 로이! 넌 아빠를 납득시킬 수 있어!

291

상대방을 격려해주는 말

Encouragement

- [ ] That's the spirit! - [ ] Go for it! - [ ] You go, girl!
- [ ] Hang tough! - [ ] You show 'em!

601

그런 정신으로 해야지!
That's the spirit!

→ **That's the way!**라고도 해요. 먼저 나 자신부터 격려하자고! 예~ That's the spirit! I can speak it like you, Susan!

A I'm going to work on this all night until I get it done.
B What a great attitude, Wesley! That's the spirit!

attitude 태도

A 밤을 새서라도 이걸 끝낼게요.
B 아주 좋은 태도일세, 웨슬리! 그런 정신으로 해야지!

602

해봐요!
Go for it!

→ **You can do it!** 뭐든 시도해보라고 용기를 줄 때 써요.

A I'm going to become a movie star!
B Go for it, Britt! Why not?

A 난 영화배우가 될 거예요!
B 해봐요, 브릿! 못할 것도 없잖아요?

용기와 열정을 북돋아 주는 생생 표현

603
잘한다!
You go, girl!

 → 특히 미국에서 많이 써요. 여성들에게만 쓰세요.

A I'm going to work on this machine until it's fixed!
B You go, girl! I know you can do it, Jasmine!

work on ~에 착수하다, 연구하다, 개선시키다

A 이 기계를 내가 고치고 말거야!
B 잘한다! 당신은 할 수 있어, 야스민!

604
굳건히 버텨요!
Hang tough!

 → 어려움이 닥쳐도 힘내라고 격려할 때 쓰는 말.

A This project is already 2 days behind!
B Just keep working at it and hang tough. You'll catch up!

catch up 따라잡다 eg. Don't skip the class. It'll be hard to catch up.

A 이 프로젝트가 벌써 이틀이나 뒤쳐졌네!
B 열심히 해요, 꿋꿋하게. 곧 따라잡을 겁니다!

605
능력을 보여줘요!
You show 'em!

 → Show your ability/capacity. 할 수 있다는 자신감을 주는 말.

A I'm going to learn to rollerblade next month!
B You show 'em what you can do!

rollerblade (v) 인라인스케이트를 타다 (n) 인라인스케이트(in-line skate)

A 다음달에 인라인스케이트를 배울 거야!
B 할 수 있다는 걸 보여줘요!

긍정적인 태도로 이끄는 말

Positive Thinking

- [ ] Chin up!
- [ ] Think positively!
- [ ] Keep on keeping on
- [ ] In it to win it!
- [ ] Buck up! / Cheer up!

606

힘내요!
Chin up!

→ **Stay positive.** 기죽지 말고 기운내라는 뜻. Keep your chin up!의 줄임말이죠.

A I'm still doing my job search. I feel hopeless.
B Chin up! Never give up!

hopeless 가망이 없는 eg. I'm a hopeless cook.

A 아직도 직장을 찾고 있어요. 난 가망이 없어요.
B 힘내요! 포기하지 말아요!

607

긍정적으로 생각해요!
Think positively!

→ **Look at the bright side!** 자주 쓸수록 좋은 말!

A I'm such a loser!
B Think positively! You can start all over at anytime!

start over 다시 시작하다   at anytime 하시라도

A 난 인생 패배자예요.
B 긍정적으로 생각해요! 언제고 다시 출발할 수 있어요!

용기와 열정을 북돋아 주는 생생 표현

Chapter 18

608
꾸준히 열심히 하세요.
Keep on keeping on

 → Continue to work hard. Stay faithful.

　A   Being a saleswoman is a tough job!
　　　B   Keep on keeping on! You'll get used to this job.

get used to ~에 익숙해 지다   eg. I'm getting used to Korean dishes.

　A   여자가 영업자가 되는 건 힘들어요!
　　　B   꾸준히 열심히 해봐요. 곧 익숙해질 테니.

609
끝까지 해야 이기죠!
In it to win it!

 → You are "in the game" to "win it"!

　A   I've been hiking for 4 kilometers. I can't go another step.
　　　B   In it to win it! We've only got 1 more kilometer to go!

　A   4킬로미터나 하이킹을 했더니, 더 이상 못 가겠군.
　　　B   끝까지 해야 이기죠! 1킬로미터만 더 가면 돼요!

610
기운내요!
Buck up! / Cheer up!

　A   I'm too tired from doing all this copying. It seems endless!
　　　B   Buck up! We're about 90% done.

endless 끝없는, 지속되는(continuous)

　A   이걸 복사하느라 죽겠어요! 끝이 없어요!
　　　B   기운내요! 90% 정도는 했잖아요.

깔끔한 동의가 맘에 들어!

Agreement
☐ I'm with you. ☐ Same here! ☐ You are so right!
☐ My thoughts exactly! ☐ You read my mind.

611
찬성이에요.
I'm with you.

→ I agree with you. '함께 한다'는 것은 동의/찬성한다는 뜻!

A I think we should all go to the park after work.
B I'm with you! The whole staff needs a break.

A 일 끝내고 우리 모두 공원에 가죠.
B 찬성이에요! 직원 모두에게 휴식이 필요해요.

612
동감입니다!
Same here!

→ I have the same opinion as you.

A I hope we don't have to work this Saturday!
B Same here! I need to have Saturday off once in a while.

don't have to ~할 필요가 없다   once in a while 가끔씩, 한 번 정도

A 이번 토요일엔 쉬고 싶어요.
B 동감입니다! 토요일엔 가끔씩 쉬어야죠.

296

용기와 열정을 북돋아 주는 생생 표현

Chapter 18

613
맞고말고요!
You are so right!

 → I couldn't agree with you more.

　A That movie wasn't even half as good as it was advertised.
　　　B You are so right! It was mostly just talk with no action.

　A 그 영화는 광고내용의 절반도 안 되게 형편없어요.
　　　B 맞아요! 액션은 없고 거의 대사로 때웠죠.

614
나도 바로 그 생각했어요!
My thoughts exactly!

 → I have the exact same thoughts/opinion that you do.

　A It's time for a cigarette break, isn't it?
　　　B My thoughts exactly! I'm dying for a cigarette.
be dying for 몹시 ~하고 싶다

　A 담배 피울 때가 되지 않았나요?
　　　B 바로 그 생각하고 있었어요! 담배가 엄청 당기더라고요.

615
내 마음을 아는군요.
You read my mind.

 → You know what I have on my mind. 상대의 마음을 '읽을 수 있다'면 얼마나 좋을까!

　A We should send an email to Mr. Chan in Singapore about that delivery.
　　　B You read my mind! We need to make sure that he got it!
make sure ~을 확실히 하다

　A 싱가포르의 찬 씨에게 배송 관련해서 메일을 보내야겠죠.
　　　B 내 마음을 아는군! 받았는지 확인해봐야지!

상대방의 기를 살려주는 쉽고 좋은 말

Support

☐ Right beside you ☐ You got my vote! ☐ I'll back you.
☐ You lead, I'll follow. ☐ I couldn't agree more.

616

옆에 있을게요.
Right beside you

→ I am standing right beside you to support you.

A I'm really worried about singing out there.
B Don't worry. We will be right beside you.

A 저기서 노래를 부를 게 너무 걱정돼.
B 염려마. 우리가 옆에서 도와줄 테니까.

617

한 표 던집니다!
You got my vote!

→ I support you so strongly, "if you were a candidate, I would vote for you". 출마한다면 찬성표를 던질 정도로 지지한다는 뜻.

A I think we need to expand this office space.
B You got my vote! There are too many people crowded into one space.

expand 확장하다, 늘리다   crowded 붐비는, 혼잡한

A 사무실을 확장해야 겠어요.
B 한 표 던집니다! 한 공간에 사람들이 너무 많아요.

용기와 열정을 북돋아 주는 생생 표현

Chapter 18

618
지지해줄게요.
I'll back you.

 → I'll support your idea/plan.

A This is a risky investment, but I'm sure it'll be profitable.
B Talk with the director again. I'll back you!

A 위험이 따르는 투자지만, 분명 수익성이 있어요.
B 전무님께 다시 말씀 드려요. 나도 지지해줄게요!

619
당신 하자는 대로 할게요.
You lead, I'll follow.

A Let's get something to eat from that street vendor.
B Right! You lead, I'll follow.

A 저 노점에서 뭘 좀 먹읍시다.
B 좋아요! 당신 하자는 대로 해요.

620
더 이상의 동의는 없어요! 그렇고 말고요!
I couldn't agree more.

 → I agree with you so much that it would be impossible to agree to a higher degree.

A We've got to have some quality time for family dinner.
B I couldn't agree more! After all, we're family!

quality time 귀중한 시간, 교류 시간

A 가족끼리 저녁 한 끼 제대로 먹을 시간은 내야죠.
B 그렇고 말고요! 우린, 어쨌든, 가족이에요!

성공과 칭찬, 누구나 듣고 싶은 말!

Success & Praise
- ☐ You're the man! ☐ You did it! ☐ Dynamite!
- ☐ Su-perb! ☐ Out of this world!

621
참 잘했어요!
You're the man!

→ You are the greatest man. You did really well! 남자에게만 써요. 남자친구, 남편, 아들에게 칭찬해 보세요!

A I finally found a way to get this program to run.
B You're the man, Alfred! I knew you could do it.

A 드디어 이 프로그램 운영 방법을 알았네.
B 잘했어요, 알프레드! 당신이 해낼줄 알았어요!

622
해냈군요!
You did it!

→ You made it! You succeeded in it.

A We managed to increase store sales 20% last quarter!
B You did it! That was always our goal, wasn't it?

manage to do 가까스로 ~하다, 그럭저럭 해내다

A 지난 분기에 점포 매출 신장이 20%에 달했습니다!
B 해냈군! 그게 늘 우리 목표였잖소?

용기와 열정을 북돋아 주는 생생 표현

Chapter 18

623
대단해!
Dynamite!

 → You did a great job, "explosively" well-done! 성공폭발!?

A I worked on this all night, and it's finally ready for submission.
B Dynamite! I knew you'd meet the deadline!

meet the deadline 마감을 지키다

A 밤샘 작업을 해서, 드디어 제출할 수 있습니다.
B 대단해! 자네가 마감을 지킬줄 알았네!

624
대성공이야!
Su-perb!

 → Well-done! '수-퍼브'로 읽어요. 뭐, 그래야 교양 있게 말하는 것이라고 하니…

A The director said he liked our presentation.
B Su-perb! That's due to your great preparation, Kail.

due to ~ 때문이다, 덕택이다(thanks to)   preparation 준비

A 부장님이 우리 프레젠테이션이 맘에 드신대요.
B 대성공이야! 카일, 자네가 잘 준비한 덕이야.

625
성공하기 힘든 일을 해냈어!
Out of this world!

 → It's so great that it seems beyond human capacity. 이 세상에서 성취하기 힘든 일을 이루었다는 극찬!

A I've got great seats for the next soccer match!
B Out of this world! It's hard to get good seats at such a late date.

It's hard to do ~하기 힘들다, 어렵다

A 다음 축구 경기를 볼 수 있는 '로얄석' 표를 구했어!
B 대단하구나! 임박해선 좋은 좌석표를 얻기 힘든데.

그대에게 아낌 없는 찬사를!

Compliment

- You're one in a million.
- No one does it like you!
- What'd I do without you?
- You're an ace!
- You're the tops.

626
당신 같은 인재는 드물어요.
You're one in a million.

 → You're so unique that only one in a million people is like you. 백만 명에 한 명 나올 수 있는 사람! 그정도로 '대단한 인재'란 뜻. 상대방을 좀 '띄워' 줄 때 써요.

A I arranged your flight to LA, along with your hotel.
B You're one in a million, Jane. Thanks for doing that.

arrange 마련하다, 정리하다   along with ~와 함께

A LA 항공편과 함께 호텔도 잡아뒀어요.
B 제인, 당신 같은 인재는 드물어! 고마워요.

627
당신이 있어 참 다행이죠?
What'd I do without you?

 → I couldn't do anything without you. I'm depending on you! 상대방이 늘 도움이 되고 필요한 존재라는 말.

A I set out coffee for Mrs. Hans, Granny.
B Thanks, Ellyn. What'd I do without you?

A 한스 부인께 차를 내드렸어요, 할머니.
B 고맙구나, 앨린. 네가 있어 참 다행이잖니?

628
당신밖에 없어!
You're the tops.

 → You're the best, the "top person in the world".

A I brought you some sandwiches, Al, since you skipped lunch.
B You're the tops! Thanks a lot, Jenny.

since (이유·원인) ~이니까   skip 건너뛰다, 빼먹다

A 앨, 샌드위치를 좀 가져왔어요. 점심을 안 먹은 것 같아서요.
B 당신밖에 없어! 고마워, 제니.

629
아무도 흉내 못내죠.
No one does it like you!

 → No one can match your style/capacity.

A I think everyone in the meeting agreed with my analyses.
B That's because you're a great talker. No one does it like you!

A 회의 참석자 모두가 내 분석에 동의한 것 같아.
B 말씀을 아주 잘하시니까요. 아무도 흉내 못내죠!

630
당신은 최고야!
You're an ace!

 → You're the best, the "top card in the deck".

A I checked the dogs before I left. They seem to be fine.
B I'm relived now. You're an ace, Joy.

ace 실력자   be relived 안심이다   eg. He's alive! Now I'm relieved.

A 떠나기 전에 개들을 점검했는데, 괜찮아 보였어요.
B 이제 안심이다. 당신은 최고야, 조이!

CHAPTER 19

Surprise and Shock

Is this the company bowling team? It sure is. Want in? Isn't this the local parents' g... I'd like to join the school French Club here. You hopping on? How long have you st... Why don't you join our research group? I'm a solo act, sorry. You're leaving our de... jumping ship. I got a better offer. Is this the company bowling team? It sure is. Want in? Isn't this the local parents' group? It is. You s... You hopping on? How long have you studied French? Can I come to your party this Friday? Of course! The more, the merrier. Aren't y... You're leaving our department? Yeah, from now on you're on your own. Why didn't you help carry our bags? Every man for himself; I'...

Susan Says...

I try to find as many thrills—in as many places—as I can.

Surprise and Shock

놀랍고 황당한
일을 당하면 쓰는
생생 표현

631 › 665

너무 갑작스러워 감당하기 힘들 때

Surprise
- [ ] You don't say? [ ] Surprise, Surprise! [ ] Boy oh boy!
- [ ] Who knew? [ ] I must be dreaming!

631
그럴리가?
You don't say?

→ I'm rather surprised, but is it true? 의외의 정보에 '약간 놀랐을 때' 써요.

A Imelda is leaving us today.
B You don't say? She seemed happy living here.

A 이멜다가 오늘 떠나겠대요.
B 그럴리가? 여기서 사는 걸 좋아했던 것 같던데.

632
놀랐겠군요!
Surprise, Surprise!

→ You're not expecting this, are you? 아이러니컬한 상황에 써요.

A My son passed an exam to enter a top university!
B Surprise, surprise! And you always doubted that he could do it!

A 내 아들이 최고 대학에 들어갔어요!
B 놀랐겠군요! 그럴 수 없을 거라고 늘 의심했죠!

633
어머나! 이 일을 어째!
Boy oh boy!

 → It may cause some trouble, though. 문제의 소지가 있는 정보를 들었을 때 써요.

A I bought a German Shepherd for my son.
B Boy oh boy! How are you going to live with that thing in your small house?

A 아들에게 독일 산 셰퍼드를 사줬어.
B 어머나! 그 작은 집에서 '그놈'과 어떻게 지내려고요?

634
누가 알았겠어요?
Who knew?

 → No one could have guessed this surprise.

A Arnold and Samantha are getting married!
B Who knew? They never seemed that serious a couple before.

serious 심각한, 진지한

A 아놀드와 사만타가 결혼한대요!
B 정말이요? 그런 사이로 전혀 보이지 않던데요.

635
세상에! 내가 꿈을 꾸나?
I must be dreaming!

 → It's totally unbelievable! Hard to believe what I've heard.

A Why are you looking like that?
B I must be dreaming. My wife just told me she's pregnant!

A 왜 그렇게 쳐다봐요?
B 내가 꿈을 꾸는 건가? 아내가 임신을 했답니다!

황당한 상황에 툭 내뱉는 말

Bewilderment

☐ I'm lost for words. ☐ That takes the cake! ☐ What in the world?
☐ Stranger and stranger! ☐ Am I going crazy?

636

말이 안 나오네요.
I'm lost for words.

 → I can not speak because of bewilderment.

A You'll be promoted to district manager next month.
B I never expected anything like that. I'm lost for words.

anything like that 그와 같은 일(것)   be lost 어찌할 바를 모르다

A 다음달에 지부장으로 승진할 겁니다.
B 전혀 기대하지 못했는데. 뭐라 말해야 할지.

637

산통 깨는군!
That takes the cake!

 → As if a "cake were taken away" from a party suddenly 뜻밖의 안 좋은 소식으로 화가 날 때 써요.

A The electricity just went down in the building!
B That takes the cake! How're we going to get our work done now?

go down (전기 등이) 나가다, 끊어지다

A 건물 내 전기가 갑자기 나갔어요!
B 산통 다 깨졌네! 지금 작업한 것은 어쩌라고?

놀랍고 황당한 일을 당하면 쓰는 생생 표현

Chapter 19

638
세상에, 이런 일이?
What in the world?

A Hey, look at this great new website I pulled up!
B What in the world are you doing? Shouldn't you be working?

pull up (인터넷) 접속하다, 접근하다 eg. My computer takes a long time to pull up sites.

A 여기, 내가 접속한 웹싸이트 좀 봐요!
B 세상에, 뭐 하는 거야? 업무 봐야 하잖아요?

639
아리송해! 뭐가 뭔지!
Stranger and stranger!

 → That's very confusing. I don't get it!

A Look! The store is going to start selling miniskirts next week.
B In the middle of winter? Stranger and stranger!

in the middle of ~의 한 가운데

A 야! 저 가게에서 다음주에 미니스커트 세일한대.
B 이 한 겨울에? 아리송하구만!

640
내가 뭐 잘못된 건가?
Am I going crazy?

 → I'm extremely confused and bewildered. 왜 이런 일이 생기는지 아리송할 때 써요.

A What the heck's wrong with you?
B I can't remember my own cell phone number! Am I going crazy?

A 당신 도대체 왜 그래요?
B 내 휴대폰 번호가 생각나지 않아! 내가 뭐 잘못된 건가?

인상깊은 일이 벌어지면

Impressiveness

- You don't see that every day!
- Get a load of that!
- That's really something else!
- Imagine that!
- I'm speechless!

641
흔한 일이 아닌데!
You don't see that every day!

 It's not a common sight. 일상과는 아주 다른 상황이 벌어졌을 때 이렇게 말해요.

A Look at the gold sports car cruising down the street!
B You don't see that every day! I wonder who owns it?

cruise 유유히 항해하다, 지나가다

A 도로를 빠져나가는 저 금색 스포츠카 좀 봐!
B 흔히 볼 수 있는 게 아닌걸! 누구 차일까?

642
저것 좀 봐요!
Get a load of that!

 Look at that amazing thing!

A What are you looking at?
B Get a load of that! There are four supermodels coming down the street.

A 뭘 보고 있어요?
B 저것 좀 봐요! 4명의 슈퍼 모델들이 거리를 내려오고 있어요.

643

정말 대단한걸!
That's really something else!

 → That's very impressive.

A Did you see the new movie, Born to Win?
B Yes, that was really something!

A '본투윈'이란 영화 봤어요?
B 예, 정말 대단한 영화죠!

644

한번 상상해봐요!
Imagine that!

A We're moving most of our IT functions to India.
B Imagine that! Our company is finally going global!

go global (규모·운영 방식 등이) 글로벌로 되다

A 대부분의 IT사업은 인도로 이전할 거예요.
B 상상이 가요! 드디어 우리 회사도 글로벌화 되네요.

645

말문이 막혀요!
I'm speechless!

 → I'm so surprised/impressed that I cannot speak.

A Honey, I'm taking you to a fancy dinner tonight for our anniversary!
B How romantic! I'm speechless!

take~ to ~를 …에 데려가다

A 여보, 오늘밤, 결혼 기념일인데 내가 근사한 저녁 살게.
B 너무 낭만적이다! 말문이 막히네요!

이렇게 황당하고 실망스럽기는 처음이야!

Dismay

- ☐ Come again? ☐ Are you serious? ☐ Are you for real?
- ☐ I don't/can't believe my eyes. ☐ Words fail me!

646
뭐라고 하셨죠?
Come again?

 → I'm dismayed. Please repeat what you said. 너무 기가 막혔을 때 써요.

A Don't you owe me $500?
B Come again? I don't recall ever borrowing money from you.

owe ~에게 빚지다, 은혜를 갚다   recall 회상하다, 기억하다

A 내게 500달러 갚을 게 있지 않나요?
B 뭐라고요? 돈을 빌린 기억이 전혀 없는데요.

647
진짜예요?
Are you serious?

A We sell only low-alcohol beer in this karaoke, sir.
B Are you serious? What's the use of having a beer if it's low-alcohol?

What's the use of ~이 무슨 소용인가?

A 본 노래방에서는 저알콜 맥주만 팝니다, 손님.
B 진짜 그래요? 저알콜이면 그게 무슨 맥주인가요?

놀랍고 황당한 일을 당하면 쓰는 생생 표현

Chapter
•• 19

648
사실인가요?
Are you for real?

 → Could this possibly be real?

A Parking in this garage is $8 per hour, ma'am.
B Are you for real? I could practically buy the parking lot for that price.

practically 실질적으로, 실제로   for that price 그 가격으로

A 본 주차장은 시간당 8달러입니다, 부인.
B 사실이요? 그 돈이면 이 주차장을 사도 되겠군.

649
눈이 의심스럽네!
I don't/can't believe my eyes.

 → You're so surprised by what you see or hear. 도저히 믿기지가 않아! 긍정적인 상황 뿐만 아니라 부정적일 때도 써요. 아니, 우리 딸이 오늘 신부가 되다니! 믿기지가 않아! — My daughter is a bride today! I can't believe my eyes!

A This new cell phone has a satellite TV function.
B Wow! I don't believe my eyes!

function 기능

A 이 신형 휴대폰엔 위성TV 기능도 있어요.
B 세상에! 믿어지지 않는데!

650
말을 못하겠군!
Words fail me!

 → 어떤 말로도 현재의 내 심경을 표현하지 못할 만큼 황당하다는 뜻.

A I'm buying a motorcycle next week.
B Words fail me! Why would a grown woman do that?

A 다음주에 오토바이를 살 거예요.
B 말을 못하겠군! 다 큰 여자가 왜 그런 게 필요해?

경외감이 들 정도로 놀라울 때

Shock & Awe
- [ ] It floored me. / I'm floored.   - [ ] It blew me away. / I'm blown away.   - [ ] It rocked me.
- [ ] It's outrageous!   - [ ] I'm thrown.

651

정말 뜻밖이네요.
It floored me. / I'm floored.

→ I'm so shocked that I fell to the floor. 쓰러질 정도로 너무나 뜻밖일 때 써요.

- A I'm studying Chinese at night nowadays.
- B I'm floored! I never knew you had any interest in languages.

- A 요즘 야간에 중국어를 공부하고 있어요.
- B 정말 뜻밖이네요! 외국어 공부에 관심 있는 줄 몰랐어요.

652

끝내줬어! 놀라웠어!
It blew me away. / I'm blown away.

→ I'm so shocked/surprised that I was "exploded into pieces".

- A Did you see our team score the winning point at the last minute?
- B Yeah! It blew me away!

- A 우리 팀이 마지막 순간에 득점하는 것 봤어요?
- B 예! 끝내줬어요!

놀랍고 황당한 일을 당하면 쓰는 생생 표현

Chapter
•• 19

653
몸이 떨릴 정도야.
It rocked me.

 → It was a powerful shock, like an earthquake, "rocked" my body.

- A How did the meeting go?
- B It rocked me. The new CEO wants to make a lot of changes.

- A 회의는 어땠어요?
- B 몸이 떨릴 정도야. 새 CEO께선 많은 변화를 원하셔.

654
있을 수 없는 일이야!
It's outrageous!

 → It's shocking and morally unacceptable. 상식적으로 납득하기 어려운 일에 써요.

- A Did you hear that a huge new casino's going to open downtown?
- B Yes, and it's outrageous! There are three already!

- A 시내에 엄청 큰 카지노가 생긴다는 소식 들었어요?
- B 예, 있을 수 없는 일이죠! 이미 3개나 있는데!

655
당혹스럽군요.
I'm thrown.

- A I'll pay for your hotel through my cell phone, Mr. Page.
- B By cell phone? I'm thrown! Technology's advancing fast!

pay for ~를 지불하다   advance 진보하다, 발전하다

- A 페이지 씨, 휴대폰으로 호텔비를 계산할게요.
- B 휴대폰으로요? 당혹스럽네요. 기술이 정말 빠르군요!

평정심을 보여주고 싶을 때

Equanimity

- [ ] Nothing new to me.
- [ ] And?
- [ ] Am I supposed to be impressed?
- [ ] I've seen better/worse.
- [ ] It's not the end of the world.

656

새로울 것도 없네.
Nothing new to me.

→ It's not impressive at all. 괜히 말한 사람만 '썰렁' 하겠죠!

A Traffic on the city bridge is so crowded!
B Nothing new to me. Traffic on here is always like this.

A 도시 교량에 교통이 엄청 밀린대요!
B 새로울 것도 없네. 여기 교통 상황은 늘 이런걸.

657

그래서요?
And?

→ And isn't there anything more? 무척 냉소적이네요!

A I just spent a week Europe!
B And? I've been to Europe four times already.

A 난, 유럽에서 일주일을 보냈어요!
B 그래서요? 난, 유럽에 4번이나 갔다왔죠.

658

그만 자랑하시죠?
Am I supposed to be impressed?

 → Please stop boasting. You don't impress me. 별로 인상적이지 않다는 뜻.

A Look at my great new luxury sedan!
B Am I supposed to be impressed? It doesn't look that luxurious to me!

A 근사한 내 세단차를 구경하세요!
B 그만 자랑하시죠? 내가 보기엔 근사하지도 않고만!

659

더한 것도 있는데요, 뭘.
I've seen better/worse.

 → It's not bothersome/impressive/moving at all. 더 성가시고/인상적이고/감동적인 일도 있다는 말. 겨우 그걸 가지고 '야단' 이냐고 꼬집을 때 써요.

A Look at the mess the guests made in the dining room.
B I've seen worse. Let's just get started cleaning it up, okay?

A 손님들이 식당을 엉망으로 해 놓았군요.
B 더한 것도 있는데요, 뭘. 자, 어서 치우기나 하죠?

660

별것도 아닌데 그래요.
It's not the end of the world.

 → Don't think too seriously about this situation. "It will not cause the world to end."

A The store declined my credit card.
B Just use cash instead. It's not the end of the world.
decline 거절하다, 거부하다

A 저 가게에서는 신용카드를 안 받아.
B 그럼, 현금으로 내요. 그런 걸 가지고 그래.

# 참는 것도 한계가 있지!

Indignation

☐ I won't stand for it! ☐ That's the last straw. ☐ I've had it!
☐ Enough is enough! ☐ That's it!

661
참고만 있지는 않겠어!
I won't stand for it!

→ I won't stand here and tolerate this situation!

A You're being demoted to section chief, Danny.
B What? I won't stand for it! I'd rather quit!

I'd rather 차라리 ~하겠다

A 데니, 과장으로 좌천될 거래요.
B 뭐요? 참고만 있을 수는 없지. 차라리 그만두겠어!

662
이번만이다!
That's the last straw.

→ That's the final indignity/insult I'll tolerate.

A Mr. Danson wants us to review these articles before they are published.
B That's the last straw! I'm really tired of him giving us last minute assignments.

give~ last minute assignments 마지막 순간에 ~에게 과제를 주다

A 댄슨 씨가 출간 전에 이 논문들을 다시 검토하래요.
B 이번만이다! 그가 마지막 순간에 일을 주는 데 지쳤어.

놀랍고 황당한 일을 당하면 쓰는 생생 표현

Chapter 19

663
더는 못하겠어!
I've had it!

 → I've tolerated enough! But not any more!

A I win again! Pay up $50!
B I've had it with this game! All I ever do is lose!

tolerlate ~을 참아내다

A 또 이겼다! 50달러 내!
B 이 게임, 더는 못하겠군! 나만 잃고있어!

664
해도 너무 하는군! 그쯤 해두지!
Enough is enough!

 → I won't tolerate this anymore. That's enough!

A The income tax is going to increase again this year.
B Again? I'm paying too much already. Enough is enough!

income tax 소득세   cf. earned/unearned income 근로/불로 소득

A 소득세가 올해 또 오른다는 군.
B 또요? 이미 엄청 내고 있는데도. 해도 너무 하는군!

665
됐어요! 그만해!
That's it!

 → I'm ready to explode because of this situation.

A I'm sorry that I forgot your birthday.
B That's it! What kind of husband are you?

A 당신 생일을 잊어서 미안해요.
B 됐어요! 당신, 남편이 맞긴 맞아요?

CHAPTER 20

Money

Is this the company bowling team? It sure is. Want in? Isn't this the local parents' group? It is. You signing up? We I'd like to join the school French Club here. You hopping on? How long have you studied French? Can I come to yo Why don't you join our research group? I'm a solo act, sorry. You're leaving our department? Yeah, from now on y offer. Is this the company bowling team? It sure is. Want in? Isn't this the local parents' group? It is. You signing up? We need more pa You hopping on? How long have you studied French? Can I come to your party this Friday? Of course! The more, the merrier. Aren't yo You're leaving our department? Yeah, from now on you're on your own. Why didn't you help carry our bags? Every man for himself; I've

Susan Says...

Yes, I've got a taste for the classical: Bach and Schubert over Beethoven, actually.

Money

생활 속 '돈'
이야기를 할 때 꼭 쓰는
생생 표현

돈에 대한 나의 생각은?

Philosophies of Money

☐ Money talks. ☐ Cash is king. ☐ Greed is good.
☐ Money changes everything. ☐ Money can't buy love.

666

돈이면 다 되죠.
Money talks.

→ Money has influence, it can "talk powerfully."

A Why do you always get good service in restaurants?
B I give tips all the time, and money talks.
all the time 늘, 항상

A 식당에서 왜 당신에겐 서비스가 좋은 거죠?
B 항상 팁을 주거든요. 돈이면 다 되죠.

667

현금이 최고지.
Cash is king.

 → The ability to pay, or pay in cash, is the most important.

A I wanted to stay at a 5-star hotel, but I didn't have the money.
B You'd better bring more next time, because cash is king!

A 최고급 호텔에서 머물고 싶었는데, 돈이 모자랐어요.
B 다음엔 더 많이 가져가요, 현금이 최고죠!

Chapter •• 20

668
돈을 좋아하는 게 곧 '선'이죠.
Greed is good.

 → **I love money.** 돈을 좋아하는 것이 나쁜 게 아니라는 미국 속담.

A You're demanding even more profit from the deal?
B As we say in New York, greed is good.

demand 요구하다   even more 훨씬 더 많은

A 여기서 훨씬 더 높은 수익을 요구하는 건가요?
B 우리 뉴욕에서는 '돈을 좋아하는 게 곧 선' 이라고 하죠.

669
돈이면 안 될 게 없어.
Money changes everything.

 → **Wealth influences a person's behavior.** 돈으로 바꾸지 못할 게 '정말' 없을까요?

A Angie moved to Hawaii after winning the lottery.
B Well, that's natural because money changes everything.

that's natural 그건 당연하다, 짐작대로다

A 앤지가 복권에 당첨되더니 하와이로 이사 갔대요.
B 뭐, 돈으로 안 될 게 없으니까요.

670
사랑을 돈으로 살 수는 없죠.
Money can't buy love.

 → **Money has a limit.** happiness나 health 같은 것도 마찬가지죠. Money can't buy happiness.

A Why is Jeff still single? He's a very wealthy man.
B He's looking for real romance, and money can't buy love.

wealthy (a) 매우 부유한(very rich)   wealth (n) 부, 재산

A 왜 제프가 아직 싱글이죠? 그는 엄청 부자인데요.
B 진정한 로맨스를 찾고 있지만, 사랑을 돈으로 살 수는 없죠.

돈이 차고 넘친다면

Surplus Money
- ☐ I'm flush! ☐ I've got a fat wallet. ☐ They've got deep pockets.
- ☐ She's got money to burn. ☐ Money is no object.

671
난 부자야!
I'm flush!

→ I have a lot of money on me. 화장실 물 내리듯 써도 남을 돈이 있다면?! 주머니 사정이 좋아져서 '부자가 된 기분'일 땐 I'm feeling flush.라고 해요. feeling하나 더 썼을 뿐인데 뉘앙스가 느껴지죠?

A You've been in a happy mood all day.
B That's because I'm flush. I just got paid.

That's because ~이기 때문이지 get paid 월급(임금)을 받다

A 오늘 기분이 아주 좋은 것 같아요.
B 돈이 많으니까. 월급 받았거든요.

672
지갑이 두둑해.
I've got a fat wallet.

→ I'm carrying a lot of money. My wallet is bulging or "fat" with cash.

A You're going to pay for the dinner and drinks tonight?
B I've got a fat wallet, so why not?

A 오늘 당신이 저녁과 술도 산다는 거야?
B 지갑이 두둑하거든. 그러니 안 될 것 없지?

673

자금 사정이 좋아요.
They've got deep pockets.

 → Big pockets that hold a lot of money. 워렌 버핏 같은 '큰손'이나 대기업 등에 주로 써요.

A Do you think it would be okay to make this loan to Brown Paint Co.?
B No problem. They've got deep pockets, so they can easily pay it back.

make a loan to ~에게 대출해주다   pay back 되갚다

A 브라운 페이트 사의 대출을 해줘도 괜찮을까요?
B 괜찮아. 자금력이 있으니 쉽게 상환할 거야.

674

돈은 태울 정도로 있어.
She's got money to burn.

 → She's got so much money that tossing it into a fire is okay.

A You just spent $300 in that bar! Aren't you worried?
B No! I've got money to burn tonight. On to the next place!

A 술집에서 300달러나 썼는데. 걱정 안 돼요?
B 전혀! 오늘밤, 돈은 태울 정도로 많아. 2차 가죠!

675

돈은 내 관심사가 못 돼.
Money is no object.

 → I have unlimited amounts of money, so money is not an object of concern. 보통 사람들은 '돈 벌어 부자 되기'가 최대 관심사인데…

A Do you want to buy that necklace? It looks so expensive!
B Money is no object, especially as this is a gift for my wife.

A 그 목걸이를 사세요? 엄청 비싸 보이던데.
B 돈은 문제가 안 되죠. 특히 아내에게 줄 선물일 때요.

돈이 떨어졌을 때 하게 되는 말

Money Shortages

☐ I'm broke.   ☐ I'm flat.   ☐ I'm on my last dollar.
☐ I'm tapped out.   ☐ My pockets are empty.

676

돈 없어요.
I'm broke.

 → I have no money on me. 가장 일반적인 말이죠. broken이라고 하지 않도록 주의!

A Let's go to an Italian restaurant.
B Sounds great, but I'm broke. Would you mind paying this time?

Would you mind + -ing? ~ 해주겠어요?

A 이탈리아 식당으로 가죠.
B 좋은데, 난 돈 없어요. 이번엔 당신이 살래요?

677

난 빈털터리야.
I'm flat.

 → No money is being carried on me, "like a flat tire".

A You'll have to pitch in to help pay for this pizza.
B Sorry, but I'm flat! I'll help out next time.

pitch in 조금 보태다, 돕다   eg. All my friends pitched in to help me.

A 피자 주문하게 돈을 보태세요.
B 미안, 난 빈털터리야! 다음엔 도울게요.

678

돈이 이것밖에 없어.
I'm on my last dollar.

 I have only a very little money on me. I'm on은 I only have의 뜻.

A Could you pay for me this time?
B I'd love to but I'm on my last dollar.

A 이번에 내 것도 계산해 줄래요?
B 그러고 싶지만, 나도 돈이 이것밖에 없어요.

679

돈이 똑 떨어졌어요.
I'm tapped out.

 I ran out of money. "My last money has flowed out, like water draining out of a tap".

A What about ordering sushi?
B I'm tapped out because of the drinks we just had. Could you pay?

because of ~ 때문에

A 스시를 주문하는 게 어때요?
B 아까 마신 술 때문에 돈이 떨어졌는데, 내주겠어요?

680

주머니가 텅 비었어.
My pockets are empty.

A You've used up all your money again, haven't you?
B Yeah, sorry. My pockets are empty today.

use up 다 써버리다

A 돈을 또 몽땅 써버렸다는 거예요?
B 응, 미안. 지갑이 텅 비었어.

누가 돈을 낼 것인지 정할 때

Paying & Treating

- [ ] It's on me.
- [ ] It's on the house.
- [ ] Check, please.
- [ ] Let's split it.
- [ ] Let's run a tab.

681

내가 낼게요.
It's on me.

→ It's my treat. I'm paying for everything. on은 pay for와 같은 뜻. — Who's this on? = Who's paying?

A I'm going to pay now.
B It's on me today. I just want to show you my appreciation.

show~ one's appreciation ~에게 감사를 표하다

A 이제 계산해야겠군.
B 오늘은 내가 낼게요. 감사의 마음을 전하는 뜻에서요.

682

주인장이 "쏩니다!"
It's on the house.

A Hey, waitress, I didn't order this drink.
B It's on the house, because you're a regular customer.

regular customer 단골 손님

A 이봐요, 난 술 주문하지 않았어요.
B 주인이 내는 거예요. 단골이시라고요.

생활 속 '돈' 이야기를 할 때 꼭 쓰는 생생 표현

Chapter 20

683

계산서 주세요.
Check, please.

 I'm ready to pay after a meal/drinks. check는 bill의 뜻.

A How was your meal?
B It's fine. We're ready to go, though. Check, please.

A 음식은 어떠셨나요?
B 맛있어요. 그만 가려고하니, 계산서 주세요.

684

나눠서 냅시다.
Let's split it.

 Let's divide the cost. 사람 수대로 나누어 내자는 뜻.

A The bill comes to $73.39
B There are five people here, so let's split it.

come to (합계) ~가 되다   split 쪼개다, 나누다

A 73달러 39센트 나왔어요.
B 우리 5명이니까 나눠서 냅시다.

685

달아놓읍시다.
Let's run a tab.

 run은 use, tab은 전표(a total list of individual purchases)를 말해요.

A Should we pay the waiter now?
B Let's run a tab instead. It's more convenient.

instead 대신에   eg. Would you like a cup of tea instead?   convenient 편리한

A 웨이터를 불러 계산해야죠?
B 그냥 달아놓읍시다. 그게 더 편하겠어.

돈 빌리고, 빌려줄 때 으레 쓰는 말

Borrowing & Lending

- [ ] Got $10 to spare?
- [ ] I can spot you.
- [ ] Short? / Are you short?
- [ ] I'll cover you.
- [ ] I've got this one.

686
10달러 여유 있어요?
Got $10 to spare?

→ **Have you got any extra money?** 여분의 돈이 있는지 묻는 말.

A Have you got $10 to spare?
B Sure, what do you need it for?

A 여분으로 10달러 있어요?
B 예, 뭐 하는 데 쓸 건데요?

687
내가 줄게요.
I can spot you.

→ **I can lend you money/pay for you.** spot은 lend money to의 뜻. 즉석에서 필요한 돈을 융통해 줄 때 써요.

A I left my purse back in the office.
B I can spot you for lunch. Don't worry about it.

A 사무실에 지갑을 놓고 왔네.
B 점심 값은 나한테 있어요. 걱정 말아요.

688

(돈이) 부족해요?
Short? / Are you short?

 → Do you lack money? short은 lacking money의 뜻.

 A These movie tickets costs $9 each? I don't think I have that much.
B Short? I can pay for you.

 A 영화표가 각각 9달러야? 그만큼은 안 될 것 같은데.
B 부족해요? 내가 내줄게요.

689

내가 대신 낼게요.
I'll cover you.

 → I'll pay for you. cover는 pay for와 같은 뜻.

 A I don't think I have enough to pay the delivery-man.
B I'll cover you. How much do you need?

enough to ~하기에 충분한

 A 배달원에게 줄 돈이 충분치 않네.
B 내가 대신 낼게요. 얼마 필요해요?

690

이건 내가 낼게요.
I've got this one.

 → I'll pay for this meal/drinks/situation. this one은 this time occasion의 뜻.

 A I want to pay for the taxi ride, but I don't have enough money.
B I've got this one, so it's no problem.

 A 내가 택시 요금을 내려고 했는데, 돈이 부족하네.
B 이번엔 내가 낼게요. 걱정 마요.

대박과 쪽박, 한두마디면 통해!

Profit & Loss
- I blew
- I hit it big!
- I came up empty.
- Zilch!
- Nada

691
(돈을) 날렸네!
I blew

→ I wasted money. I let money "blow away on the wind". 오, 아까운 내 돈!

A Why do you look so blue?
B I blew $800 in a casino. My wife's going to kill me!

A 왜 그렇게 우울해요?
B 카지노에서 800달러나 날렸어. 아내가 날 가만 안 두겠군!

692
한 건 했어요!
I hit it big!

→ I earned big money success. 한국말과 같은 표현이죠!

A Why are you looking so happy?
B I hit it big! I earned $300 in a card game.

earn (돈을) 벌다, 획득하다

A 뭐 때문에 그렇게 기뻐해요?
B 한 건 했죠! 카드 게임에서 300달러 땄어요.

생활 속 '돈' 이야기를 할 때 꼭 쓰는 생생 표현

693
허탕으로 끝났어요.
I came up empty.

 → I lost money/failed to earn money. 노력에도 불구하고 아무런 수익도 얻지 못했을 때 써요.

A How did your sales calls go this morning?
B I came up empty. I didn't manage to sell a single item!

sales call (텔레 마케팅) 상품 판매를 위해 거는 전화

A 오전에 마케팅 전화 결과는 어땠어요?
B 허탕으로 끝났어요. 한 개도 팔지 못했어요!

694
제로예요!
Zilch!

 → I've got nothing/zero. 'zilch'는 'zero'를 뜻하는 말.

A How much did your fund earn this year?
B Zilch! I wish I hadn't invested!

I wish (that) I+과거(완료)시제 ~하지 않는 편이 나았을 걸 그랬다

A 올해 펀드 수익을 얼마나 올렸어요?
B 제로예요! 투자하지 말 걸 그랬어요!

695
공짜예요.
Nada

 → 스페인어에서 차용된 영어. Nothing!과 같은 뜻.

A How much did this CD cost you?
B Nada: it came with the book.

A 이 CD를 얼마주고 샀어요?
B 공짜예요. 책에 끼어서 온 겁니다.

돈을 내 놓으라고? 그게 문제일 때

Collecting/Demanding Payment

- [ ] Cough it up!
- [ ] Show me the green
- [ ] Put up or shut up
- [ ] Time to pay the piper
- [ ] There's no free lunch.

696
지금 뱉어내요!
Cough it up!

 I demand strongly the money owed. 한국말과 비슷한 비유죠? 없으면 입에 든 것이라도 뱉어 내라는 말. 강력하게 요구할 때 써요.

A Don't I owe you $700?
B You do! Cough it up!

cough~ up (억지로라도) ~을 지불하다

A 내가 700달러 갚을 게 있지 않아요?
B 그래요! 지금 뱉어내요.

697
돈이 있는지 보여줘.
Show me the green

 green은 미국 달러를 가리켜요. 지폐 달러의 색깔 때문에 생긴 말. 구어체로 자주 쓰이니 알아두세요.

A I think I'm ready to buy these sunglasses.
B Okay, show me the green and they're all yours.

be all yours ~은 네 소유다, 네가 알아서 해도 좋다

A 이 선글라스를 사야겠군.
B 그래요, 돈이 있어야 당신 것이 되죠.

698
말은 필요없어요.
Put up or shut up

 → Stop talking and pay what you owe. put up은 give the money의 뜻.

A Can I get an extension on my bill?
B No! Put up or shut up! You have to pay now!

get an extension on ~에 대한 기한을 연장 받다

A 지불 기한을 연장해줄 수 있나요?
B 안됩니다! 말은 필요 없고, 지금 지불해주시오!

699
돈 갚을 때가 됐어요.
Time to pay the piper

 → You've got to pay your debt. 예전에 피리 연주를 듣고 그 대가로 돈을 지불하던 데서 비롯된 말.

A Are you the collection agent?
B Yes I am. Time to pay the piper!

collection agent 수금 요원 cf. collection agency 수금 대행업체

A 수금하러 오셨나요?
B 그렇소. 돈 갚을 때가 됐습니다!

700
세상에 공짜는 없죠.
There's no free lunch.

 → There is no free thing in the world.

A Can't you reduce the shipping costs on these items?
B There's no free lunch. Sorry, but you'll have to pay full price.

reduce (가격)낮추다, 깎다 shipping costs 선적(운송) 단가

A 이 물품 선적 단가를 내려줄 수 없겠어요?
B 세상에 공짜는 없죠. 정가대로 지불하셔야 합니다.

CHAPTER 21

Gossip and Rumor

Is this the company bowling team? It sure is. Want in? Isn't this the local parents' group? I'd like to join the school French Club here. You hopping on? How long have you studied? Why don't you join our research group? I'm a solo act, sorry. You're leaving our department? jumping ship. I got a better offer. Is this the company bowling team? It sure is. Want in? Isn't this the local parents' group? It is. You s You hopping on? How long have you studied French? Can I come to your party this Friday? Of course! The more, the merrier. Aren't y You're leaving our department? Yeah, from now on you're on your own. Why didn't you help carry our bags? Every man for himself; I'

Susan Says...

Don't be afraid of the measuring tape: let it motivate you to exercise harder!

Gossip and Rumor

생활 속 소문의
현장에 꼭 등장하는
생생 표현

701 › 735

세상의 비밀은 모두 알고 싶어!

Secrets

☐ Got anything juicy? ☐ Give me the skinny (on) ☐ What's the lowdown (on)?
☐ Got anything ☐ What's the 411 (on)?

701
뭐 '재밌는' 얘기 있어?
Got anything juicy?

→ Have you got anything enjoyable to hear? juicy는 ripe secret란 뜻.

A I overheard Cynthia and Irene talking about their boyfriends.
B Got anything juicy on them?

overhear 우연히 엿듣다 eg. Sorry, I couldn't help overhearing.

A 우연히 신시아와 아이린이 '남친' 얘기하는 것을 들었어.
B 뭐 '재밌는' 얘기 있어?

702
있는 대로 다 말해봐.
Give me the skinny (on)

→ Tell me real facts. 말에 '옷'을 입히지 말고 마른 몸 그대로 보여달라는 비유. skinny는 core facts의 뜻.

A It's a secret, but Hansu is going to quit for a better offer.
B Is that so? Give me the skinny on it.

A 비밀인데, 한수가 더 좋은 제안을 받고 그만둘거래.
B 그래요? 있는 대로 다 말해봐요.

703

내막이 뭔데요?
What's the lowdown (on)?

 → Give me the most important information on that. 남들은 잘 모르는 실질적이고 중요한 정보를 나한테만 귀띔해 달라는 뜻. lowdown은 the most realistic and important facts의 뜻.

A I heard this area is going to be designated as green-belt!
B Is that true? What's the lowdown?

be designated as ~로 지정되다

A 이 지역이 그린벨트로 묶인대요.
B 사실이에요? 내막이 뭔가요?

704

~에 대해 아는 게 있어요?
Got anything on

 → Have you got any information on that? 사람과 상황에 모두 써요.

A Got anything on our rivals?
B I think they may be entering a market ahead of us.

ahead of ~에 앞서서

A 경쟁사에 대해 아는 게 있어요?
B 우리보다 먼저 시장진입을 할 것 같아요.

705

중요 정보가 뭔데요?
What's the 411 (on)?

 → '411'은 미국의 '정보제공 안내 번호'를 말해요. 일반 명사로도 사용되어 information, gossip의 뜻으로 써요. 특히 비밀리에 구전되는 내부정보(inside information)를 말해요.

A I see you've been talking to a lot of people today. What's the 411?
B I'll tell you later. Now's not a good time.

411 정보, 소문 eg. I heard the 411 on her possible divorce.

A 오늘, 많은 사람들에게 뭔가 말하던데. 중요 정보가 뭔데요?
B 나중에 말해줄게요. 지금은 좀 곤란해요.

'소문난 잔치에 먹을 게 없다' 지만

Rumors

- [ ] What's going around?
- [ ] Have you heard the latest?
- [ ] Just between you and me
- [ ] That's just talk.
- [ ] That's just hot air.

706
돌고 있는 얘기가 뭐죠?
What's going around?

There's a rumor circulating among people.

A What's going around? There's a lot of quiet talk here.
B There's a rumor that the New Year's Party will be canceled.

There's a rumor (that) ~라는 소문이 있다

A 돌고 있는 얘기가 뭐죠? 여기서 엄청 소곤대던데.
B 신년 파티가 취소된다는 얘기가 있어요.

707
방금 소식 들었어요?
Have you heard the latest?

latest는 latest news를 말해요.

A Have you heard the latest? There's a big fire downtown.
B That's awful! How bad is it?

A 방금 소식 들었어요? 시내에 대형화재가 났어요.
B 저런! 얼마나 심각하대?

340

708
우리끼리만 얘기인데
Just between you and me

 → Keep this a secret between you and me.

A Aren't Mr. and Mrs. Connor going to buy a new apartment?
B No, just between you and me they decided to delay for another year.

delay 연기하다 another year 한 해 더(one more year)

A 코노 씨 부부가 새 아파트를 사지 않는다죠?
B 예, 우리끼리만 얘기인데 1년 더 미루기로 했대요.

709
그냥 소문이었어요.
That's just talk.

 → 여기서 talk는 empty talk의 뜻. 잘못된 정보를 말할 때 써요.

A There's going to be a visit by the mayor tomorrow!
B That's just talk. Why would the mayor come here?

A 내일 시장님이 방문하신다면서요!
B 그냥 소문이었어요. 시장이 여길 왜 오겠어요?

710
그건 허풍이야.
That's just hot air.

 → That's an exaggeration. hot air는 breathed words without meaning의 뜻.

A Michelle says she owns 4 sets of diamonds!
B That's just hot air. She doesn't even own a single ring.

own 소유하다 not even ~조차도 아니다

A 미셸이 그러는데 다이아몬드가 4세트나 있대요!
B 그냥 허풍이야. 반지도 하나 없는 애야.

일파만파 번지는 소문!

Rumor Spreading

☐ It's on the grapevine. ☐ Rumor has it (that). ☐ Word is
☐ People talk. ☐ It's on the wire.

711
소문이 무성합니다.
It's on the grapevine.

 → There's a rumor spreading among people in a network. 포도덩굴이 마구 뻗어 나가는 것에 비유한 말.

A How did you get your information?
B Alicia told me, but it's on the grapevine. Haven't you heard?

A 그걸 어떻게 알았어요?
B 앨리샤 한테요. 한지만 소문이 무성하대요. 못 들었어요?

712
소문에요
Rumor has it (that)

 → A current rumor suggests blah blah blah. has it은 suggests의 뜻.

A Why is everyone going downstairs?
B Rumor has it that a movie star is in the lobby!

A 왜 모두 아래층으로 내려가는 거죠?
B 로비에 영화배우가 와 있다는 소문이 있어서요.

713
~라는 소문이 있어.
Word is

 → The current rumer is that... 현재 돌고 있는 소문을 말해요.

A Why doesn't Milo have a girlfriend?
B Word is he might be gay!

A 밀로는 왜 여자친구를 안 사귀는거야?
B 소문에 그가 게이라는데!

714
누군가 말했겠죠.
People talk.

 → People are always talking and spreading various rumors.

A Wow! Where did you hear that Tyler won an award?
B You know how it is: people talk.

win an award 상을 타다

A 그래! 타일러가 상을 탔다는 것을 어디서 들었어?
B 그거야, 누군가 말했겠죠.

715
누구나 아는 얘기야.
It's on the wire.

 → Everybody knows as if it were part of the news wire. 인터넷 뉴스 보도(news wire)처럼 모두에게 알려진 내용이란 뜻.

A How did you know I studied in Japan?
B It's on the wire. I studied there too, actually.

A 내가 일본에서 공부했다는 것을 어떻게 알았어요?
B 모두 알던데요. 실은 나도 거기서 공부했어요.

결국엔 들키게 될 거짓말

Lies

☐ There's nothing to that. ☐ That's bull! ☐ Who'd believe that?
☐ That's a crock! ☐ Talk sense!

716

사실 무근이에요.
There's nothing to that.

→ There's no truth to that rumor or that talk. nothing은 no truth의 뜻.

A I heard that Elise was married three times!
B She's never been married. There's nothing to that.

A 엘리제가 3번이나 결혼했다며!
B 그녀는 결혼한 적 없어요. 사실 무근이에요.

717

순전히 거짓말이야!
That's bull!

→ That's complete nonsense. That's simply not true. bull은 lie, nonsense의 뜻.

A Hey, weren't you in jail for a while, Kurt?
B That's bull! I've never done anything bad like that!

in jail 교도소에 가다/있다   do anything bad 뭔가 나쁜 짓을 하다

A 이봐, 커트, 교도소에 한동안 있었다며?
B 순전히 거짓말이야! 난 나쁜 짓을 한 적이 없어!

718
그걸 누가 믿겠어요?
Who'd believe that?

 → Nobody believes that. It's just hot air.

A The company's going to fly us to Spain First Class!
B Who'd believe that? They'll send us by coach as usual!

by coach 버스로(by bus)   as usual 늘 그렇듯

A 회사에서 1등석 항공편으로 스페인에 보내준대요!
B 그걸 누가 믿겠어요? 평소처럼 버스로 보낼 텐데!

719
그건 헛소리야!
That's a crock!

 → **That's ridiculous!** crock은 empty bowl의 뜻. 쓸모 없는 것을 나타내요.

A Did you know that Dean's a heavy drinker?
B That's a crock! He doesn't drink anything but water!

anything but ~외에는 절대로 아닌   eg. He never does anything but sleep.

A 딘이 술을 엄청 마신다면서요?
B 그건 헛소리야! 물밖에 못 마시는 친구인걸!

720
납득이 가는 말을 해요!
Talk sense!

 → You don't speak in a reasonable way. That's nonsense. 합리적으로, 이성적으로 설득력이 없는 얘기를 할 때 써요.

A Su-mi says she spent last week in Hollywood!
B Talk sense! She doesn't even own a passport.

A 수미는 지난주를 할리우드에서 보냈대요!
B 납득이 가는 말을 해요! 그녀는 여권조차 없어요.

소문의 진상을 알고 보니

Exposure

- [ ] Your story's out. [ ] You got me. [ ] Now you know.
- [ ] Aha! [ ] It's front page news.

721
모두가 알고 있어요.
Your story's out.

→ It's not a secret anymore. 세상에 비밀이 어디 있나요?!

A Your story's out. You got engaged, didn't you?
B Shhh! Keep it quiet, please.

A 모두가 알고 있어요. 약혼했다면서요?
B 쉿! 제발 조용히 하세요.

722
(헉) 들켰군.
You got me.

→ 우연히 상대방에게 '비밀'이 발각된 경우에 써요. 반대는 I got you!가 되겠죠.

A You're trying to leave work early for the soccer game, aren't you?
B You got me. Don't tell the boss, though.

A 축구 보려고 일찍 퇴근하려는 거, 맞죠?
B 들켰군. 사장님께는 말하지 말아줘.

Chapter 21

723
당신도 알게 됐군요.
Now you know.

 → I've failed in keeping it a secret. 냉소적으로 툭 던지는 말이에요.

A You're planning a surprise party for Jill, aren't you?
B Now you know! Keep it a secret!

keep~ a secret ~를 비밀에 부치다

A 질에게 '깜짝 파티' 열어줄 거니?
B 너도 알게 됐구나! 비밀로 해야 돼!

724
알았다!
Aha!

 → I know why! I've exposed your secret!

A I don't feel too well this morning.
B Aha! You drank too much last night, didn't you?

A 오늘 아침 몸이 영 안 좋은데.
B 알았다! 어젯밤 엄청 마셨죠, 그렇죠?

725
1면 기사감인데요, 뭘.
It's front page news.

 → Everyone knows, as if it were a newspaper story.

A How did you find out I got a charity award?
B It's front page news, Bonnie. You should be proud!

charity 봉사, 자선   proud 자랑스런, 뿌듯한

A 내가 봉사상을 받았다는 걸 어떻게 알았어요?
B 1면 기사감인데요, 보니. 뿌듯하겠어요!

비밀, 너 딱 걸렸어?!

Hidden Secrets

- [ ] You hiding something?
- [ ] You know something I don't?
- [ ] Keeping something from me?
- [ ] What are you trying to pull?
- [ ] You don't fool me.

726
뭐 숨기는 것 있어요?
You hiding something?

→ You are hiding something, aren't you?

A What's up, Tom? You hiding something?
B Don't tell anyone, but I think I lost the keys to Dad's car.

A 무슨 일이야, 톰? 뭐 숨기는 것 있니?
B 아무한테도 말하지마. 아빠 차 열쇠를 잃어버린 것 같아.

727
내가 모르는 비법이라도 있니?
You know something I don't?

→ Are you hiding any secret I don't know about/should know about?

A You've gotten Mr. Wang to approve all of your designs, but I haven't. You know something I don't?
B It's just my personal skill. That's all.

approve 인정하다, 승인하다

A 왕 부장이 당신 디자인만 승인해주고, 내 것은 안 해주셔. 내가 모르는 비법이라도 있어요?
B 나만의 능력이죠. 그뿐입니다.

생활 속 소문의 현장에 꼭 등장하는 생생 표현

Chapter 21

728
나한테 감추는 것 있죠?
Keeping something from me?

 → 여기서 something은 any secret의 뜻.

A Keeping something from me? You've been talking quietly on the phone all day.
B It's nothing you need to know about.

keep~ from ···에게 ~을 막다, 금지시키다

A 나한테 감추는 것 있죠? 종일 전화로 소곤대고 있잖아요.
B 당신이 알 바 아니에요.

729
뭘 속이려는 거야?
What are you trying to pull?

 → What kind of deception are you trying to use against me? pull은 pull a trick/deceive someone의 뜻.

A Your cell phone has a lot of guys' numbers on it! What are you trying to pull?
B Nothing, Al, those are all just old classmates of mine.

of mine 나의 ~중에 eg. two friends of mine.(내 친구들 중 두 명) deceive 속이다, 기만하다

A 당신 휴대폰에 남자들 번호가 많이 있던데! 내게 속이는 게 뭐야?
B 별것 아니야, 앨, 모두가 옛 동창들 번호야.

730
날 속일 생각은 마세요.
You don't fool me.

 → Don't make a fool of me. fool 은 trick의 뜻이죠.

A You don't fool me. You're not really sick, are you?
B I am! I've got the flu!

A 날 속일 생각은 마요. 진짜 아픈 거 아니죠?
B 정말이에요! 독감에 걸렸어요!

창피하고 굴욕스런 순간이 닥치면

Humiliation

- ☐ My name is mud.
- ☐ I want to crawl into a hole.
- ☐ I could die.
- ☐ Just shoot me
- ☐ I feel six inches tall.

731
엄청 창피했어요.
My name is mud.

→ I feel low and dirty, like mud because of an embarrassment or mistake I made.

A Didn't you knock over the cake at the wedding?
B Yes, that's why my name is mud.

A 결혼식에서 당신이 케이크에 넘어졌다면서요?
B 예, 그래서 엄청 창피했어요.

732
쥐 구멍에라도 들어가고 싶군.
I want to crawl into a hole.

→ I'm so embarrassed! I want to escape this humiliating situation.
쥐란 말은 없지만 한국말과 뉘앙스가 거의 같죠!

A Brent, the whole class saw you fall down yesterday.
B I was so embarrassed. I want to crawl into a hole.

embarrassed 창피한, 수치스러운   crawl into ~안으로 기어들어가다

A 브렌트, 어제 반 전체가 네가 넘어지는 걸 봤다면서.
B 어찌나 창피하던지. 쥐 구멍에라도 들어가고 싶었어.

733
죽고 싶었어요.
I could die.

 → I need death to escape this humiliation. can이 아니라 could를 쓴 점에 유의하세요!

A How do you feel after the boss shouted at you?
B I could die! That's how I feel.

shout at ~을 크게 꾸짖다, 소리 지르다

A 부장님한테 큰 소리로 혼나니 어때?
B 죽고 싶었지! 바로 그런 기분이야.

734
차라리 날 죽여요.
Just shoot me

 → Please kill me so I can escape this humiliation.

A Mr. Watson says your presentation was horrible.
B Okay, just shoot me.

horrible 형편 없는(terrible, aweful)

A 왓슨 씨 말이 네 프레젠테이션이 형편없대.
B 그래요, 차라리 날 죽이라죠.

735
초라해진 느낌이었어.
I feel six inches tall.

 → I feel beneath others, or "as if I have physically shrunk" because of my humiliation. 굴욕을 당하면 왠지 '작아지는' 느낌이 들지요!

A You wore a casual outfit to the formal company dinner!
B I'm sorry. I feel six inches tall.

casual outfit 평상시 의상(casual clothes)

A 회사공식 파티에 평상복을 입었다면서요!
B 그래. 아주 초라해진 느낌이 들더군.

CHAPTER 22

Responsibility and Management

Is this the company bowling team? It sure is. Want in? I'd like to join the school French Club here. You hopping me out. Why don't you join our research group? I'm a solo act, sorry. You're leaving our department? Yeah, from now on you're on your own. company bowling team? It sure is. Want in? Isn't this the local parents' group? It is. You signing up? We need more parents. This is th You hopping on? How long have you studied French? Can I come to your party this Friday? Of course! The more, the merrier. Aren't You're leaving our department? Yeah, from now on you're on your own. Why didn't you help carry our bags? Every man for himself; I

Susan Says...

I got my MBA for a reason—and it wasn't to do charity work.

Responsibility and Management

성공의 키워드,
책임과 관리에 쓰는
생생 표현

736 > 770

결정의 순간이 찾아 오면

Decisions

- [ ] Get off the fence
- [ ] It's your call.
- [ ] The ball's in your court.
- [ ] It's decision time.
- [ ] What's it gonna be?

736
그만 결정을 내려요.
Get off the fence

 → You've got to make a decision. 한국말로 '양다리' 걸치지 말고 결정을 내리라고 촉구할 때 써요.

  A We'd better hold another meeting on this issue.
B Won't you just get off the fence and decide?

hold a meeting on ~에 대한 회의를 열다

  A 이 문제에 대해 한번 더 회의하죠.
B 그만 결정을 내려야 하지 않겠어요?

737
당신이 결정해요.
It's your call.

 → You are the one to make the decision. 경기에서 심판이 최종 판결(referee's call)을 내리는 것에 비유.

  A Shouldn't we put these new dresses on display?
B It's your call. I think we could wait a day or two, though.

put~ on display ~을 진열하다, 전시하다

  A 새 의상들을 진열해야 하지 않을까?
B 당신이 결정해요. 난, 하루 이틀 더 있다 해도 될 것 같은데.

738
공은 당신에게 넘어갔어요.
The ball's in your court.

 정치 뉴스에서 많이 듣는 말이죠? 영어 표현 그대로입니다.

A This salary you're offering is too low.
B You can take it or go. The ball's in your court.

take it or go/leave 수락하든지 말든지 뜻대로 하다

A 제안하신 월급은 너무 낮습니다.
B 수락 여부를 결정해요. 공은 당신에게 넘겨진 상태니까요.

739
결정할 시간입니다.
It's decision time.

 It's time to make a decision. It's not possible to go over this issue again.

A These reports still don't give us any good answers.
B It's decision time. I think we just have to make a choice.

A 이 보고서만으로는 해결책이 보이지 않아요.
B 결정할 시간입니다. 이제 선택을 해야죠.

740
어떤 선택을 해야하죠?
What's it gonna be?

 여기서 what은 what choice를 말해요.

A There are over 14 movies in this theater.
B We can't see all of them. What's it gonna be?

A 여기서 상영하는 영화가 14개나 돼요.
B 다 볼 수는 없고, 어떤 걸로 봐야 할까요?

내 책임이 아니라고 강조하고 싶다면

Non-Responsibility

- [ ] It's not my area.
- [ ] Nothing to do with me.
- [ ] What's it to me?
- [ ] Don't come to me about it.
- [ ] Do I look like someone who cares?

741

내가 할 일이 아닙니다.
It's not my area.

→ **It's not my responsibility.** area는 field of responsibility의 뜻.

A Are you supposed to help us set up the meeting room?
B Sorry, it's not my area. Please speak to someone else.

set up 준비하다, 마련하다   speak to ~에게 말하다, 부탁하다

A 회의실 정리를 도와줄 거죠?
B 미안하지만, 내가 할 일이 아니에요. 다른 사람에게 부탁하시죠.

742

나와는 무관합니다.
Nothing to do with me

→ **It doesn't interest me. I have no business in it.** 참 많이 쓰는 말이니 꼭 사용해 보세요.

A Are you going with us to see the Shanghai Motor Show?
B No, that's got nothing to do with me.

A 상하이 모터쇼에 같이 갈래요?
B 아뇨, 나와는 무관한 일이에요.

743

그게 뭐 중요한가요?
What's it to me?

 What importance would it have to me?

A Bus fare is going up this month!
B What's it to me? I catch the subway to work every day.

go up 인상되다   catch/take the subway 지하철을 타다

A 이달에 버스 요금이 인상된대요!
B 그게 뭐 중요한가요? 난 매일 지하철로 출근하는데.

744

내게 부탁하지 마세요.
Don't come to me about it.

 그 일로 내게 오지 말라니… 부탁하러 오지 말란 뜻이에요.

A We need some more help moving this furniture.
B I don't work here so don't come to me about it.

I (don't) work here. 여기 직원이다(아니다)

A 이 가구 옮기는 것 좀 더 도와주세요.
B 난 여기 직원이 아니에요. 그러니 내게 부탁하지 마세요.

745

내가 도와줄 사람 같아요?
Do I look like someone who cares?

 Your problem has no interest to me! 내 코가 석자이니 당신 문제에 신경쓸 수 없다는 말. 상황에 따라서는 아주 쌀쌀맞게 들릴 수도 있겠죠.

A My computer is down again!
B Do I look like someone who cares? I have my own computer problems!

A 내 컴퓨터가 또 다운되었네!
B 내가 도와줄 사람으로 보여요? 내 것도 문제가 있어요!

책임소재를 밝힐 때 쓰는 말

Management
- [ ] The buck stops here. [ ] That'd be me. [ ] This is my turf.
- [ ] Who's the head honcho? [ ] Who runs this place?

746
제가 모든 책임을 지죠.
The buck stops here.

→ **I take all responsibility.** 책임을 전가하지 않겠다는 의지 표현. 반대로 pass the buck은 책임을 회피한다는 의미가 돼요.

A Who's in charge of this place?
B I am. The buck stops here. What do you need?

be in charge of ~을 책임지다

A 여기 책임자가 누굽니까?
B 접니다. 제가 모든 책임을 지죠. 무슨 문제인가요?

747
접니다.
That'd be me.

→ I am the person in charge. The person in charge is me.

A Who can I talk to about this broken TV?
B I'm on the customer service desk so I guess that'd be me.

customer (service) desk 고객센터

A TV 고장 문제는 누구에게 말해야 하나요?
B 고객센터에 근무하니, 제게 말씀하시면 됩니다.

748

여긴 내 영역입니다.
This is my turf.

 I am the boss here. turf는 territory의 뜻.

A So they made you head of Personnel, eh?
B Yeah, I guess this is my turf now.

A 인사부 수장이 되었다고요?
B 예, 이제 이곳은 내 영역이죠.

749

누가 최고 책임자죠?
Who's the head honcho?

 honcho 스페인어에서 온 말로 boss란 뜻. 미국에 스페인 사람들이 많은 만큼 영어에도 영향을 줘요.

A I've got a complaint I want to make. Who's the head honcho here?
B Ms. Hanson is in charge. She's on the 3rd floor.

A 불만 사항이 있는데, 누가 최고 책임자인가요?
B 한슨 씨예요. 3층으로 가세요.

750

여기 운영자가 누구죠?
Who runs this place?

A I can't find a single person in charge. Who actually runs this place?
B Please speak to Mr. Dearden over at that cubicle. He can help you.

cubicle (사무실) 구획, 칸막이 eg. I have a cubicle next to my boss!

A 책임자가 아무도 없군. 여기 실질적인 운영자가 누구죠?
B 저쪽 구역의 도드 씨에게 말하세요. 도와줄 겁니다.

책임감을 고취시키는 말

Assigning Responsibility

- [ ] Hold the fort
- [ ] It's all yours.
- [ ] It's your baby.
- [ ] Take it and run
- [ ] The place is all yours.

751

잘 지키게.
Hold the fort

 → Take care of everything in here. Protect everything in here. 마치 요새를 사수하듯 책임 있게 잘 보호하고 관리하란 뜻.

A I'm going out to lunch. Can you hold the fort for me while I'm gone?
B Sure, Mr. Foster, no problem.

A 점심 식사하러 나갈 건데. 내가 없는 동안 여길 잘 지킬 수 있죠?
B 그럼요, 포스터 씨, 걱정 마세요.

752

당신이 맡아서 하세요.
It's all yours.

 → I'm turning over responsibility for this place/thing/event to you.

A I'm making you leader of this team. From now on, it's all yours.
B Thanks, sir. I'll do my best in the position.

do one's best in ~에서 최선을 다하다

A 자네가 주장이 될 거야. 이제부터 모두 알아서 하게.
B 감사합니다, 감독님. 임무에 최선을 다하겠습니다.

360

성공의 키워드, 책임과 관리에 쓰는 생생 표현

Chapter 22

753

잘 돌보세요.
It's your baby.

 → It's a precious thing you must take care of. 아기를 돌보듯 정성을 다해서 잘 처리하란 뜻.

A You're in charge of this event. It's your baby, so make sure it succeeds.
B I'll be certain to do that, Ms. Sutton.

make sure 확실히 ~하다(be sure/certain to)

A 자네가 이번 행사 책임자니까. 만전을 기해서 꼭 성공시키게.
B 반드시 그렇게 하겠습니다, 써튼 씨.

754

맡아서 잘 해줘요.
Take it and run

 → Take a task/project/assignment and move it toward success.

A You're in charge of this construction. Take it and run.
B I won't disappoint you, Mr. Brown.

construction (건설)공사　disappoint 실망시키다

A 이번 공사를 책임지고 있죠. 잘 해주시오.
B 실망시키지 않을 겁니다, 브라운 씨.

755

여긴 당신 책임입니다.
The place is all yours.

 → The facility/area/office is all yours. You are the boss here.

A I'm making you manager here. The place is all yours.
B You've really honored me, Ms. Murphy.

honor 넝쩡되게 하다, 기회를 주다

A 당신이 이곳 관리자가 되니까, 이젠 여긴 당신 책임입니다.
B 영광입니다, 머피 씨.

무책임을 따끔하게 질책하는 말

Irresponsibility

- [ ] Were you asleep at the wheel?
- [ ] Out to lunch
- [ ] It went right by you.
- [ ] You fell on your face.
- [ ] You botched it.

756

도대체 뭘 하고 있었죠?
Were you asleep at the wheel?

→ Were you not paying attention? 운전 중에 잠을 잔 것에 비유. 중대사를 제대로 처리하지 못한 경우에 써요.

A Were you asleep at the wheel? Our costs rose all last year!
B I'm sorry, sir, but I did my best.

A 도대체 뭘 하고 있었죠? 작년 비용이 모두 증가했잖소!
B 죄송합니다, 사장님, 하지만 최선을 다했습니다.

757

어디에 한눈을 판 거요.
Out to lunch

→ You should've paid attention to this! 일을 챙기지 못하고 점심 먹으로 나간 것에 비유한 말.

A You must be out to lunch! This machine should have been turned off.
B I'm sorry, ma'am. I'll do it right now.

should have+p.p. (유감) ~했어야 했는데(실제는 그렇지 못한 경우)

A 어디에 한눈을 판 거요! 이 기계를 껐어야지요.
B 죄송합니다, 사장님. 바로 하겠습니다.

758

정신을 어디다 둔 거요.
It went right by you.

→ You didn't notice important information!

A Didn't you notice that customer was angry? It went right by you!
B I'm sorry, Mrs. Potter. I'll talk to him right away.

notice 알아채다 eg. I didn't notice that.

A 저 고객이 화난 게 안 보여요? 정신을 어디다 둔 거요!
B 죄송합니다, 포터 씨. 바로 상담하겠습니다.

759

웃음거리가 됐어요.
You fell on your face.

→ You made a huge/ridiculous mistake.

A I gave you an opportunity but you fell on your face.
B I'm sorry, sir. It won't happen again.

gave~ an opportunity ~에게 기회를 주다

A 당신에게 기회를 줬는데, 웃음거리가 됐어요.
B 죄송합니다. 다시는 그런 일 없을 겁니다.

760

큰 실수를 했어요.
You botched it.

→ You made a big mistake! botch는 make a big mistake의 뜻.

A You said that you would bring my bags to the airport, but you botched it!
B I'm so sorry, Betty. My mind was somewhere else, I guess.

My mind was somewhere else. 넋 놓고 있다, 딴 생각하다

A 공항으로 가방을 가져오겠다고 해놓고, 실수했잖아요!
B 너무 미안해, 베티. 넋 놓고 있었나봐.

믿고 맡길 건지 고민된다면

Grooming for Responsibility

- Are you man/woman enough?
- Are you up for this?
- You're a big boy/girl now!
- This is the big time.
- I'm giving you the ball.

761
해낼 자신 있어요?
Are you man/woman enough?

Are you prepared enough in character and skills to do this job?
인성과 능력 면에서 제대로 일을 감당할 수 있는지 묻는 말. 상대에 맞게 man/woman을 써요.

A I'm making you a director. Are you woman enough for it?
B I am, Mr. Embry. Please trust me.

A 당신에게 전무 자리를 줄 텐데, 해낼 자신 있어요?
B 예, 엠버 씨. 믿어 보세요.

762
준비는 되었나요?
Are you up for this?

up for는 prepared의 뜻. 정말 많이 쓰이는 말이에요!

A Today's our 5-kilometer run. Are you up for this?
B Sure! And I bet I finish before you do!

I bet (that) ~을 확신하다(I'm sure that)

A 오늘은 5킬로미터 뛸 건 데. 준비는 됐어요?
B 그럼요! 당신보다 내가 앞설걸!

763

어른답게 처신해요!
You're a big boy/girl now!

 → You should act like an adult! You should know better. 어른답게 행동하란 뜻.

A I've had a bad headache all day.
B You're a big girl now. Endure it.

endure 참다, 인내하다 eg, I won't endure a three-hour delay.

A 하루종일 두통이 심해요.
B 어른답게, 참아봐요.

764

지금이 중요합니다.
This is the big time.

 → This is big chance/challenge.

A Wow! This is my first time on Wall Street.
B Yes, this is the big time. You'd better stay smart if you want to succeed here.

stay smart 똑똑히 처신하다

A 대단하군! 월스트리트는 처음이라서요.
B 예, 지금이 아주 중요하죠. 여기서 성공하려면 정신 똑바로 차려야 해요.

765

성공할 기회를 주겠소.
I'm giving you the ball.

 → I'm giving you the chance to score a big success. 중요 경기에서 득점 기회를 만들어준다는 것에 비유.

A I'll be floor manager from next week?
B You earned it through your hard work, so I'm giving you the ball.

floor manager (백화점 등의) 매장 책임자

A 다음주부터 내가 매장감독이 된다구요?
B 당신이 열심히 일한 덕이죠. 이제 성공할 기회를 준 겁니다.

책임을 전가할 때 으레 쓰는 말

Shifting Responsibility

- Don't look at me.
- I wasn't the only one.
- Why blame me?
- I'm not the one.
- Could you have done better?

766

난 아니에요.
Don't look at me.

→ Don't think of me as the person who's responsible for this. 책임소재를 지적할 때 먼저 상대를 똑바로 쳐다 보게 되죠? 그래서 나온 말.

A Didn't you approve this loan that went bad?
B I don't work in the loan department, so don't look at me!

A 잘못된 대출 승인을 당신이 했나요?
B 대출부서에서 근무하지 않아요. 그러니 난 아니죠!

767

나만 그런 것은 아닙니다.
I wasn't the only one.

→ Everyone else was also doing this bad thing. 공동책임이란 뜻.

A You've been using the company car for personal reasons, haven't you?
B Yes, but I wasn't the only one.

for personal reasons 개인 사유(용도)로

A 회사차량을 개인 용도로 사용했죠?
B 예, 하지만 나만 그런 것은 아닙니다.

성공의 키워드, 책임과 관리에 쓰는 생생 표현

Chapter 22

768
왜 나만 탓하세요?
Why blame me?

 → You're not treating me fairly. It's not fair enough. 나만 꼭 집어 탓하지 말라는 항의!

A This report was almost 2 weeks late!
B Why blame me? The whole team was responsible.

A 이 보고서는 2주나 늦었어요!
B 왜 나만 탓하세요? 팀 전부가 책임이죠.

769
내가 한 일이 아닙니다.
I'm not the one.

 → I'm not the one responsible for this. You have the wrong person.

A Didn't you order these supplies? They cost over $800!
B No, Mr. Cozy. I'm not the one.

supplies 물품, 공급할 물건 **cost** 비용이 들게 하다

A 이 물품을 주문하지 않았어요? 800달러가 넘어요!
B 아뇨, 코지 씨. 내가 한 일이 아닙니다.

770
좀 더 잘할 수 있잖아요?
Could you have done better?

 → Could you have performed better? Could you have created a greater success?

A You took over 6 hours to get those trucks loaded? Could you have done better?
B My staff worked as hard as they could.

as hard as one could/possible 최대한 열심히

A 그 트럭들을 싣는 데 6시간이나 걸렸네요. 좀 더 잘할 수 있잖아요?
B 직원들은 최선을 다했습니다.

CHAPTER 23

Foolishness and Wisdom

Is this the company bowling team? It sure is. Want in? Isn't this the loca[l] I'd like to join the school French Club here. You hopping on? How long Why don't you join our research group? I'm a solo act, sorry. You're lea[ving] company? Yeah, I'm jumping ship. I got a better offer. Is this the company bowling team? It sure is. Want in? Isn't this the local paren[t] You hopping on? How long have you studied French? Can I come to your party this Friday? Of course! The more, the merrier. Aren't y[ou] You're leaving our department? Yeah, from now on you're on your own. Why didn't you help carry our bags? Every man for himself; I'[m]

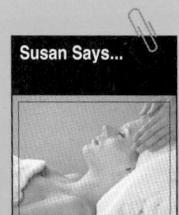

Susan Says...

There are heavens on earth: the private spas and saunas of New York City.

is. You signing up? We need more parents. This is the company union desk, right? Right! In or out? All emplo yees should join.
rench? Can I come to your party this Friday? Of course! The more, the merrier. Aren't you going to stay with our group? Sorry, you have to count me out.
nt? Yeah, from now on you're on your own. Why didn't you help carry our bags? Every man for himself; I've got no time to help you guys. You're leaving the
signing up? We need more parents. This is the company union desk, right? Right! In or out? All emplo yees should join. I'd like to join the school French Club here.
th our group? Sorry, you have to count me out. Why don't you join our research group? I'm a solo act, sorry.
lp you guys. You're leaving the company? Yeah, I'm jumping ship. I got a better offer.

Foolishness and Wisdom

똑똑함과 어리석음은
종이 한장 차이

771 ▸ 805

똑똑한 사람을 좋아하세요?

Intelligence

- ☐ You're sharp. ☐ You're a quick one. ☐ Great thinking!
- ☐ You're a regular Einstein. ☐ You're a whiz!

771
아주 똑똑해요.
You're sharp.

→ You are very smart. 원어민들은 sharp도 많이 써요.

A I figured out this problem we were working on, Mr. Price.
B Good job, Jo. You're sharp!

figure out 알아내다, 해결하다

A 프라이스 씨, 고민하던 문제를 해결했어요.
B 잘했네, 죠! 아주 똑똑해요!

772
두뇌 회전이 빠르세요.
You're a quick one.

→ Say this to a person whose brain works quickly. '머리가 좋다'는 한국말과 같아요!

A This is a way we can meet all the customer requests.
B Way to go, Ralph. You're a quick one!

meet (요구 등에) 부응하다, 맞추다

A 이렇게 하면 고객의 요구를 충족시킬 수 있어요.
B 그러자고, 랄프. 자넨 두뇌 회전이 빨라!

773
훌륭한 생각이야!
Great thinking!

 → It's a marvelous/excellent idea!

A I found a way to persuade the investors, sir. Here's my plan.
B This looks clever. Great thinking!

persuade 설득하다   clever 영리한, 설득력 있는

A 투자자들을 설득할 방안이 있어요. 바로 이겁니다.
B 먹힐 것 같군. 훌륭한 생각이야!

774
아인슈타인이 따로 없네.
You're a regular Einstein.

 → A person "as brilliant as Einstein" 아인슈타인 만큼이나 천재성이 있다는 비유. 남이 생각하지 못한 기발한 착상에 대한 칭찬이지만 상황에 따라 '비아냥'으로 들리기도 해요. "어이, 우리 아인슈타인이 해결해 보시지!"

A I found a way to make our products safer.
B Wow! You're a regular Einstein.

cf. a regular Romeo   로미오처럼 잘 생긴 남자(자칭 미남)

A 우리 제품을 더 안전하게 해줄 방안이 있어요.
B 와! 아인슈타인이 따로 없군.

775
당신은 천재야!
You're a whiz!

 → You are a very brilliant person! You're a genius! whiz는 wizard와 같아요.

A This is my plan for the new store.
B Looks great! You're a whiz!

plan for ~에 대한 계획/기획

A 새 점포 기획안입니다.
B 훌륭해요! 당신은 천재야!

그런 '꼼수'에는 안 속아요!

Slyness
- [ ] You think you're slick? [ ] You snake! [ ] Pulling a fast one?
- [ ] Trying to sneak one over? [ ] What's your game?

776

속을 줄 알아요?
You think you're slick?

→ You are evading honesty. But I exposed you. '뺀들거리며' 잔머리를 굴리는 사람에게 써요.

[듣기]
A You think you're slick? You're hiding information from me!
B No, I'm not.

[말하기]
A 속을 줄 아나? 나한테 뭘 숨기고 있지!
B 아, 아닙니다.

777

비열한 사람 같으니!
You snake!

→ 동서양을 막론하고 뱀은 교활의 상징인가 봐요. 영어에서 snake는 성경 속 에덴동산의 '그 교활한 동물'—low, tricky animal, as in the devil—로 연상되곤 하죠.

[듣기]
A You snake! Are you seeing another woman behind my back?
B No, honey, I love only you.

behind one's back ~의 뒤에서, 안 보는 데서

[말하기]
A 비열한 사람 같으니! 나 모르게 다른 여자를 만나고 있죠?
B 아니야, 여보. 난 당신 만을 사랑해.

778

재빨리 빠져나가려고?
Pulling a fast one?

 → You think you're moving quickly to trick people?

A Pulling a fast one? Why didn't you report to me when you came in?
B I'm sorry. I thought you were busy.

report to ~에게 보고하다 eg. Let's report to the police.

A 재빨리 빠져나가려고? 왜 들어 왔을 때 보고 안 했죠?
B 죄송해요, 바쁘신 것 같아서요.

779

은근슬쩍 넘어가려고요?
Trying to sneak one over?

A You're interviewing at a different company? You're trying to sneak one over?
B Not at all, sir, I'm not interviewing anywhere.

A 다른 회사 면접을 보고 있죠? 은근슬쩍 넘어가려고요?
B 아닙니다. 아무 데도 면접 보는 곳 없어요.

780

꿍꿍이가 뭡니까?
What's your game?

 → What deceitful strategy are you using?

A What's your game? You're always trying to chat with the secretaries!
B No, just some of the time.

chat with ~와 잡담하다   some of the time = sometimes

A 꿍꿍이가 뭡니까? 늘상 여비서들과 농담 따가나 하고!
B 그렇지 않습니다. 어쩌다가 그래요.

해결책, 내 손안에 있소이다!

Problem Solving

- [ ] Nothing to it
- [ ] No sweat!
- [ ] It's child's play.
- [ ] I've/you've got it!
- [ ] No problemo

781

뻔한 일이죠.
Nothing to it

→ **There is no hard work.** 아주 손쉽게 할 수 있는 일이란 뜻.

A What's the best way to get to Atlanta from here?
B We can either fly or take an express bus. Nothing to it!

either A or B A 또는 B 중 택일

A 아틀랜타까지 가는 최선의 방법은 뭐죠?
B 항공편이나 고속버스로 가면 되죠. 뻔한걸요!

782

수고할 것도 없죠!
No sweat!

→ It's so easy that I won't have to sweat in order to do it.

A Can you get that ball down from the roof?
B I'll just use a ladder. No sweat!

A 지붕 위의 저 공을 내려줄 수 있어요?
B 사다리를 이용하죠. 수고랄 것도 없죠!

374

783

아주 쉬워요!
It's child's play.

 It's so simple a child could do it. 아이들도 할 수 있을 만큼 쉽다는 뜻.

A How can I get this software to run properly?
B Just click this icon here. It's child's play!

properly 제대로, 적절하게

A 이 소프트웨어를 작동시키려면 어떻게 하죠?
B 여길 클릭해요. 아주 쉽죠!

784

알았다! 그렇지!
I've/you've got it!

 영화나 시트콤에서 자주 듣는 말이죠. 정말 자주 쓴답니다.

A Shouldn't we use a hammer to fix this board?
B You've got it! That's exactly what we should do!

That's exactly ~는 바로 그거야. eg. That's exactly what I'm saying.

A 망치를 사용해야 판넬을 고칠 수 있잖아요?
B 그렇지! 바로 그렇게 해야겠군!

785

그러죠. 문제 없어요.
No problemo

 No problem. 이탈리아/스페인어를 그대로 쓰는 예가 꽤 있죠? 미국인이 많이 쓰니까 알아두세요.

A Can you repair this broken copier for me?
B No problemo! I'll be there in a minute.

A 복사기 고장난 것 좀 수리해줄 수 있어요?
B 그러죠. 바로 갈게요.

머리는 좀 떨어지지만

Weak Intelligence

- [ ] She's got half a loaf.
- [ ] He doesn't have it together.
- [ ] He's clueless.
- [ ] She's no genius.
- [ ] He's a bit slow.

786

머리가 절반밖에 안 돼.
She's got half a loaf.

 → **She's not that smart.** loaf of bread는 brain의 뜻. half a loaf of bread라면 half a brain이 되겠죠. 먹고 살 '빵'을 구하려면 '똑 소리' 나는 머리가 필요하듯 말이죠.

A Do you think Erica's smart?
B Her? Nah…she's just got half a loaf!

A 에리카가 똑똑한 것 같아요?
B 그녀요? 아뇨, 머리가 절반밖에 안 돼요!

787

지능이 떨어져요.
He doesn't have it together.

 → **Mentally weak and disorganized** have it together는 smart/organized의 뜻. not을 빼면 반대로 지능이 뛰어나다는 말. He's really got it together.= He's really smart/organized.

A Jack's always acting weirdly.
B He's nice, but he doesn't have it together.

weirdly (ad) 이상하게, 엉뚱하게 (a) weird 이상한, 납득이 안되는

A 잭은 항상 엉뚱한 행동을 해요.
B 사람은 좋은데, 지능이 좀 떨어져요.

788
적응력이 없어요.
He's clueless.

 → He has "no clues" to reality. There's no knowledge of anything around him/her.

A Kevin never knows what's going on.
B He doesn't pay attention to his work! He's clueless!

pay attention to ~에 주의하다, 귀 기울이다

A 케빈은 언제나 뭘 하는지 이해를 못해요.
B 공부에 신경 쓰지도 않고요. 적응력이 없어요.

789
영특하지 못해요.
She's no genius.

 → She's not that smart at all. 천재가 아니라고 하는 게 듣기엔 좀 더 나은가요?

A Why hasn't Gill figured out a way to analyze the data?
B She's no genius, that's why.

analyze 분석하다

A 왜 질이 데이터 분석 방안을 못 내놓는 거죠?
B 천재가 아니거든요.

790
그는 좀 둔해요.
He's a bit slow.

 → He's "slow-minded." He/She's not intelligent.

A Why hasn't Frank been promoted in over 5 years?
B He's a bit slow. He could never be a manager.

in over+숫자/기간 ~넘게 지나도록

A 왜 프랭크는 5년이 넘도록 승진이 안 되죠?
B 좀 둔해요. 지배인은 못될 겁니다.

어리석음, 그대를 어찌할꼬?!

Foolishness
- [ ] She's out of her mind.
- [ ] He's certified.
- [ ] Nobody's home.
- [ ] Nothing's upstairs.
- [ ] She's not all there.

791

제 정신이 아닌가봐요.
She's out of her mind.

 → Say this when someone you know is acting very crazily! 가끔 평소와 달리 행동할 때도 있죠. 그것도 아주 멍청하게. 그럴 때 일반적으로 쓰는 말.

A Why hasn't Eunice come into work? It's almost 10:00!
B She's out of her mind!

A 수가 아직도 왜 출근을 안 하지? 10시가 다 됐는데!
B 제 정신이 아닌가봐요.

792

(정신질환) 환자잖아요.
He's certified.

 → He's "certified to be crazy" by a psychiatrist. 비유적으로 사용되요.

A Al is screaming out the window for no reason!
B That's typical. He's certified!

psychiatrist 정신과 의사   That's typical. 늘 있는 일이다.

A 앨이 이유없이 창 밖을 향해 소릴 질러대요.
B 늘 그래요. 환자잖아요!

793
머리가 텅 비었죠.
Nobody's home.

 → A person with no brains, like "an empty house."

A Nelson can't even figure out which subway line to catch home!
B Look at him! Nobody's home!

A 넬슨은 집에 갈 때 어느 지하철을 타는지도 몰라요!
B 보세요! 머리가 텅 비었죠!

794
(공부) 머리가 없어요.
Nothing's upstairs.

 → 사람의 머리가 제일 위에 있듯이, 집의 꼭대기 방에 뭐가 있을까요? Brain! 재밌는 비유죠?

A Steve always dresses so well every day!
B Yeah, but he's got nothing upstairs.

A 스티브는 매일같이 옷을 잘 입죠!
B 그래요, 하지만 머리는 없는 친구죠.

795
생각이 모자라요. 약간 이상해요.
She's not all there.

 → She's slightly stupid or strange.

A Mary is always just staring at other people!
B I guess it's because she's not all there!

stare at ~을 응시하다, 뚫어지게 보다

A 메리는 항상 사람들을 뚫어지게 봐요!
B 생각이 좀 모자라서 그러는 것 같아요!

꼬인 문제로 난감할 때

Problem Frustration
- ☐ I'm going in circles. ☐ Knocking my head against a wall. ☐ I can't make head or tails.
- ☐ What's what? / What's going on? ☐ It's Greek to me.

796

제자리 걸음이에요.
I'm going in circles.

I'm getting no solution just like "going around in a circle aimlessly." 해결책이 보이지 않고 진척이 전혀 안 될 때 써요.

A Have you got a plan worked out yet?
B No, I believe I'm going in circles!

A 기획안 준비 다 됐어요?
B 아뇨, 제자리 걸음이에요!

797

머리만 쥐어박고 있어요.
Knocking my head against a wall

I'm stuck. I'm doing a futile thing. 한국말과 같죠!

A Don't you have those numbers totaled up yet?
B Sorry, I'm so confused. I think I'm knocking my head against a wall.

total up 총 합산하다(sum up)

A 그 숫자 총계가 아직 안 됐나요?
B 그게, 뒤죽박죽이 되어서요. 머리만 쥐어박고 있어요.

798

도무지 하나도 모르겠어요.
I can't make head or tails.

 I can't understand where something begins or ends. 머리와 꼬리가 어딘지 조차 모를 정도로 암담한 상황!

A You look so confused. What's the matter?
B I can't make head or tails out of this memo we just got.

confused 이해가 잘 안 되는, 혼란스러운

A 혼란스러워 보이는데요. 왜 그래요?
B 방금 받은 이 메모 내용을 도무지 모르겠어요.

799

뭐가 뭔지
What's what? / What's going on?

 I don't understand it at all. I don't know what to do.

A Have you made a choice among those dresses?
B No, they're so mixed up I can't see what's what.

be mixed up 뒤 섞이다, 혼란스럽다

A 그 옷들 중에서 결정하셨나요?
B 아뇨, 다 뒤섞여서 뭐가 뭔지 모르겠어요.

800

전혀 모르겠어요.
It's Greek to me.

 It's not understandable at all, like a foreign language. 미국인에게 그리스어로 말한다면? 뻔하겠죠. 원어민들이 즐겨 사용하는 말이에요.

A Do you understand this computer graphic information?
B Sorry, it's Greek to me.

A 이 컴퓨터 그래픽 정보를 이해하겠어요?
B 미안해요, 전혀 모르겠어요.

언변이 뛰어난 사람에게 한마디!

Intelligent Speaking

- ☐ He's a smooth talker.
- ☐ She's got a way with words.
- ☐ She knows what to say.
- ☐ Her words grab you.
- ☐ He knows what he's saying.

801
그는 말이 유창해요.
He's a smooth talker.

→ His words persuade people easily.

A How did Ben convince the client?
B You know how he is: he's a smooth talker.

A 벤이 어떻게 고객을 납득시켰나요?
B 그를 알잖아요. 말이 유창하니까요.

802
말의 달인이에요.
She's got a way with words.

→ She's very good at words. get a way with는 very skilled란 뜻.

A How did Cindy become the company's top saleswoman?
B She's got a way with words. Customers are always convinced by her.

be convinced by ~에게 설득되다, 납득되다

A 신디는 어떻게 회사의 최우수 영업자가 되었죠?
B 말의 달인이에요. 그녀에게 안 넘어가는 고객이 없어요.

803
뭘 말하면 되는지 알죠.
She knows what to say.

 → She knows how to convice people.

A Are you going to vote for that woman?
B Maybe. She knows what to say.

vote for 찬성 투표하다   what to say 말해야 할 것

A 저 여자에게 찬성 투표할 거요?
B 그러게요. 뭘 말해야 할지 아는데요.

804
그녀의 말에 사로잡혀요.
Her words grab you.

 → She speaks so well that the words "grab" your attention/emotion.

A Do you think Marion is a good presenter?
B Of course! Her words really grab you.

grab ~을 움켜 잡다   presenter 발표자

A 마리온이 훌륭한 발표자라고 생각해요?
B 그럼요! 그녀의 말에 사로잡히잖아요.

805
그의 말에는 설득력이 있어.
He knows what he's saying.

 → He's very knowledgeable. His words are very convincing/persuasive.

A Was the seminar persuasive? How was the speaker?
B He knows what he's saying.

persuasive 설득되는, 알기 쉬운

A 세미나는 알아듣겠던가요? 발표자는 어땠어요?
B 말에 설득력이 있더군.

CHAPTER 24

Groups and Individuals

Is this the company bowling team? It sure is. Want in? Isn't this the local parents' group? I'd like to join the school French Club here. You hopping on? How long have you studied French? Yeah, I'm jumping ship. I got a better offer. Is this the company bowling team? It sure is. Want in? Isn't this the local parents' group? It You hopping on? How long have you studied French? Can I come to your party this Friday? Of course! The more, the merrier. Aren't you You're leaving our department? Yeah, from now on you're on your own. Why didn't you help carry our bags? Every man for himself; I've Why don't you join our research group? I'm a solo act, sorry. You're leaving

Susan Says...

No matter what, you've got to find at least sometime for yourself to do nothing at all.

You signing up? We need more parents. This is the company union desk, right? Right! In or out? All employees should join. ...nch? Can I come to your party this Friday? Of course! The more, the merrier. Aren't you going to stay with our group? Sorry, you have to count me out. ... Yeah, from now on you're on your own. Why didn't you help carry our bags? Every man for himself; I've got no time to help you guys. You're leaving the company? ...p? We need more parents. This is the company union desk, right? Right! In or out? All employees should join. I'd like to join the school French Club here. with our group? Sorry, you have to count me out. Why don't you join our research group? I'm a solo act, sorry. help you guys. You're leaving the company? Yeah, I'm jumping ship. I got a better offer.

Groups and Individuals

크고 작은 조직
생활에서 꼭 쓰는
생생 표현

806 > 840

참여의사, 가장 쉽게 묻기

Making Groups

- [ ] Want in?
- [ ] Signing up?
- [ ] In or out?
- [ ] (You) Hopping on?
- [ ] The more, the merrier

806

참여할래요?
Want in?

→ Do you want to come into a group/project/situation? 친한 사이에 일반적으로 쓰는 말. 주어를 넣어 You want in?라고 해도 좋아요.

A Is this the company bowling team?
B It sure is. Want in?

Is this~? 이 곳이 ~(하는 데) 인가요? eg. Is this the personnel department?

A 사내 볼링팀인가요?
B 그래요. 참여할래요?

807

가입할래요?
Signing up?

→ Are you signing a document to join a project/team? 입회서에 정식으로 서명을 하고 가입할 때 써요.

A Isn't this the local parents' group?
B It is. You signing up? We need more parents.

A 학부형 모임인가요?
B 예, 가입할래요? 인원이 더 필요하거든요.

808
들어 올래요, 말래요?
In or out?

 → Are you going to join or not? 직역해도 뜻이 짐작되는 쉬운 표현이죠. 격의 없이 자주 쓰는 말.

A   This is the company union desk, right?
B   Right! In or out? All employees should join.

(union) desk (노조 가입) 접수/안내 데스크   eg. Customer service desk

A   회사 노조 접수처인가요?
B   맞는데요. 가입할래요? 모두 가입해야 해요.

809
들어올래요?
(You) Hopping on?

 → Are you joining the team? hopping on은 깡충 뛰어서 들어오다는 뜻. 동아리 모임 등에 참가여부를 물을 때 쓰는 친근한 말. Coming onboard도 좋아요.

A   I'd like to join the school French Club here.
B   You hopping on? How long have you studied French?

I'd like to~ ~하고 싶다   How long have you+과거분사 얼마동안 ~했나요?

A   교내 불어 동아리에 들려고 하는데요.
B   가입하게요? 불어는 얼마나 배웠나요?

810
많을수록 더 재밌죠.
The more, the merrier

 → The more people that join, the more fun it will be. 참여자가 많을수록 재미도 더하다는 뜻. 게임이나 파티 등에 참여를 유도할 때 자주 써요.

A   Can I come to your party this Friday?
B   Of course! The more, the merrier.

the+비교급, the+비교급 ~할 수록 더욱 …하다

A   이번 금요일 파티에 나도 가도 돼?
B   그럼! 사람이 많을수록 더 재미있는 법이니까.

탈퇴의사, 가장 쉽게 말하기

Leaving/Declining Groups
- [ ] Count me out
- [ ] I'm a solo act.
- [ ] You're on your own.
- [ ] Every man for himself
- [ ] I'm jumping ship.

811
나는 빼세요.
Count me out

→ Don't include me in your group/project. 참여하지 않겠다고 할 때 가장 편하게 쓰는 말.

A Aren't you going to stay with our group?
B Sorry, you have to count me out.

stay with ~와 함께 하다(머물다)

A 우리 팀에 있지 않을 건가요?
B 미안하지만, 전 빼세요.

812
혼자 하는 게 좋아요.
I'm a solo act.

→ I like working alone. 팀의 일원보다는 독립적으로 행동하는 편을 택할 때 쓸 수 있는 말. I like performing solo.도 좋아요.

A Why don't you join our research group?
B I'm a solo act, sorry.

A 우리 연구팀에 들어오는 게 어때요?
B 난 혼자 하는 게 편해요, 미안합니다.

Chapter 24

크고 작은 조직생활에서 꼭 쓰는 생생 표현

813
네 힘으로 해야지.
You're on your own.

→ You have to handle a situation by yourself. 스스로 알아서 해야 한다는 사실을 다짐해 둘 때 써요.

A You're leaving our department?
B Yeah, from now on you're on your own.

from now on 지금 부터는, 앞으로는

A 우리 부서를 떠나신다면서요?
B 그래, 이제부터는 자네 힘으로 잘 꾸려나가게.

814
자기 일은 자기가 해야지.
Every man for himself

→ Every person should tend only to their own interests. 타인에 대한 배려나 관심보다 자신의 일에 우선순위를 두겠다고 말하는 것. It's time to be selfish.도 좋아요.

A Why didn't you help carry our bags?
B Every man for himself. I've got no time to help you guys.

I've got no time to ~할 시간이 없다

A 왜 가방 나르는 것을 도와주지 않았어요?
B 자기 일은 자기가 해야지. 난 남들을 도와줄 시간이 없소.

815
난 그만둘래요.
I'm jumping ship.

→ I'm leaving the group. 함께 타고 있던 배에서 갑자기 뛰어내린다는 뜻이니, 중에 그만두겠다는 '탈퇴 선언' 이죠. jumping은 leave suddenly의 뜻.

A You're leaving the company?
B Yeah, I'm jumping ship. I got a better offer.

A 회사를 그만둘 건가요?
B 예, 그만두려고 해요. 더 나은 제안을 받았거든요.

389

단도직입적으로 '어느 편'인가요?

Picking Sides

☐ Whose side are you on?   ☐ With us or against us?   ☐ Know where you came from?
☐ Hopping the fence?   ☐ Changing horses?

816

누구 편이죠?
Whose side are you on?

 잘 알고 계신 표현이죠? 끝에 on을 붙이는 것 잊지 마세요.

A   I'm going to help Beatrice.
B   She works for a rival department. Whose side are you on?

work for ~에 근무하다

A   난 비어트리스를 돕겠어요.
B   그녀는 경쟁 부서에서 일하잖아요. 누구 편이죠?

817

찬성이요, 아니면 반대요?
With us or against us?

 Do you support or oppose us? with는 찬성을 뜻하는 for와 같아요.

A   I have a lot of complaints about this group.
B   With us or against us? Just be quiet and help.

have a lot of complaints about ~에 불만이 많다

A   이 팀에 불만이 아주 많아요.
B   우리에게 찬성이요, 아니면 반대요? 조용히 돕기나 해요.

818

근본을 잊지 말아야죠?
Know where you came from?

 → You must remember your personal roots.

A: I'm not going to visit my hometown anymore.
B: Won't visit? Don't you know where you came from?

come from ~ 출신이다

A: 고향엔 다시 안 올 거야.
B: 안 온다고? 근본을 잊지는 않았겠지?

819

이적을 하겠다고요?
Hopping the fence?

 → '자기 집' 담에서 뛰어 내려 다른 집으로 간다는 비유.

A: I'm not going to play on this team anymore.
B: Hopping the fence? We'll miss you.

A: 이 팀에서 더 이상 뛰지 않을 겁니다.
B: 이적을 하겠다고요? 많이 보고싶겠군요.

820

방향을 바꿀 거요?
Changing horses?

 → You are taking a now style/area/job. 말을 갈아타듯 방향전환을 하겠다는 말.

A: I'm switching from national to international customers.
B: That'll be a big challenge. Ready for changing horses?

switch from A to B A에서 B로 바꾸다

A: 국내고객에서 국제고객으로 바꿀 생각이야.
B: 큰 도전이 될 텐데요. 방향을 바꿀 준비는 됐어요?

협동심을 북돋아 주는 말

Group Encouragement

☐ Let's pull together.   ☐ All for one!   ☐ Where's your team spirit?
☐ Let's stick together.   ☐ There's no "I" in "team!"

821
함께 힘을 모읍시다.
Let's pull together.

 → Let's "pull all of our resources together" to succeed.

  A How can we get this cargo loaded in time?
B Let's pull together, and we can do it!

cargo 화물   load 선적하다   in time 제 시간 내에

  A 이 화물들을 어떻게 시간 내에 선적하죠?
B 함께 힘을 모으면, 할 수 있어요!

822
하나로 뭉쳐요!
All for one!

 → Everyone unites.

  A Do you think we can really win this basketball game?
B Sure we can! All for one!

  A 이번 농구 경기에서 이길 수 있을까요?
B 그렇고말고! 하나로 뭉치면 돼!

크고 작은 조직생활에서 꼭 쓰는 생생 표현

Chapter 24

823
팀 정신은 어디 갔나요?
Where's your team spirit?

 → It's worth working as a team.

A I want to make sure I get credit for this work.
B This is a group project, Gary. Where's your team spirit?

make sure (that) ~을 확실히 하다   get credit for ~에 대해 인정을 받다

A 이번 일에서 제가 확실히 인정받고 싶어요.
B 이건 팀 작업이야, 게리. 팀 정신은 어디간 거지?

824
다 같이 하는 거야.
Let's stick together.

 → We're in this situation together, so we have to work hard as a team and help each other. 함께 팀워크를 이뤄 노력한다는 말.

A My tennis skills are awful. We're going to lose this match!
B Just play as best as you can. Let's stick together.

A 내 테니스 실력이 엉망이에요. 경기에서 질 거예요!
B 그저 최선을 다하게. 다 함께 하는 경기일세!

825
개인행동은 안 돼!
There's no "I" in "team!"

 → Act as a team member. We don't need an individual mindset. 조직에서 개인적인 성취만 내세울 때 써요.

A Why do I have to work with the rest of you guys?
B There's no "I" in "team!" You can't work by yourself.

the rest of ~의 나머지   by oneself 홀로(alone)

A 왜 내가 남들과 같이 일해야 해요?
B 개인행동은 안 돼! 자네 혼자 해낼 수는 없어.

팀워크 방해꾼에겐 따끔한 충고를!

Misfits

- [ ] You're on the wrong team.
- [ ] You don't fit in.
- [ ] You're the weak link.
- [ ] You're the black sheep.
- [ ] You're dragging us down.

826
번지수가 틀린 것 같네.
You're on the wrong team.

 → Who needs you? You should leave our group. 차라리 떠나는 게 나은 조직원도 있겠죠?

A You're on the wrong team. All you do is mess things up.
B Okay, I'd be happy to leave.

mess~ up ~를 망치다   I'd be happy to 기꺼이 ~하다

A 자넨, 번지수가 틀린 것 같네. 일을 망치기만 하잖나.
B 알겠어요, 기꺼이 나가죠.

827
여기에 맞지 않아요.
You don't fit in.

 → You don't belong here. 반대로 내가 맞지 않을 때는 I don't fit in.라고 하세요.

A Why do I have to leave the club?
B You don't fit in. You'd better join a different one.

had better ~하는 편이 낫다   different 다른

A 왜 내가 여길 나가야 한다는 거죠?
B 여기에 맞지 않아요. 다른 클럽을 찾는 게 나아요.

828
결속력을 약화시켜요.
You're the weak link.

 → You're not a team player. weak link는 weakest link in a chain을 말해요. 멤버 간에 신뢰감을 저해한다는 뜻.

A Why can't you let me stay with you guys?
B Sorry, but you're the weak link, that's why.

A 왜 내가 계속 있으면 안 된다는 거야?
B 미안하지만, 너로 인해 결속력이 떨어지거든.

829
우리와는 달라. 왕따야.
You're the black sheep.

 → Someone who sticks out too much 모두가 흰색 양들인데 혼자만 검은색이니… 함께 어울릴 수 없는 사람에게 써요.

A I'm being expelled from the association?
B I think you're the black sheep. You should find someplace else.

be expelled 추방되다, 쫓겨나다

A 내가 협회에서 쫓겨나는 건가요?
B 당신은 우리와 다른 것 같소. 다른 곳을 찾아봐요.

830
당신은 도움이 안 돼요.
You're dragging us down.

 → You're making us weak. You are dragging down our performance.

A Why am I being left on my own?
B You're dragging us down, Lucy. You can't stay with us.

on one's own 홀로, 단독으로 eg. I can't do it on my own.

A 왜 나만 홀로 남겨진 거죠?
B 당신은 도움이 안 돼요, 루시. 함께 할 수 없어요.

강점과 약점, 긍정적으로 말하기

Group Strength & Weakness

- [ ] You're point.
- [ ] He's a wildcard.
- [ ] You're the glue of this team.
- [ ] You're the heart of this place.
- [ ] You're our go-to guy/gal.

831

당신이 선봉장이야.
You're point.

→ You're the leader. 행진의 선봉에 서는 기수처럼 핵심 역할을 한다는 뜻.

A I'm really happy you're on our team. You're point for our next assignment.
B Thanks. I'lll do the best I can.

A 자네가 우리팀에 와서 기쁘네. 다음 임무의 선봉장이야.
B 감사합니다. 최선을 다하겠습니다.

832

그가 와일드카드죠.
He's a wildcard.

→ A person who can greatly help or harm a group. 긍정적인 역할과 부정적인 영향에 모두 써요.

A Should we keep Walter in our sales department? He acts a little strange.
B He's a wildcard, but I think his performance will improve.

performance (업무) 수행력   improve 개선되다

A 우리 영업부에 월터를 계속 둬야 하나요? 행동이 아닌데요.
B 와일드카드인 셈이지. 하지만 그도 역량이 나아지겠지.

크고 작은 조직생활에서 꼭 쓰는 생생 표현

Chapter 24

833
덕분에 조직이 탄탄해져요.
You're the glue of this team.

 → A person helping the group stay strong, like glue. 접착제처럼 조직의 결속을 공고히 해주는 사람!

A Mom, you're the glue of this family.
B Very sweet of you to say so, Jim. Thanks.

(It's) nice/sweet of you to say so. ~라고 말해 주니 고맙다/기쁘다

A 엄마 덕에 우리 가족이 화목해요.
B 짐, 그렇게 말해주니, 정말 고맙구나.

834
이곳에 심장 같은 존재예요.
You're the heart of this place.

 → You add warm human importance to a group. 따뜻한 피가 흐르게 하는 심장 같은 사람이 되게 하소서!

A You always make everyone smile, Alicia. You're the heart of our choir.
B Thanks, reverend.

A 앨리샤, 당신은 항상 모두를 미소짓게 해줘요. 우리 합창단에겐 심장 같은 존재예요.
B 감사합니다, 목사님.

835
우리의 버팀목 이에요.
You're our go-to guy/gal.

 → A person that people can "go to" for a job to be done correctly. 문제라도 생기면 가서 의논하고 싶은 사람!

A You really made the whole team successful. You're our go-to guy, Carl.
B Oh, it was nothing, sir.

A 덕분에 팀이 성공했어요. 칼, 당신은 우리의 버팀목이에요.
B 이런, 한 것도 없는데요, 감독님.

팀원들 사이에 생기는 사소한 일들

Intra-Group Dynamics

- [ ] We're falling apart.
- [ ] We're killing each other.
- [ ] We're rolling.
- [ ] We're becoming close.
- [ ] We're creaking along.

836
뿔뿔이 각자예요.
We're falling apart.

→ We're losing spirit. We're like a "structure falling apart."

A Are you happy working on the marketing campaign?
B No, nothing's getting done. In fact, we're falling apart.

work on ~를 힘써 하다/활동하다

A 홍보 마케팅 일은 재밌어요?
B 아뇨, 되는 게 없어요. 사실, 팀원들도 뿔뿔이고요.

837
서로에게 상처를 줘요.
We're killing each other.

→ We're harming each other a lot, instead of helping each other. '서로 못 잡아먹어 안달이다' 란 말이지요!

A Aren't you and your wife happy at home?
B Sometimes, yes. But then at other times I think we're killing each other.

Sometimes~ at other times... ~할 때도 있고, …할 때도 있다

A 집에서 아내와 사이가 좋지 않나요?
B 그럴 때도 있고, 서로 못 잡아먹어 안달일 때도 있죠.

크고 작은 조직생활에서 꼭 쓰는 생생 표현

Chapter 24

838
잘 굴러가고 있어요.
We're rolling.

 → We're moving successfully. 뭐든 잘 굴러간다(rolling)는 것은 긍정적이죠!

A So your marketing team is doing well?
B We're rolling. I think we'll get the product released on time.

release 출시하다   on time 제때에

A 그래 마케팅 팀 일은 잘 되나요?
B 잘 굴러가고 있어요. 제때에 제품 출시도 될 것 같고요.

839
친해지고 있어요.
We're becoming close.

 → We're getting to know each other better as time goes by.

A How do you like working with Julie and Mark?
B We're becoming really close, and have accomplished a lot of work.

accomplish 성취하다, 이루다

A 줄리와 마크와 같이 일하는 게 어때요?
B 정말로 친해지고 있어요. 많은 것을 함께 이루었죠.

840
삐걱대면서도 가고 있어요.
We're creaking along.

 → We're moving slowly but steadily, like an old wagon moves "creakily."

A Isn't your study group learning a lot?
B Not really, we're just creaking along.

A 스터디 그룹에서 배운 것은 많니?
B 꼭 그렇지는 않지만, 삐걱대면서도 가고 있어요.

CHAPTER 25

Alcohol

Is this the company bowling team? It sure is. Want in? Isn't this the local parents' group? It is. You signing up? I'd like to join the school French Club here. You hopping on? How long have you studied French? Can I come Why don't you join our research group? I'm a solo act, sorry. You're leaving our department? Yeah, from now offer. Is this the company bowling team? It sure is. Want in? Isn't this the local parents' group? It is. You signing up? We need more p You hopping on? How long have you studied French? Can I come to your party this Friday? Of course! The more, the merrier. Aren't You're leaving our department? Yeah, from now on you're on your own. Why didn't you help carry our bags? Every man for himself; I'

The perfect dinner: tasty, delicious and not a single gram of fat or cholesterol.

Alcohol

어울리는 재미 · 술자리의 천태만상, 생생 표현

841▶875

나만의 술주문 방식은?

Ordering Drinks

- [ ] I'll have a round of beer.
- [ ] Make mine a double
- [ ] Easy on the Soju
- [ ] I want a man's drink.
- [ ] Give me a cold one

841

맥주로 주세요.
I'll have a round of beer.

 → I'll have several drinks. 이때 round는 여러 잔 마시게 되는 술의 한 회를 말해요.

- A What would you like, sir?
- B I'll have a round of beers for me and my coworkers.

- A 뭘로 드시겠어요?
- B 나와 동료들에게 맥주로 주세요.

842

더블로 한 잔 더요.
Make mine a double

 → Extra strength, 2-shots of liquor, "make my drink a double-shot one"

- A Vodka straight up?
- B Yes, and make mine a double, please.

straight up (위스키) 스트레이트로

- A 보드카 스트레이트로요?
- B 예, 더블로 한 잔 더 줘요.

843
소주는 조금만 넣어요.
Easy on the Soju

 → Only a little portion of Soju/whiskey/rum, etc. in the drink. 종류를 섞어 마실 때 써요.

A Boilermakers?
B Yes, but easy on the Soju. Make mine mostly beer.

boilermakers 폭탄주　mostly 거의, 대부분

A 폭탄주로 드려요?
B 예, 소주는 조금만 넣어요. 거의 맥주로요.

844
독한 걸로요.
I want a man's drink.

 → I want drink strong enough for man. 성별로 술의 강도가 아무래도 좀 다르죠? 약한 술은 a lady's drink라고 해요. 너무 독한 것 말고, 약한 것으로 한 잔! — I want a lady's drink. Nothing too powerful!

A Are you ready to order, sir?
B Yes, but I want a man's drink! Something strong!

A 주문하시겠어요?
B 예, 독한 걸로 줘요! 아주 독한 걸로!

845
찬 맥주로 주세요.
Give me a cold one

 → I want a beer, a "cold beer".

A Are you ready for drinks?
B Yeah, give me a cold one. A British ale would be great!

ale 전통적인 영국 맥주

A 술 드시겠어요?
B 예, 찬 맥주로 줘요. 영국 맥주 있으면 좋고요!

나의 음주 스타일은?

Drinking Styles

☐ Bottom's up!   ☐ I'm nursing this one.   ☐ Down that!
☐ I want to pound a few.   ☐ I'm going to get hammered.

846

원샷!
Bottom's up!

→ 한국의 "One shot!"에 해당되는 말.

A Finally, we've got our drinks!
B I know! Bottom's up!

A 드디어, 술이 나왔어요!
B 그렇군! 원샷!

847

천천히 마시고 있어요.
I'm nursing this one.

→ I'm drinking slowly. 아기 보듯 천천히 여유있게 마시겠다는 뜻.

A Is that still your first beer?
B Yeah, I'm nursing this one.

A 아직도 맥주 첫째 잔이에요?
B 예, 천천히 마시고 있습니다.

848
들이켜요!
Down that!

 → Drink it quickly! 찔끔거리지 말고 '죽' 한방에 들이켜 마실 때 써요. 여기서 down은 drink와 같은 뜻.

A Hey, Brad, down that glass of cognac!
B I don't want to drink so fast!

A 이봐, 브래드, 그 코냑 잔을 들이켜 마시게!
B 난 급하게 마시고 싶지 않아.

849
잠깐 술 몇 잔 하고 싶네.
I want to pound a few.

 → I want to drink a few drinks quickly! pound는 술을 빨리 마실 때 써요.

A What do you want to do after work?
B I want to pound a few. I need to relieve my stress.
relieve one's stress 스트레스를 풀다

A 퇴근하고 뭐 할 건가?
B 잠깐 술 몇 잔 하려고요. 스트레스도 풀 겸.

850
진창 마실 거야.
I'm going to get hammered.

 → I'm going to get drunk. 망치로 머리를 한 대 얻어맞은 것처럼 '진창' 술독에 빠져 보겠다는 말씀!

A You're drinking so fast!
B I'm going to get hammered. I had a bad day today.
have a bad day 일진이 좋지 않다

A 너무 빨리 마시고 있어요!
B 진창 마실 거야. 오늘은 재수 옴 붙은 날이었거든.

술 마시는 장소도 가지가지!

Drinking Locations

- [ ] It's a dive.
- [ ] It's a meat market!
- [ ] Wall to wall people!
- [ ] It's a professionals' hangout.
- [ ] It's a dance spot.

851

싸구려 술집이야.
It's a dive.

→ It's a small and dirty place. dive는 허름한 장소를 말해요.

A Don't you want to stay here?
B No, it's a dive! Let's find someplace else!

A 여기가 별로인가요?
B 아뇨, 싸구려 술집이네요. 다른 곳으로 가요!

852

파트너 구하러 가는 곳이군!
It's a meat market!

→ A bar or club where many singles go to find partners quickly.

A Do you like going to the new nightclub on the East Side?
B No! In my opinion, it's just a meat market!

A 이스트 사이드에 있는 새로운 나이트클럽에 가볼래?
B 싫어! 거긴 파트너 구하러 가는 데야!

853
발 들여 놓을 데도 없네!
Wall to wall people!

 → The place is completely crowded, "from one wall to another".

A Don't you like crowded dance clubs?
B Not this crowded! There are wall to wall people here!

A 북적이는 댄스클럽이 좋지 않니?
B 이렇게 많은 것은 말고! 여긴 발 들여 놓을 데가 없어!

854
지식인들이 자주 가는 데지.
It's a professionals' hangout.

 → hangout은 '자주 가는 장소'를 말해요.

A What about drinking over at Bozbo's Pub?
B Sounds good. It's a professionals' hangout.

professional (변호사, 의사 등) 전문직 종사자, 지식인

A 보즈보 펍에서 한 잔 하는 게 어때?
B 좋아, 지식인들이 자주 가는 데지.

855
춤 추는 곳이야.
It's a dance spot.

A What do you think of going to Barnaby's Disco?
B I like the idea. It's a great dance spot.

spot 장소, 건물

A 바나비 디스코로 가는 게 어때?
B 좋아. 거긴 춤추기 좋은 데야.

취하면 누구나 튀어나오는 말

Drunks & Drunkenness

- [ ] I'm wasted. [ ] She drinks like a fish. [ ] The room's spinning.
- [ ] He can't hold his liquor. [ ] I'm going to lose it.

856

엄청 취했어요.
I'm wasted.

→ I'm dead drunk. I'm so drunk that my body can be "laid waste". 쓰레기처럼 내다 버려도 모를 정도로 취했다는 뜻.

A Do you want to order another drink?
B No more! I'm really wasted.

A 한 잔 더 할래요?
B 더는 못해요! 이미 엄청 취했어요.

857

그녀는 술고래죠.
She drinks like a fish.

→ She's a heavy drinker. 잘 알고 계신 표현이죠!

A Why is Blair drinking so much?
B Didn't you know? She usually drinks like a fish!

A 블레어가 왜 저렇게 마셔대죠?
B 몰랐어요? 그녀가 술고래란걸!

858
방이 빙빙 돌아요.
The room's spinning.

 → I'm so drunk the room appears to be turning. 취객의 행태는 동서양이 비슷한 듯!

A You drank three bottles of Soju!
B I know! The whole room's spinning!

A 너, 소주를 3병이나 마셨어!
B 알아요! 방 전체가 빙빙 돌아요!

859
통제가 안 돼.
He can't hold his liquor.

 → He can't control himself. 술버릇이 나쁘거나 신체적으로 고통을 겪게 되는 상황에 써요.

A Why does Phil always fight after he drinks?
B He can't hold his liquor. After he drinks, he goes crazy!

liquor 주류, 술   go crazy 제정신이 아니다

A 필은 술 마시면 왜 싸우는거죠?
B 그는 통제가 안 돼. 술만 마시면 '개' 가 돼요!

860
토할 것 같아.
I'm going to lose it.

 → I'm going to throw up. lose it은 lose control of one's stomach의 뜻.

A What's the matter with you?
B I drank too much. I think I'm going to lose it.

A 왜 그래요?
B 너무 많이 마셨어요. 토할 것 같아요.

고약한 술버릇에 일침을 주는 말

Bad Drinking Behavior

☐ You don't know when to stop (drinking)!   ☐ You're cut off!
☐ He's a mean drunk.   ☐ A couple and she's gone.   ☐ Sleep it off!

861

자신의 주량도 모르는군요!
You don't know when to stop (drinking)!

→ Don't drink so much that you can't control yourself. 주량을 넘어 폭음을 할 때 써요.

A One more round of beers!
B No more! You don't know when to stop!

A 맥주 한 잔만 더 하죠!
B 더 이상은 안 돼요! 자신의 주량도 모르는군요!

862

그만 마셔요!
You're cut off!

→ No more drinks for you. 대개 바텐더가 손님에게 하는 말.

A Waiter, another pitcher of beer for me and my friends!
B You're cut off. You guys are all too drunk to continue.

A 여기, 내 친구들에게, 맥주 피처로 하나 더요!
B 그만 마셔요. 이제 더는 못 마실 정도로 취했어요.

863
술버릇이 고약해요.
He's a mean drunk.

 → A person that becomes mean, loud, violent, or cruel after drinking.

A Drake always shouts at people after drinking!
B He's a mean drunk, so I don't like to drink with him.

A 드레이크는 술만 마시면 고함을 쳐대요!
B 술버릇이 고약해서, 난 같이 술 마시기 싫다니까.

864
한두 잔에도 '가죠'.
A couple and she's gone.

 → She does wild things after drinking. gone은 gone crazy의 뜻으로 나쁜 술버릇을 꼬집는 말.

A Why is Cameron crying all of a sudden?
B You know how she is: a couple and she's gone.

A 카메론이 왜 갑자기 울어요?
B 알잖아요. 한두 잔에도 '가잖아요'.

865
가서 그만 잠이나 자게!
Sleep it off!

 → Go home and sleep off your drunkonness!

A Another bottle of Soju!
B No, you've had enough. You'd better sleep it off.

A 소주 한 병 더 하죠!
B 안 돼, 많이 마셨어. 가서 그만 잠이나 자게.

분위기에 따라 달리 건배하기

Toasts

☐ Here's to ☐ Hear! Hear! ☐ I propose a toast
☐ Let's raise a glass to ☐ To Yoojin: Best wishes!

866
~를 위해 건배!
Here's to

> I'd like to make a toast to... A toast to... 잘 아는 표현이죠! 이어서 'for+건배목적'을 붙여 말해요. 나의 자상한 남편이 되어준, 석준 씨를 위해 건배! — Here's to Sukjoon, for being my loving husband!

A Here's to Mrs. Durby, for 25 years of service to our company!
B To Mrs. Durby!

A 25년간 회사에 봉직하신, 더비 씨를 위해 건배!
B 더비 씨에게 건배!

867
여기도, 건배!
Hear! Hear!

> A polite audience reply to a toast. Cheers! 청중들이 주인공을 위해 건배를 제창하면서 던지는 말. 흥겹게 술잔이 부딪히는 장면이 떠오르네요!

A A toast, to our everlasting friend, Torby!
B Hear! Hear! To Torby!

A 우리의 영원한 친구, 토비를 위해 건배!
B 여기도, 건배! 토비를 위해!

어울리는 재미 · 술자리의 천태만상, 생생 표현

Chapter 25

868
~에게 건배 합시다
I propose a toast

 → Allow me to toast... 격식을 갖춘 자리에서 사용해요. 사랑스런 신랑과 신부에게 건배 합시다! — I propose a toast, to the lovely bride and groom!

A I propose a toast to Coach Jackson, who led our team to victory!
B To Coach Jackson!

lead~ to a victory ~를 승리로 이끌다

A 우리 팀을 승리로 이끈, 잭슨 코치를 위해 건배!
B 잭슨 코치를 위하여!

869
~를 위해 잔을 듭시다!
Let's raise a glass to

 → Say this in a semi-formal setting. 적당히 격식을 갖춘 분위기에 써요.

A Let's raise a glass to Mr. and Mrs. Fowler, for staying married over 50 years!
B To Mr. and Mrs. Fowler!

stay married for/over (결혼하여) ~동안/넘게 해로하다

A 50년 넘게 해로하시는, 파울러 씨 부부를 위해 잔을 듭시다!
B 파울러 씨 부부를 위하여!

870
유진에게, 행운을 빌어!
To Yoojin: Best wishes!

 → A toast to Yoojin! My best wishes to her! 멀리 떠나거나, 새로운 일을 시작하는 주인공을 위해 건배할 때 써요.

A To Yoojin: best wishes on her return to Korea!
B To Yoojin!

A 유진에게, 한국으로 돌아온 걸 축하해요!
B 유진을 위하여!

413

술의 유혹으로부터 '말짱' 하려면

Sobriety

- [ ] Sober up!
- [ ] None for me, thanks.
- [ ] I'm driving. / I'm the DD.
- [ ] I'm on/off the wagon.
- [ ] I'm not over last night.

871

술을 깨야지!
Sober up!

→ **You don't drink anymore.** 만취한 친구에게 '정신 버쩍 들도록' 크게 한마디 해줘요. 딱 한 잔만 더! —Just one more drink! 안 돼! Sober up!

A I'd like a few more beers.
B No! Sober up! It's time to go home!

A 맥주 몇 잔만 더 마시자.
B 안 돼! 술을 깨야지! 집에 가야지!

872

난 안 마셔.
None for me, thanks.

→ **I don't want any drinks.** 술자리에 참석했지만 왠지, 술이 '당기지 않거나' 마실 수 없는 상황일 때 써요.

A Aren't you going to have a drink?
B None for me, thanks. I have a test tomorrow.

A 술 안 마실 거야?
B 난 안 마셔. 내일 시험이 있거든.

873

운전해야 해. 대리운전해야 해.
I'm driving. / I'm the DD.

 DD means "Designated Driver." 마시기 싫을 때 '좋은 핑계'가 될 수도 있겠네…

A Why aren't you having any drinks?
B I'm the DD. I'll just have juice.

designated 지정된　cf. 음주운전 DUI (driving under the influence (of alcohol))/ drinking and driving

A 왜 술을 전혀 안 마셔요?
B 대리운전해야 해요. 그냥 주스로 주세요.

874

술 끊었어요. 끊었다가 다시 마셔요.
I'm on/off the wagon.

 I stopped drinking/started drinking again. wagon은 wagon of sobriety 란 의미.

A You're having soda instead of liquor?
B Right, because I'm on the wagon.

A 술 대신 소다수 마시는 거예요?
B 예, 술 끊었어요.

875

어젯밤 술이 안 깼어.
I'm not over last night.

 I haven't recovered from last night's drinking. over는 recovered from(회복하다)의 뜻.

A Come on and have a drink!
B Sorry, I'm not over last night! I drank too much then!

A 자, 이리 와서 한 잔 해요!
B 미안, 어젯밤 술이 안 깼어! 엄청 마셨거든!

CHAPTER 26

Wild and Crazy

Is this the company bowling team? It sure is. Want in? Isn't this the local parents' group? It is. I'd like to join the school French Club here. You hopping on? How long have you studied French? Why don't you join our research group? I'm a solo act, sorry. You're leaving our department? ship. I got a better offer. Is this the company bowling team? It sure is. Want in? Isn't this the local parents' group? It is. You signing up? You hopping on? How long have you studied French? Can I come to your party this Friday? Of course! The more, the merrier. Aren't y You're leaving our department? Yeah, from now on you're on your own. Why didn't you help carry our bags? Every man for himself; I'v

Susan Says...

I believe that every woman has her
soulmate out there somewhere; but
you'll never find him by sitting at home.

We need more parents. This is the company union desk, right? Right! In or out? All employees should join.
your party this Friday? Of course! The more, the merrier. Aren't you going to stay with our group? Sorry, you have to count me out.
n you're on your own. Why didn't you help carry our bags? Every man for himself; I've got no time to help you guys. You're leaving the company? Yeah, I'm jumping
parents. This is the company union desk, right? Right! In or out? All employees should join. I'd like to join the school French Club here.
with our group? Sorry, you have to count me out. Why don't you join our research group? I'm a solo act, sorry.
elp you guys. You're leaving the company? Yeah, I'm jumping ship. I got a better offer.

Wild and Crazy

일탈을 꿈꾸는 당신을 위한 생생 표현

876 › 910

쉬운 말로 '작업' 걸기

Pick-up Lines

☐ Come here often? ☐ Buy you a drink? ☐ Ask me to dance?
☐ My place or yours? ☐ Can I get your number?

876

여기 자주 와요?
Come here often?

→ When a man tries to pick up a girl, he usually says this.

A You look familiar. Come here often?
B No, I've never been here before.

I've never been here/there before. 전에는 여기/거기에 가본 적이 없다. 즉 '처음'이란 뜻.

A 낯이 익어 보이는데. 여기 자주 와요?
B 아니오. 처음이에요.

877

술 한 잔 살까요?
Buy you a drink?

→ 한국말과 똑같죠? 술로 유혹을 하시겠디!

A Buy you a drink? I'd like to get to know you.
B No thanks. I'm here with my boyfriend.

A 술 한 잔 살까요? 사귀고 싶어서요.
B 고맙지만 사양합니다. 남자친구와 같이 왔어요.

878
나와 춤 출래요?
Ask me to dance?

 → Why don't you ask me to dance? Shall we dance? 젊은이들이 잘 쓰는 표현으로 주로 여성이 남성에게 '작업' 걸 때 써요. 반면 남자는 Dance?라고 합니다.

A This is my favorite song. Ask me to dance?
B Okay. Why not!

A 내가 제일 좋아하는 곡이에요. 나와 춤 출래요?
B 좋아요. 그러죠!

879
내 집이나 당신 집으로 자리를 옮길까요?
My place or yours?

 → Should we leave this place and go to your apartment or mine? 남녀가 데이트하면서 '2차'로 직행할 때 쓰는 말. 영화나 시트콤에서 종종 듣죠? 하지만 현실에서 섣불리 썼다간 '큰 코' 다칠 수 있는 주의하세요!

A We seem to be getting on well. My place or yours?
B Sorry, I'm not that kind of girl.

A 우린 꽤 친해지는 것 같은데. 내 집이나 당신 집으로 자리를 옮길까요?
B 미안하지만, 전 그런 여자가 아니에요.

880
전화번호가 어떻게 되죠?
Can I get your number?

 → Can you let me know your phone number? 여기서 number는 전화번호를 말해요.

A It was nice meeting you, but I have to go home.
B I'd like to contact you later. Can I get your number?

A 만나서 반가웠어요. 이젠 가봐야겠어요.
B 나중에 연락하고 싶은데. 전화번호가 어떻게 되죠?

한판 붙어볼까?

Fighting Words

- [ ] Meet me outside!
- [ ] You're asking for it!
- [ ] How about a knuckle sandwich?
- [ ] I'll scratch your eyes out!
- [ ] Say your prayers

881
밖에서 한판 붙자!
Meet me outside!

→ **Meet me outside so we can fight!** 무작정 호기부리는 데야 동서양이 다르지 않겠죠?

A You idiot! Get out of my way.
B Idiot? Meet me outside, and I'll show you who's an "idiot."

get out of ~벗어나다, 비키다

A 이 머저리! 저리 비켜.
B 머저리? 밖에서 한판 붙자! 누가 그런지 알게 해주지.

882
붙어보자는 거군!
You're asking for it!

→ **You're provoking me to violence against you. You're "asking" me to beat you up.** 상대방이 자청한 '싸움'이란 뜻.

A Get out of my chair! Quick!
B Watch your mouth! You're asking for it.

ask for ~을 요청하다

A 내 자리에서 나와! 어서!
B 입 닥쳐! 붙어보자는 거군.

일탈을 꿈꾸는 당신을 위한 생생 표현

Chapter 26

883

한방 먹어볼래?
How about a knuckle sandwich?

 → What about putting my fist into your mouth? 상대방의 입술 사이로 주먹이 들어간 모습이 꼭 샌드위치 같나요? 싸움판에서나 쓰는 말.

A How about giving your girlfriend to me?
B How about a knuckle sandwich?

knuckle 손가락 관절, 마디

A 나한테 네 여자친구를 넘기는 게 어때?
B 한방 먹어 볼래?

884

나한테 한번 당해볼래!
I'll scratch your eyes out!

 → 여성들이 쓰는 말. 눈을 할퀴면 정말 괴롭겠죠!

A Jennie, I heard you were dating every boy on campus.
B What?! Yoojin, I'll scratch your eyes out!

scratch 할퀴다, 긁다

A 진, 학교의 모든 남자들과 데이트 한다며?
B 뭐라고? 유진, 나한테 한번 당해볼래!

885

기도나 하시지.
Say your prayers

 → You should pray/prepare to be beaten to death and meet God. 참, 싸우는 마당에 무슨 말인들 못하겠어요!

A I'm ready to fight you!
B Is that so? Well, say your prayers.

prayer 기도, 소원 빌기   eg. I say my prayers before going to bed.

A 자, 싸울 준비됐어!
B 그렇단 말이지? 좋아, 기도나 하시지.

421

게으름의 유혹에 빠지고 싶을 때

Sloth

- [ ] I'm going to veg out. [ ] I'm gonna crash (out). [ ] I'm a couch potato.
- [ ] Just chill out. [ ] I'm zoned.

886

그냥 빈둥거릴 거야.
I'm going to veg out.

 → I'm going to be lazy. I'm just relaxing. veg는 vegetate의 줄임말. 식물처럼 가만히 앉아 있거나 누워서 빈둥거릴 때 써요.

A What are you going to do all weekend, Joe?
B Me? I'm just going to veg out.

veg 하릴 없이 보내다 eg. I just veged out in front of TV yesterday.

A 죠, 주말 내내 뭐 할 거예요?
B 나요? 그냥 빈둥댈 거야.

887

잠이나 푹 자야지.
I'm gonna crash (out).

 → I'm going to sleep heavily. 잠자리 갖출 것도 없이 푹 쓰러져 자겠다는 뜻. 몹시 피곤해서 '잠 자는 게 낙'처럼 느껴질 때 써요.

A Will you come out to the restaurant with us?
B Sorry, but I'm gonna crash.

A 우리와 외식하러 가지 않을래요?
B 아니, 잠이나 푹 잘 거야.

888
'방콕'할 거야. 엉덩이가 붙었나봐.
I'm a couch potato.

 I'm gonna lie around the house lazily, watching TV or surfing the Internet on the couch. 도통 움직이고 싶지 않을 때 써요.

A You've just been lying around all day!
B Sorry! I guess I'm a couch potato.

A 하루 종일 누워 있기만 하는군요!
B 미안! 엉덩이가 붙었나봐.

889
그냥 조용히 쉴래.
Just chill out.

 Relax. Be calm, cool/chill. 태도나 자세, 행동에 모두 써요.

A You aren't going to play soccer with us?
B No, I'm too tired. I'm going to just chill out for the rest of the day.

for the rest of the day 남은 하루 동안

A 우리와 축구하지 않을 건가요?
B 아니, 너무 피곤해. 남은 하루는 그냥 좀 쉴래요.

890
피곤 그 자체인걸.
I'm zoned.

 I'm too tired/exhausted/distracted, in a "zone of distraction/exhaustion."

A What about joining me for a game of ping pong?
B I'm zoned. Maybe later.

A 탁구 한 게임 하는 게 어때요?
B 피곤해요. 나중에 하죠.

끝없는 욕망을 드러내는 쉬운 말

Ambition & Ruthlessness

- [ ] All's fair!   [ ] It's never enough.   [ ] Anything goes.
- [ ] Whatever it takes   [ ] Winning is everything.

891
성공만 하면 돼!
All's fair!

 → Success justifies everything! Short for proverb "All's fair in love and war." '사랑과 전쟁에서 최후의 승자가 되면 모든게 정당화된다' 는 격언에서 온 말.

A How could you trick me into losing money?
B All's fair! I aim to win.

aim to do ~하는 게 목표다

A 어떻게 나를 속여서 돈을 잃게 할 수 있어요?
B 성공하면 그뿐이지! 난 이기는 게 목표야.

892
결코 만족 못해요.
It's never enough.

 → I want everything. I want the whole world. 욕망에는 끝이 없다고 하죠? ― Is desire endless?

A Aren't you satisfied? You've got everything.
B It's never enough. I want even more.

satisfied 만족하는   eg. Are you satisfied now?

A 당신은 만족하지 않나요? 모든 걸 가졌잖아요.
B 결코 만족하지 못하죠. 더 많이 원하게 되니까요.

424

893

수단과 방법을 안 가려요.
Anything goes.

 → Any method to succeed is acceptable. 지나친 성공 집착이 문제입니다!

A You took my material for your report!
B In business, anything goes. You should know that.
material 자료, 재료

A 당신 보고서에 내 자료를 이용했군요!
B 사업에선, 수단과 방법을 안 가리죠. 그 점을 아셔야죠.

894

어떤 대가를 치르더라도
Whatever it takes

A Did you avoid paying taxes last year?
B Maybe. I do whatever it takes to avoid them.
avoid+-ing ~하는 것을 회피하다

A 작년에 탈세를 하셨죠?
B 그럴지도 모르죠. 세금을 피하는 일이라면 뭐든 하니까요.

895

승리가 전부예요.
Winning is everything.

 → Winning is the most important thing. 승자가 모든 것을 독식하니까요! — The winner takes it all!

A You're such a hardworking person.
B Winning is everything to me. That's why I'm like that.
such a/an+형용사+사람 대단히 ~한 사람 eg. He's such a nice man!

A 정말로 열심히 하시는군요.
B 내겐 승리가 전부예요. 그래서 열심이죠.

좌절과 절망도 쉬운 말로 담담하게

Tragedy

- [ ] It's the end of the world.
- [ ] How can I go on?
- [ ] It's up in smoke.
- [ ] I've lost everything!
- [ ] The chance slipped away!

896
세상이 끝난 기분이야.
It's the end of the world.

→ **I'm hopeless now.** 이런 사람에겐 반대로 It's not the end of the world!라고 말해 보세요!

A What's wrong with you, Joy?
B I just lost my job. It's the end of the world!

A 조이, 무슨 일이야?
B 막 실직을 했어요. 세상 끝난 기분이야.

897
어떻게 살아가죠?
How can I go on?

→ **How can I continue living?** go on은 live의 뜻.

A What happened to you, Jim?
B I lost all my money in stocks. How can I go on?
happen to ~에게 발생하다, 일어나다

A 짐, 무슨 일이 생긴 거예요?
B 주식으로 돈을 몽땅 잃었는데, 어떻게 살아가죠?

898
다 물거품이 되었어.
It's up in smoke.

 My goal/plan is destroyed. 영어에선 물거품 대신 다 타버리고 연기 속으로 사라진 것에 비유해요.

A How did your Biology class go?
B Go? It's up in smoke! I got an "F."

A 생물학 과목은 어땠어?
B 어떠냐고? 다 물거품이 되었어! F학점 받았거든.

899
모든 걸 잃었어요!
I've lost everything!

 I've got nothing to rely on. I don't know how to live on.

A Why do you look so down?
B My store collapsed. I've lost everything!

collapse 무너지다, 좌절되다, 실패하다

A 왜 그렇게 우울해요, 로버트?
B 가게가 망했어요. 난 모든 걸 잃었어요!

900
기회가 달아났어요!
The chance slipped away!

 Some goal/object "slipped from my grasp." 목표, 기회, 또는 원하는 사람이 주어로 와요. 난, 그만 제인을 놓치고 말았네. → Jane slipped away! She married someone else.

A I know you've always wanted to be a good lawyer, Tim.
B Yeah, but I failed again! The chance slipped away!

I've always wanted to ~하는 게 소원이었다

A 당신은 훌륭한 변호사가 되길 원했죠, 팀.
B 그래, 하지만 또 낙방을 했으니! 기회가 사라졌이!

실수와 후회할 때 툭 던지는 말

Remorse & Mistakes

☐ Uh-oh! ☐ I wasn't thinking. ☐ Now I've done it.
☐ I shot myself in the foot. ☐ I cut my own throat.

901
이런!
Uh-oh!

 뭔가 잘못 되었을 때 툭 튀어 나오는 의성어에요.

A You look stunned!
B Uh-oh! I left my keys and wallet at home!

leave (물건을) 남겨 두다, 놓다

A 정신 없어 보이는데!
B 이런! 열쇠와 지갑을 집에 두고 왔네!

902
무심코 있었네!
I wasn't thinking.

 넋 놓다가 '사고' 터지면 원어민들이 툭 던지는 말. 그런데, 연쇄 살인범도 잡힌 뒤에 "왜 죽였어!"물으면, 십중팔구 답변은 — I wasn't thinking!이라죠.

A Water's flooded the bathroom, Honey!
B Uh-oh! I forgot to turn off the water. I wasn't thinking!

forget to do ~할 것을 잊다 eg. I forgot to bring a bottle of wine!

A 목욕탕에 물이 넘쳤어요, 여보!
B 이런! 수도를 잠근다는 걸 잊었어. 무심코 있었네!

일탈을 꿈꾸는 당신을 위한 생생 표현

Chapter 26

903
일 냈어! 사고 쳤어!
Now I've done it.

 done it은 made a big mistake의 뜻이에요.

A Now I've done it. I lost an important file!
B Too bad, Jim. It can happen to anyone.

A 중요한 파일을 잃었어요!
B 안 됐군요, 짐. 하지만 누구나 있는 일이에요.

904
내가 자초한 일이야.
I shot myself in the foot.

 I hurt myself badly by mistake! 자기 발에 총을 쏜 것과 같다는 비유. 어처구니 없는 실수에 써요.

A Why did you buy so many things with your credit card?
B You're right: I shot myself in the foot by using it too much!

A 왜 신용카드로 그렇게 많은 것을 샀소?
B 당신 말이 옳아요. 과다하게 사용해서 화를 자초했네요.

905
기회를 망쳤어요.
I cut my own throat.

 I killed my own opportunity. 자기 목을 벤 것만큼이나 중대한 실수를 했을 때 써요.

A Did the job interview go well?
B No, I cut my own throat by talking too much, I think.

go well 잘 되다, 성공적이다

A 구직 면접은 잘 했나요?
B 아뇨, 말을 너무 많이 해서 망친 것 같아요.

용기와 자신감을 드러내는 말

Courage & Competence

- [ ] You get things done.
- [ ] I love trouble.
- [ ] Bring 'em on!
- [ ] I'm confident enough!
- [ ] No fear!

906

어려운 일을 성사시켰네!
You get things done.

→ You achieve the impossible job! Well done!

A Great job with the new client! You get things done.
B Thank you. I always try my hardest.

A 신규 고객을 잘 잡았네! 어려운 일을 성사시켰어.
B 감사합니다. 전, 항상 일을 성사시키려고 애씁니다.

907

도전적인 일이 좋아요.
I love trouble.

→ I enjoy risk or danger. I like to challenge myself.

A Can you handle this risky job for me?
B I love trouble. Depend on me.

risky 위험한, 어려운(difficult)

A 이 힘든 일을 좀 해주겠어요?
B 난 힘든 일이 좋아. 나만 믿어요.

908
덤벼!
Bring 'em on!

 → I'm ready for conflict! You'd better challenge me. 대단한 각오죠!

A I'm concerned about our new rivals.
B I don't care. Bring 'em on! We're bound to win.

be bound to ~하게 되어 있다

A 새 경쟁자가 걱정이 되요.
B 난 상관없어요. 오라고 해요! 우리가 이길 테니까.

909
충분히 자신 있어요!
I'm confident enough!

 → I can do it easily/fearlessly. You can rely on me.

A Can you work until midnight?
B I'm confident enough! I can work all night if I have to.

confident 자신 있는, 확신하는   if I have to 꼭 그래야 한다면

A 자정까지 일할 수 있어요?
B 자신 있어요! 필요하다면 밤샘도 할 수 있어요.

910
못할 것도 없지!
No fear!

 → I have no fear about it. 두려워하지 않고 과감히 도전해보겠다는 의지 표명.

A It seems dangerous driving so fast.
B No fear! I'm ready to drive even faster!

A 너무 빨리 달리면 위험하잖아요.
B 괜찮아! 훨씬 더 속도를 낼 건데!

CHAPTER 27

Communication

Is this the company bowling team? It sure is. Want in? Isn't this the local parents' group? It is. I'd like to join the school French Club here. You hopping on? How long have you studied French? Why don't you join our research group? I'm a solo act, sorry. You're leaving our department? ship. I got a better offer. Is this the company bowling team? It sure is. Want in? Isn't this the local parents' group? It is. You signing up? You hopping on? How long have you studied French? Can I come to your party this Friday? Of course! The more, the merrier. Aren't You're leaving our department? Yeah, from now on you're on your own. Why didn't you help carry our bags? Every man for himself; I

Susan Says...

If a problem seems impossible,
give it to a woman: she'll solve it.

Communication

의사소통할 때
빠지지 않는
생생 표현

911 › 945

납득 여부를 확인할 때 쓰는 말

Comprehension

- [ ] I (don't) get you. [ ] I see. [ ] It's clear as a bell.
- [ ] Clear? [ ] Understood

911
이해가 돼요. 안 돼요.
I (don't) get you.

 → I (don't) understand what you're saying. get은 understand의 뜻.

  A Do you understand the plan I've outlined?
    B Yes, I get you. I'll carry it out right away.
    outline 약술하다, 대충 설명하다   carry~out ~를 실행(수행)하다

  A 약술한 기획 내용을 알겠어요?
    B 예, 무슨 말인지 알겠어요. 당장 실행하겠습니다.

912
예. 알았어요.
I see.

 → 이미 알고 계시죠? 그래도 막상 말하려면 입이 '꽁꽁' 얼어붙잖아요. Just say it!

  A I want you to get this entire warehouse clean.
    B I see, Mr. Bright. Will you send us any help, though?
    warehouse 창고, 물품 보관소   though (문장 끝에 씀) 그러나, 하지만

  A 이 물품 보관소 전체를 청소해 놓으세요.
    B 예, 브라이트 씨. 한데, 추가 인력을 보내주실 거죠?

434

913
명확히 이해했어요.
It's clear as a bell.

 → I understand it because it "rings loudly and clearly," like a bell. 추가 설명은 사절이란 뜻.

 A Do you have any questions about this assignment?
B No, Mrs. Grick. It's clear as a bell.

 A 이번 과제에 대해 질문 있어요?
B 아뇨, 그릭 씨. 명확히 알았어요.

914
알겠소?
Clear?

 → Is it clear/understandable to you?

 A Take these up to the third floor. Clear?
B Yes, I'll take them up right away.

clear 명료한, 이해가 가는(understandable)

 A 이걸 3층으로 가져가요. 알겠죠?
B 예, 지금 당장 옮기겠습니다.

915
그렇게 하죠.
Understood

 → I got it. I'll do it right away. 다소 '상명하달'의 냄새가 나는 상황에 써요.

 A Get all of my bags packed. I'm ready to leave.
B Understood. Would you like me to call you a taxi, too?

call~ a taxi ~에게 택시를 불러주다 eg. Call me a taxi, please.

 A 내 짐을 모두 갖다줘요. 떠날 채비가 됐으니.
B 그렇게 하죠. 택시도 불러드릴까요?

궁금증을 설명해주고 싶다면

Explanations

- [ ] I'll spell it out?
- [ ] Read between the lines
- [ ] Picture this
- [ ] Run it by me
- [ ] Shoot!

916
구체적으로 설명드려요?
I'll spell it out?

I'll give a detailed explanation as in spelling out a basic word. 철자를 쓰듯 하나하나 설명한다는 뜻. 자, 앉아요, 하나하나 설명할 테니. — Have a seat next to me and I'll spell it out for you.

A What's this new policy mean?
B Do I have to spell it out? No more taking smoke breaks during work.

policy 규칙, 규정   during ~동안

A 새로운 사규라는 게 뭔가요?
B 구체적으로 설명하라고요? 업무시간 중에 흡연휴식은 불가합니다.

917
속내를 파악해요.
Read between the lines

Try to understand his/her real feelings or intentions. 표면적인 말 속에 담긴 '진짜 속내'를 알아내란 뜻.

A Is the boss really angry with all of us?
B A little, but read between the lines: I think he's trying to motivate us, too.

angry with/at ~에게 화난   motivate 동기 부여를 하다

A 사장님이 우리 모두에게 화가 나셨나요?
B 약간은, 진짜 속내는 우리에게 동기 부여를 해주려는 거죠.

918
상상을 해봐.
Picture this

 → **Imagine this!** 상대방의 호기심을 잔뜩 이끌어내면서 말할 때 써요.

A How should we spend our next vacation?
B Picture this: how about 2 weeks in Tahiti?

A 다음 휴가는 어떻게 보낼까요?
B 이런 걸 상상해봐. 타히티에서 2주를 보내는 건 어떨까?

919
다시 설명해봐요.
Run it by me

 → **Please explain it to me.** 여기서 run은 '다시 설명하다'는 뜻. 아, 지금은 바쁘니 나중에 다시 설명해줘요. — I'm busy right now; run it by me later.

A Mr. Zane, this is the new budget proposal.
B Oh yeah? Run it by me.

A 제인 씨, 새로운 예산안입니다.
B 아, 그래요? 다시 설명해줘요.

920
어서 말해봐요!
Shoot!

 → **Ask a question now. "Shoot" the question at me.** 우물쭈물 대지 말고 '빨리' 물어보란 뜻.

A Mr. Grant, do you have a few minutes? I'd like to ask you something.
B Okay, Cameron, shoot!

A 그랜트 씨, 시간 좀 있으세요? 여쭤볼 게 있는데요.
B 그러죠, 카메론, 어서 말해봐요!

마지못해 동의할 때 쓰는 말

Reluctant Agreement

- [ ] If you say so
- [ ] It's not my first choice.
- [ ] If you insist
- [ ] If I have to
- [ ] Not because I want to

921

그리 말씀하시니
If you say so

 → If that is what you order/tell me to do, I'll do so.

A From now on, I want everyone to wear a suit to work.
B Okay, if you say so.

A 지금부터 모두가 정장하고 출근하세요.
B 알겠습니다, 그리 말씀하시니.

922

애초에 원했던 바는 아니지만.
It's not my first choice.

 → If I had a chance, I'd choose something else. 차선을 택하면서 처음 것에 대한 미련이 있을 때 써요.

A Don't you think this dress would look good on me?
B Well, actually it's not my first choice. But it might be okay.

look good on ~에게 잘 어울리다

A 이 옷이 잘 어울리지 않나요?
B 글쎄, 사실 애초에 원했던 것은 아닌데. 괜찮겠어요.

923
정 그러시다면
If you insist

 If you say it firmly... 타협의 여지 없이 강경 입장을 내세울 때 써요.

　A　Let's cancel the fishing trip. I've got things to finish during the weekend.
　　　B　Okay, if you insist, Robert.

　A　낚시 가기로 한 것 취소하죠. 주말에 끝내야 할 일이 있어요.
　　　B　그래, 로버트, 정 그렇다면야.

924
꼭 그래야 한다면
If I have to

 If it is necessary   have to는 must(~해야 한다)와 같은 뜻.

　A　I need you to drive me over to store #13 this afternoon.
　　　B　Okay, Mrs. Buckley, if I have to.

drive~ over to　~까지 태워주다　eg. Can you drive me over to the school?

　A　오늘 오후에 13호점까지 태워줘요.
　　　B　예, 버클리 부인, 꼭 그래야 한다면요.

925
원해서가 아니라
Not because I want to

 I'm being forced to do something.

　A　You're going to study at a women's college?
　　　B　Yeah, but not because I want to. My parents insist.

be forced to　억지로 ~하다　eg. I'm being forced to leave this country.

　A　여자대학으로 진학할 거야?
　　　B　응, 내가 원해서가 아니야. 부모님이 강경하셔서.

# 소통이 잘 안 될 때 튀어나오는 말

Miscommunication

- [ ] Were you listening?
- [ ] Once more
- [ ] Could you speak up?
- [ ] Am I talking to a brick wall?
- [ ] Get to the point

926

내 말 듣고 있어요?
Were you listening?

→ Were you paying attention at all? 다소 짜증난 어투로 들리는 말이에요.

A So, I should go to Room 2C, right?
B Were you listening? I told you to go to Room 3A.
tell+사람+to do (가벼운 명령) ~에게 …하라고 말하다

A 2C 방으로 가란 말씀이죠?
B 내 말 듣고 있어요? 3A 방으로 가라고 했습니다.

927

한 번 더 말하는데
Once more

→ I'll repeat it again. 여러번 반복해서 다소 언짢을 때 써요.

A These will cost $65 each, won't they?
B Nancy, listen! Once more: $67 each!

A 이것들 각각이 65달러라는 건가요?
B 낸시, 잘 들어요! 한 번 더 말하는데, 각각 67달러예요!

928
크게 말씀해주시겠어요?
Could you speak up?

 → You are talking so softly that I can't hear anything.

A What I'd like to focus…
B Could you speak up? We can't hear at the back.

at the back (of) (~의) 뒤에, 후면에   eg. He sat at the back of the bus.

A 제가 강조하는 점은…
B 크게 말씀해 주시겠어요? 뒤에서는 안 들려요.

929
벽 보고 말하는 것도 아닌데?
Am I talking to a brick wall?

 → Am I speaking to someone who doesn't listen at all? 벽 보고 말하는 것처럼 답답하다는 심경 표현.

A So our flight leaves from Phoenix?
B From Tucson! Am I talking to a brick wall?

A 그럼 항공편이 피닉스에서 출발하나요?
B 투손에서 입니다! 귀가 먹었나요?

930
요점만 말해요.
Get to the point

 → What's your point? State the "point" that you are trying to make.

A So, in conclusion, my idea is…uh…
B Get to the point! We can't wait here all day!

in conclusion 결론적으로

A 그래서, 결론적으로, 제 말씀은…
B 요점만 말해요! 종일 여기서 기다릴 수 없잖소!

말하는 데 문제가 있나요?

Speaking Problems

- [ ] Cat got your tongue?
- [ ] I have a stammer.
- [ ] Cut the jibber-jabber!
- [ ] Talk! Talk! Talk! / Blah! Blah! Blah!
- [ ] I'm stuck for a word.

931
입을 열지 않을 거요?
Cat got your tongue?

→ Has cat got hold your tongue? Are you unable to speak correctly? 상대방이 말을 시원하게 하지 않아 답답할 때 써요.

A Mr. Duvall, I just wanted to…uh…uh…uh…
B Tell me what you want, Kate. Cat got your tongue?

A 듀발 씨, 저어… 저는 다만…
B 케이트, 원하는 게 뭔데요? 입을 열지 않을 거요?

932
말을 더듬어요.
I have a stammer.

→ I've got stammering problems while speaking. 지나친 긴장이나 공포감 등으로 말을 더듬을 수 있죠. 그럴 때 써요. 정도에 따라 a bit of, a lot of 를 넣어 말해요. 반면에 선천적으로 생긴 경우엔 stutter란 단어를 써요.

A I have a bit of a stammer. How can I get rid of that?
B You should read out loud. Like magazines, poetry, etc.

get rid of ~을 제거하다

A 말을 좀 더듬는데, 어떻게 해야 없어지나요?
B 큰 소리로 읽으세요. 잡지나 시 같은 것을요.

Chapter 27

933
우물우물하지 마요!
Cut the jibber-jabber!

 → Quit mumbling/avoiding main point. Jibber-jabber는 아이들의 의미없는 말. Why the mumbo-jumbo?라고도 해요.

A So...I...uh...my main meaning...is that...
B Tell us your plan, Aron, and cut the jibber-jabber!

A 그러니까… 제가 말하려는 것은…
B 계획을 말해 봐요, 아론. 우물우물하지 말고요!

934
말은 많은데
Talk! Talk! Talk! / Blah! Blah! Blah!

 → Just a lot of talk, but no content. 알맹이 없이 말이 많은 경우에 써요.

A Therefore, it stands to reason that....
B Talk! Talk! Talk! Do you have any real information?

it stands to reason that ~하는 것은 당연하다, 이치에 맞다

A 그러므로, 당연히…
B 말은 많은데… 진짜 정보가 있긴 해요?

935
적당한 말이 생각나지 않아요.
I'm stuck for a word.

 → I don't know which word I should use for this. 적절한 단어가 생각나지 않을 때 써요.

A Dan, speak up! What's on your mind?
B I'm stuck for a word to describe my feelings for you.

stuck 막힌, 닫힌   describe 묘사하다

A 댄, 말해봐요! 마음에 있는 게 뭐에요?
B 당신에 대한 내 감정을 표현할 말이 생각나지 않아요.

피드백과 승인 받을 게 있다면

Feedback & Approval

☐ Bounce it off Sam ☐ He gave it the nod. ☐ Get his two cents
☐ Get her stamp on it ☐ My boss has to OK it.

936

샘에게 물어 보지.
Bounce it off Sam

→ See what he thinks, as if "bouncing a ball off a wall" to see what it does. 제 3자의 의견을 구할 때 써요.

A Do you think we should use this advertisement?
B I don't know. Bounce it off Sam in Marketing.

A 이 광고로 가야 할까요?
B 모르겠어요. 마케팅 부의 샘에게 물어보죠.

937

고개를 끄덕였어요.
He gave it the nod.

→ "nod one's head in approval" of something 한국말과 똑같죠! give the nod는 approve와 같은 뜻.

A Did Ms. Crane say we could start this project?
B Yes, she gave it the nod last week.

nod 묵례, 승인   eg. The CEO gave the nod of approval.

A 크레인 씨가 이 프로젝트를 해도 된대요?
B 예, 지난주에 승인했어요.

938

조언을 받아요.
Get his two cents

 → How about getting his advice on this issue. two cents는 advice의 뜻.

A Do you think my blueprints look accurate?
B Yeah, but get Mr. Manson's two cents before you start working.

blueprint 청사진, 설계도   accurate 정확한

A 내 설계도가 정확한 것 같아요?
B 예, 하지만 시작하기 전에 맨슨 씨 조언을 받아요.

939

승낙을 받으세요.
Get her stamp on it

 → We need her signature. stamp는 한국의 도장에 해당되는 것.

A Will we be able to take this trip to Poland?
B I think so, but we have to get mom and dad's stamp on it.

be able to ~할 수 있다   take a trip to ~로 여행가다

A 이번 폴란드 여행 가는 거죠?
B 그래, 하지만 엄마와 아빠의 승낙을 받아야 해.

940

사장님이 OK 해야죠.
My boss has to OK it.

 → 생활영어에는 나름의 어법이 있죠? OK가 그대로 동사로 사용된 예!

A Won't this purchase go through?
B I think so, but first my boss has to OK it.

go through (공식적으로) 수락되다, 인정되다

A 이 구매요청서 승인날 것 아닌가요?
B 그런 건데, 우선 사장님 OK를 받아야죠.

에둘러서 반대하는 말

Rebuttals

- [ ] That's what you think. 　- [ ] Can I have my say? 　- [ ] I beg to differ/disagree.
- [ ] Talk is cheap. 　- [ ] Nice speech

941

(그건) 당신 생각이죠.
That's what you think.

→ I think your opinion is wrong.

A It's going to be a long summer.
B That's what you think. I heard it's going to be short.

A 여름이 길 거라는데요.
B 당신 생각이죠. 난 짧을 거라고 들었는데.

942

내 말도 들어보시죠?
Can I have my say?

→ Can I tell my side of the story? 여기서 say는 opinion/words의 뜻.

A And that's what I think!
B Now that you've talked, can I have my say?

now that ~이니까(since)

A 그게 내 생각이에요!
B 당신이 말했으니, 내 얘기도 들어보시죠?

의사소통할 때 빠지지 않는 생생 표현

Chapter 27

943
의견이 다릅니다.
I beg to differ/disagree.

 정중하게 반대 입장을 밝힐 때 써요.

A I guess this plan is going to work out in Korea.
B I beg to differ with you on that point.

differ ~와 다르다(from/with)

A 이 계획은 한국에서 먹힐 겁니다.
B 전 그 점에서 의견이 다릅니다.

944
말만 하면 뭘 해요.
Talk is cheap.

 Your talk has no value. Nothing you say will matter. 행동이 따라야 한다는 뜻. "Actions speak louder than words!"

A Wasn't my presentation persuasive?
B A little, but talk is cheap.

persuasive 설득력 있는   eg. She's a very persuasive speaker.

A 내 PT가 설득력이 있었지요?
B 약간은, 하지만 말만 하면 뭘 해요.

945
잘 들었어요.
Nice speech

 상대방의 말에 동조하지 않는다는 것을 냉소적으로 표현하는 말. 천천히 냉소적인 기분을 담아서 말해보세요.

A And that concludes my topic.
B Nice speech. Now, I've going to give my side.

give one's side ~에게 자신의 의견[입장]을 말하다

A 그게 내 결론입니다.
B 잘 들었어요. 이젠, 내 의견을 말하죠.

CHAPTER 28

Weather

Is this the company bowling team? It sure is. Want in? Isn't this the local parents' group? It is. You signing up? I'd like to join the school French Club here. You hopping on? How long have you studied French? Can I come? Why don't you join our research group? I'm a solo act, sorry. You're leaving our department? Yeah, from now better offer. Is this the company bowling team? It sure is. Want in? Isn't this the local parents' group? It is. You signing up? We need m You hopping on? How long have you studied French? Can I come to your party this Friday? Of course! The more, the merrier. Aren't yo You're leaving our department? Yeah, from now on you're on your own. Why didn't you help carry our bags? Every man for himself; I've

Susan Says...

My friends make life worth living!

Weather

대화의 물꼬를
터주는
생생 날씨 표현

덥고 추운 날씨에 으레 쓰는 말

Extremely Hot & Cold

☐ Hot enough for you?   ☐ I'm frozen stiff.   ☐ You could fry an egg.
☐ You can see your own breath!   ☐ Windchill makes you feel colder.

946
엄청 덥지요?
Hot enough for you?

 → Isn't it extremely hot? 나만 더운 게 아니라 상대도 그런지 동의를 구하는 상황에 써요. 친한 사이엔 you대신 ya로도 말해요.

A Hot enough for you?
B Yeah! It must be over 33°C!

must be ~임에 틀림 없다

A 엄청 덥죠?
B 예! 33도가 넘을 겁니다!

947
(몸이) 꽁꽁 얼었어요.
I'm frozen stiff.

 → I'm so cold that I can't move. 또는 I'm an icicle!로 표현하는 사람도 있어요.

A Your entire face looks almost blue!
B That's because I'm frozen stiff!

stiff (구어) 사람, 녀석 eg. You lucky stiff, Jimmy.

A 얼굴이 아주 파래졌어요!
B 몸이 꽁꽁 얼었거든요!

대화의 물꼬를 터주는 생생 날씨 표현

Chapter 28

948
달걀 부쳐 먹어도 될 정도예요.
You could fry an egg.

 → It's extremely hot outside! 얼마나 더우면 도로에서 달걀을 부쳐도 될까요?

A It's so hot outside today!
B It is! It's so hot you could fry an egg.

A 오늘 너무 더워요!
B 맞아! 달걀 부쳐 먹어도 된다니까.

949
입김이 다 보여요!
You can see your own breath!

 → It's so cold that my own breath is visible. '호호' 내 입김이 다 보일 정도로 춥다는 말.

A I've never seen it this cold in Busan!
B Me neither. You can see your own breath!

this (부사) 이렇게   neither ~도 아니다

A 부산에서 이렇게 춥기는 처음이야!
B 나도요. 입김이 다 보이잖아요!

950
바람이 세서 더 춥죠.
Windchill makes you feel colder.

 → 같은 온도라도 바람이 불면 체감온도가 더 내려가죠. — That's called windchill factor.

A It's just 2 degrees outside, but it feels like minus 5 or 6.
B Windchill makes you feel much colder.

windchill (기상) 풍속 냉각   feel like ~처럼 느끼다

A 외부온도가 2도인데도 영하 5~6도인 것 같아요.
B 바람이 세서 더 춥게 느껴지죠.

날씨의 변화를 예측할 때 쓰는 말

Weather Changes

- [ ] The mercury's rising/falling.
- [ ] We're in for rain.
- [ ] It's gonna be a hot one!
- [ ] It won't hold.
- [ ] Look for clear skies today.

951

수은주가 올라요 / 떨어져요.
The mercury's rising/falling.

 → It's getting hotter/colder.

A Do you think it might snow?
B Maybe, the mercury's been falling all day.

A 눈이 올까요?
B 그럴지도, 수은주가 종일 떨어지니까요.

952

비가 오겠습니다.
We're in for rain.

 → Rain/snow is coming/expecting. '비/눈 안으로 들어간다'는 말이니 어렵지 않죠. 원어민들은 자주 씁니다.

A What kind of weather will we have today?
B The TV says that we're in for rain.

A 오늘 날씨가 어떻대요?
B TV에서 비가 올 거라는군.

953
더운 날이 되겠군!
It's gonna be a hot one!

 → 여기서 one은 day를 뜻해요. hot/cold/windy/chilly 등 골라 써보세요.

A   I hope it's a little warmer today.
B   No, it's gonna be a cold one.

A   오늘은 좀 따뜻했으면 좋겠는데.
B   아뇨, 추운 날이 될 거예요.

954
계속 이렇지는 않겠지.
It won't hold.

 → The weather won't continue as it is. hold는 continue의 뜻.

A   It's really stormy today.
B   It won't hold. I heard it'll be over by noon.

A   오늘 폭풍이 대단하네요.
B   계속 불지는 않을 겁니다. 정오에는 멈춘대요.

955
(오늘은) 맑을 겁니다.
Look for clear skies today.

 → We're expecting rain/snow/humidity/etc. today. look for는 expect와 같은 뜻.

A   Do you think we'll have high humidity?
B   No, look for clear skies and dry weather today.

humidity 습도   cf. hot and humid 습도가 높고 더운

A   습도가 높을까요?
B   아뇨, 오늘은 맑고 건조할 겁니다.

비 오고, 눈 오는 날이면 쓰는 말

Rain & Snow

- [ ] It's raining cats and dogs!
- [ ] It's really coming down.
- [ ] All I see is white!
- [ ] You'll have to swim to work/school!
- [ ] Looks like the North Pole

956

비가 억수로 와요!
It's raining cats and dogs!

 It's raining heavily. The rain is so heavy it's as if "cats and dogs" were falling from the sky. 하늘에서 개와 고양이가 쏟아져 내리듯 '엄청난 비'를 만나본 적 있으세요? 개인적으로 참 한심한 비유라고 생각하지만, 여전히 쓰는 말!

A Can we have our picnic today?
B No way! It's raining cats and dogs out there!

pour 쏟아 붓다

A 오늘 소풍 갈 수 있는 거죠?
B 안 돼! 밖에 비가 억수로 오는걸!

957

정말 쏟아붓네요.
It's really coming down.

 It's raining/snowing hard. It's pouring (down) rain/snow. 눈과 비에 모두 써요.

A It's been snowing all day, hasn't it?
B It's really coming down, but may stop later.

pour (down) 쏟아붓다/내리다

A 종일 눈이 내리잖아요?
B 정말 쏟아붓네요. 그래도 나중엔 멈추겠죠.

958

바깥이 온통 하얗네!
All I see is white!

 → There's a lot of snow outside. 눈으로 하얗게 뒤덮인 세상!

　A　Did it snow last night?
　　　　B　Yes, all I see is white out the window.

all I see 보이는 것 전부　cf. all I hear 들리는 소식 전부

　A　간밤에 눈이 왔나요?
　　　　B　예, 창밖이 온통 하얗네!

959

수영해서 가야 해!
You'll have to swim to work/school!

 → There is a lot of water outside during a morning commute. 출근/등교 시간에 비가 많이 내린 경우에 써요.

　A　Still raining hard outside, eh?
　　　　B　Yes, you'll have to swim to school.

you'll have to ~해야 할 것이다　eg. You'll have to learn Spanish as well.

　A　밖에 아직도 비가 많이 오죠?
　　　　B　그래, 학교까지 수영해서 가야겠다.

960

북극에 온 것 같아요.
Looks like the North Pole

 → It looks icy/cold outside.

　A　Has the snow melted?
　　　　B　No, it still looks like the North Pole.

melt 녹다

　A　눈이 녹았나요?
　　　　B　아니, 여전히 북극에 온 것 같아.

극한의 날씨를 표현하고 싶다면

Weather Extremes

- [ ] It's hot as the Sahara!   [ ] It's like pea soup!   [ ] I wouldn't let a dog out!
- [ ] You'll roast!   [ ] Don't blow away!

961
사하라 사막 같아!
It's hot as the Sahara!

→ **It's extremely hot, hot as the Sahara Desert.** 사하라 사막보다 더 더운 곳이 있나요? 어쨌든 땡볕 더위를 이렇게 말해요.

A It's getting much hotter outside, isn't it?
B You bet! It's hot as the Sahara!

get+비교급 점점 ~해 지다   eg. It's getting cooler.

A 점점 더 더워지는 것 같죠?
B 맞아요! 사하라 사막 같아!

962
안개가 잔뜩 꼈어요.
It's like pea soup!

→ **There's thick fog like pea soup.** 콩 수프처럼 안개가 자욱한 상태라? Picture this! 한국말로는 딱히 없는 것 같은데… 원어민들은 자주 쓴답니다.

A Can you see anything out the car window?
B No, it's like pea soup!

A 차 밖으로 뭔가 보여요?
B 아뇨, 안개가 잔뜩 껴서요!

963
날씨가 아주 고약해!
I wouldn't let a dog out!

 → The weather is too severe to even permit a dog to enter it.

A Mom, can I go out to play?
B I wouldn't let a dog out! Look at how stormy it is!

let~ out ~을 밖으로 내놓다 severe 지독한, 심한

A 엄마, 나가 놀아도 돼요?
B 날씨가 아주 고약해! 폭풍이 얼마나 심한지 보렴!

964
'통구이' 가 될걸!
You'll roast!

 → It's too hot to go out! 얼마나 덥길래 '통구이' 가 될까?

A I'm going out to skateboard.
B In this weather? You'll roast out there!

out there 밖에, 저기, 거기(붙여서 한단어처럼 씀)

A 난 스케이트보드 타러 나갈 거야.
B 이런 날씨에? 밖에 나가면 '통구이' 가 될걸!

965
(날아가지 않도록) 조심해!
Don't blow away!

 → The wind is so strong that it might "blow you away." 날씬한 사람만 해 당될까요? 주머니에 돌이라도 넣고 외출하시길!

A I'm leaving for work.
B Don't blow away! It's windy today!

leave for work 출근하다(go to work)

A 출근합니다.
B 조심하세요! 오늘 바람이 아주 세요!

난, 어떤 계절과 날씨를 좋아하지?

Weather Preferences & Changes

- [ ] Give me spring anytime!
- [ ] Spring is around the corner.
- [ ] I'll take summer over spring.
- [ ] The season's turning.
- [ ] Won't last forever

966
언제나 봄이 좋죠!
Give me spring anytime!

→ I prefer spring/summer/fall/winter. 좋아하는 계절을 넣어 말해보세요.

A Don't you like May?
B It's okay, but give me winter anytime!

A 5월이 좋지 않나요?
B 괜찮긴 하지만, 난 겨울이 언제나 좋아요!

967
곧 봄이 와.
Spring is around the corner.

 → **Spring is coming soon.** around the corner는 can almost see it의 뜻. 앞에 just를 넣어도 좋아요. 곧 내 생일이야. — My birthday is just around the corner.

A It's getting warmer, isn't it?
B That's because spring is around the corner.

A 점점 따뜻해지지 않니?
B 봄이 곧 되니까 그렇죠.

968
봄보다 여름이 좋아.
I'll take summer over spring.

 여기서 take는 prefer의 뜻이에요.

　A Don't you like spring?
　　　B It's okay, but I'll take summer over spring.

　A 봄이 좋지 않나요?
　　　B 괜찮지만, 난 봄보다 여름이 좋아요.

969
계절이 바뀌고 있군.
The season's turning.

 봄에서 여름으로, 가을에서 겨울로… 문득 계절의 변화가 감지될 때 써요.

　A All the flowers are finally blooming.
　　　B It's beautiful! The season's turning!

bloom 꽃이 피다

　A 온갖 꽃들이 피었네요.
　　　B 아름다워라! 계절이 바뀌고 있네!

970
영원히 가지는 않아.
Won't last forever

 주어 자리에 Spring/Winter/Summer/Fall을 넣어 말해요.

　A I really hate this cold weather.
　　　B Don't worry. Winter won't last forever!

last forever 영원히 지속되다   eg. My love will last forever!

　A 이렇게 추운 날씨가 너무 싫어.
　　　B 걱정 마. 영원히 겨울이진 않을 테니까!

날씨에 따라 건강을 챙길 때

Weather Caution and Danger

- ☐ Don't get soaked.   ☐ Stay warm!   ☐ Wear something light
- ☐ Bundle up!   ☐ Put something on your head!

971

(비에) 젖지 않도록 해요.
Don't get soaked.

→ Don't get too wet outside. soak를 쓰면 '흠뻑 비에 젖다'는 뜻입니다.

A Darn! I have to drive to work in this rain!
B Don't get soaked! Wear a raincoat!

A 제기랄! 이 비 속을 운전해서 출근하다니!
B 젖지 않도록 해요. 우비를 입어요!

972

따뜻하게 해요!
Stay warm!

→ Take care of yourself and keep yourself warm.

A Stay warm! You'd better wear this underwear.
B No, I don't want to look bulky.

bulky 부피가 큰, 뚱뚱해 보이는

A 따뜻하게 해야지! 이 내복을 입어라.
B 아뇨, 뚱뚱해 보이기 싫어요.

973

가볍게 입어요.
Wear something light

 → You'd better wear light clothing.

A Should I take this jacket with me?
B No, it's hot today. You'd better wear something light.

A 이 자켓을 가져 가야 할까요?
B 아뇨, 오늘 더워요. 가볍게 입는 게 좋죠.

974

잔뜩 껴 입어요!
Bundle up!

 → Wear heavy clothing. Wear "a bundle" of clothing. 많이 껴 입을수록 따뜻해!

A Is there still snow and ice on the ground?
B Yes, so you'd better bundle up before you go out.

bundle up 꾸러미로 싸다

A 땅에 아직도 눈과 얼음이 있나요?
B 그래, 잔뜩 껴 입고 외출하거라.

975

머리에 뭐 좀 써요!
Put something on your head!

 → You'd better wear a hat!

A Put something on your head! It's freezing and windy outside.
B All right, bring me that red hat.

freezing 꽁꽁 얼 정도로 추운

A 머리에 뭐 좀 써요! 밖에 바람도 불고 엄청 추워요.
B 알았소, 그 빨간 모자를 줘요.

날씨에서 나온 유용한 생활표현

Weather Idioms

- [ ] A storm is brewing.
- [ ] Seasons change.
- [ ] It'll blow over.
- [ ] A little rain must fall.
- [ ] We're at the boiling point.

976
폭풍 전야야.
A storm is brewing.

→ Big trouble is coming/expecting.

A Why is the office so tense today?
B A storm is brewing. I think the director may get fired.

tense 긴장된

A 오늘 사무실 분위기가 왜 싸늘해요?
B 폭풍 전야죠. 전무님이 해고될 건 가봐요.

977
계절은 바뀌게 마련이지.
Seasons change.

→ People/things change, like the seasons. 하늘 아래 변하지 않는 게 없다고 했던가요? 비유적으로 자주 쓰는 말.

A You don't work for Tech Soft Inc. anymore?
B No, seasons change.

A 이젠 터크 소프트 사에서 일하지 않아요?
B 안 해요, 계절은 바뀌게 마련이죠.

대화의 물꼬를 터주는 생생 날씨 표현

Chapter 28

978
사라질 겁니다.
It'll blow over.

 → Anger/sensation/fame eventually dies down. 좋고 나쁜 모든 일들이 결국엔 바람에 '휙' 날려가버릴 것이란 비유.

A Everyone loves that new pop star!
B For now, but sooner or later it'll blow over.

for now 당분간, 지금은 eg. Good-bye for now.

A 모두가 그 신인 가수를 좋아해요!
B 지금은 그렇지만 조만간 사라지겠죠.

979
궂은 날도 있는 법이지요.
A little rain must fall.

 → Trouble must come sometimes, comes from proverb, "into every life, a little rain must fall." 성경 구절 "The rain falls on the just and the unjust alike."에서 비롯된 말.

A I failed my college entrance exams!
B A little rain must fall. You'll get over it.

get over 극복하다, 회복하다

A 대학입시에서 떨어졌어요!
B 궂은 날도 있는 법이지. 넌 극복해낼 거야.

980
끓어 오를 대로 올랐죠.
We're at the boiling point.

 → We're about to explode from anger.

A Are you and your wife getting along well?
B No, I think we're at the boiling point nowadays.

get along well 잘 지내다, 사이가 좋다 eg. Are you and Tom getting along well?

A 부부 사이는 좋습니까?
B 아뇨, 최근엔 서로 끓어 오를 대로 올랐죠.

CHAPTER 29

Special Corners

Is this the company bowling team? It sure is. Want in? Isn't this the local parents' group? It i[s] I'd like to join the school French Club here. You hopping on? How long have you studied Fre[nch] Why don't you join our research group? I'm a solo act, sorry. You're leaving our department[?] jumping ship. I got a better offer. Is this the company bowling team? It sure is. Want in? Isn't this the local parents' group? It is. You sig[n] You hopping on? How long have you studied French? Can I come to your party this Friday? Of course! The more, the merrier. Aren't yo[u] You're leaving our department? Yeah, from now on you're on your own. Why didn't you help carry our bags? Every man for himself; I've

Susan Says...

One day, this entire street will be female-owned!

? We need more parents. This is the company union desk, right? Right! In or out! All emplo yees should join.
he to your party this Friday? Of course! The more, the merrier. Aren't you going to stay with our group? Sorry, you have to count me out.
w on you're on your own. Why didn't you help carry our bags? Every man for himself; I've got no time to help you guys. You're leaving the company? Yeah,
ed more parents. This is the company union desk, right? Right! In or out? All emplo yees should join. I'd like to join the school French Club here.
with our group? Sorry, you have to count me out. Why don't you join our research group? I'm a solo act, sorry.
help you guys. You're leaving the company? Yeah, I'm jumping ship. I got a better offer.

Special Corners

여성・10대・
전업주부・샐러리맨…
그들의 아우성!

981›1000

요조숙녀는 이렇게 말하지!

Ladies Corner

- [ ] Anything for a lady?
- [ ] I need to take a powder.
- [ ] Aren't there any gentlemen here?
- [ ] I'm counting calories.
- [ ] I'm not your average girl.

981

여성용품 있나요?
Anything for a lady?

→ Are you selling anything fit for ladies? 쇼핑할 때 써요. Anything for a man/kid/senior 등도 넣어 응용해보세요.

A Do you have anything for a lady in this shop?
B We certainly do. Right his way, Miss.

A 이 상점에 여성용품 있나요?
B 그럼요. 자 이리로 오세요.

982

화장 좀 고치고 올게요.
I need to take a powder.

→ I need to go to the bathroom. 품위 있는 여성이길 원한다면 '화장실 가겠다'는 말 대신 이렇게 말해요.

A I need to take a powder. Excuse me for a moment.
B I'll wait here for you.

A 화장 좀 고치고 올게요. 잠시 실례할게요.
B 여기서 기다리겠습니다.

983

도와 줄 신사분 없나요?
Aren't there any gentlemen here?

 → Can't any gentleman assist me? 대단한 요조숙녀 올시다!

A Aren't there any gentlemen here? I need help with my bags.
B I'd be happy to help you, miss.

be happy to 기꺼이 ~하다

A 도와줄 신사분 없나요? 가방 운반을 도와줘야겠어요.
B 제가 기꺼이 도와드리죠, 아가씨.

984

칼로리에 신경써야 해요.
I'm counting calories.

 → I'm on a diet. 대신 써요.

A Would you like to sample our cake?
B No thanks. I'm counting calories.

sample 시식하다

A 케이크 좀 시식해 보시겠어요?
B 됐어요. 칼로리에 신경써야 해요.

985

난 평범한 여자가 아니죠.
I'm not your average girl.

 → I'm an exceptional woman. 현모양처감을 생각했다면 '잘못 찍었어요!'

A Wow! I didn't know you were a black belt in Taekwondo.
B I'm not your average girl!

average 평범한, 보통의   exceptional 예외적인

A 와! 태권도 검은띠인 줄 몰랐어요.
B 난 평범한 여자가 아니죠!

칙칙폭폭! 10대의 인생 열차

Teen Corner

☐ Growing up is hard to do.   ☐ I'm older than I look.   ☐ I'm ready for the world.
☐ Don't treat me like a kid.   ☐ That's old-fashioned.

986
어른이 되는 게 쉽지 않아.
Growing up is hard to do.

→ I'm experiencing hardships in becoming an adult.

A How're your grades?
B Terrible! Growing up is hard to do!

A 성적은 어떠니?
B 엉망이에요! 어른이 되는 게 쉽지 않아요!

987
보기보다 나이 들었어요.
I'm older than I look.

→ 반대로 말하려면 I'm younger than I look.

A You're only 16, aren't you?
B No, I'm older than I look.

A 너 16살 밖에 안 먹었지?
B 아뇨, 보기보다 나이 들었어요.

988
세상에 나갈 준비가 됐어요.
I'm ready for the world.

 → I'm prepared for anything! 할 수 있다(can-do)는 정신이 가상하네요! Getting을 살짝 넣으면 지금 열심히 '준비 중'이란 뉘앙스가 생겨요.

A Are you studying hard, Barry?
B Yes, mom, I'm getting ready for the world.

A 배리, 공부 열심히 하고 있니?
B 예, 엄마, 세상에 나갈 준비를 하고 있어요.

989
어린애 취급 마세요.
Don't treat me like a kid.

 → I can take care of myself! 어느날 아들 녀석이 이런 말대꾸를 하더라도 너무 놀라지 마세요!

A Let me wipe your mouth for you, Frank.
B Please don't treat me like a kid, mom.

treat (like) (~처럼) 대접하다, 대우하다 eg. Don't treat me like your girl.

A 프랭크, 입을 닦아줄게.
B 엄마, 제발 어린애 취급 마세요.

990
구식이잖아요.
That's old-fashioned.

 → 생각, 말, 행동이 유행에 뒤쳐질 때 툭 던지는 말. 사람을 주어로 써도 돼요. — I'm the kind who loves only one. So the boys say I'm old fashioned.(난 단 한 사람을 사랑하는 그런 남자. 모두들 내가 구식이래요.)

A Why don't you use the house phone sometimes?
B That's old-fashioned, grandpa. I only use my cell phone.

Why don't you~ (권유)~하는 게 어때요?

A 가끔은 집 전화를 사용하지 그러니?
B 그건 구식이에요, 할아버지. 난 휴대폰만 써요.

가정주부의 '거룩한' 일상

Housewife Corner

- [ ] I'm a full-time mother.
- [ ] I've been running around all day.
- [ ] I've got my in-laws with me.
- [ ] We're an empty nest.
- [ ] We're through having kids!

991

전업주부에요.
I'm a full-time mother.

→ Although I don't have a career, being a mother takes up all of my time.

A What do you do for a living, Joan?
B I'm a full-time mother.

What do you do for a living?=What's your job?

A 조안, 무슨 일을 하세요?
B 전업주부에요.

992

종일 이 일 저 일로 분주했죠.
I've been running around all day.

→ I'm very active doing various things. 집안에서 할 일이 얼마나 많겠어요!

A You need to take a break, dear.
B I know. I've been running around all day: shopping, cleaning, things like that.

things like that 뭐 그런 것들(stuff like that)

A 여보, 좀 쉬어요.
B 그래요. 종일 분주했어요. 쇼핑에 빨래하고 뭐 그런 걸로요.

470

993

시댁 식구와 같이 살죠.
I've got my in-laws with me.

 → My in-laws live with me. with는 living with의 뜻.

A How many people are there in your home?
B Six: My husband, and 2 kids. Plus, I've got my in-laws with me.

A 댁에 몇 명이 살아요?
B 여섯이요. 남편과 두 아이. 그리고 시댁 식구도 함께 살죠.

994

애들은 다 출가했어요.
We're an empty nest.

 → Children have grown up and moved away.

A So your kids are all grown?
B Yes, we're an empty nest now. We really miss them.

nest 보금자리(가정), 울타리

A 자녀분들이 다 성장했지요?
B 예, 다들 출가했는데. 애들이 보고싶어요.

995

아이는 그만 낳을 겁니다!
We're through having kids!

 → We have no plans to get pregnant again.

A Don't you want to have another son?
B No, we're through having kids.

be through 끝내다, 마치다

A 아들 하나 더 안 낳으세요?
B 아뇨, 아이는 그만 낳아야죠.

샐러리맨의 고충이 느껴질 때면

Salaried Worker Corner

☐ How's the rat race? ☐ My job's a grind. ☐ Same-old, same-old.
☐ Working hard? Or hardly working? ☐ Home fires are burning.

996
직장생활은 어때요?
How's the rat race?

 → rat race는 직장생활의 고달픔을 뜻하는 말.

A How's the rat race? Company life okay?
B It's keeping me busy, but at least I have a job!

keep~ busy ~를 바쁘게 하다   at least 최소한

A 직장생활은 어때요? 회사에선 별일 없죠?
B 일로 바쁘지만, 최소한 직장은 잡은 셈이죠!

997
먹고 살기 힘들군.
My job's a grind.

 → I've got a grinding/difficult lifestyle. 힘들여 맷돌을 갈듯 애써서 겨우 살아간다는 뜻.

A Are you enjoying your job, Griffin?
B Actually, my job's a grind.

actually 실은, 정말이지

A 그리핀, 일하는 게 어때요?
B 정말이지 먹고 살기 힘들어요.

998

늘 똑같죠.
Same-old, same-old.

 → Eeverything remains the same. Nothing new or interesting ever happens.

A Getting along at work okay?
B Same-old, same-old.

A 직장 일은 잘 돼요?
B 늘 똑같죠.

999

열심히 하는 거요, 아니면 대충 때우는 거요?
Working hard? Or hardly working?

 → Are you working diligently or just relaxing?

A Stanley, what's up? Working hard? Or hardly working?
B Look at all these papers on my desk! What do you think?

hardly 거의 ~하지 않는   diligently 부지런히   relax 쉬다

A 스탠리, 어때? 열심히 하는 건가, 아니면 대충 때우는 건가?
B 책상 위의 이것들을 보세요! 무슨 소리 하세요?

1000

가정도 생각해야죠.
Home fires are burning.

 → Wife and kids are waiting for me at home. 전기가 없던 시절, 밖에서 일하고 돌아올 남편을 위해 불을 밝혀 두었던 데서 비롯된 말.

A Rushing off?
B Yes, the home fires are burning, so I'd better leave.

home fire 가정생활   rush off 서두르다, 급히 가다

A 서둘러 가야 해요?
B 예, 집에서 기다려요. 그만 가야겠어요.

Appendix

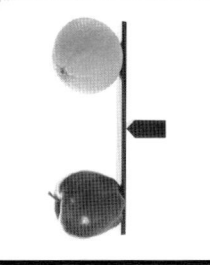

Winning & Living English Tips!

살아있는 영어, 따라해 보자

Is this the company bowling team? It sure is. Want in? It's sure is. Isn't this the local parents' group? It is. You signing up? We need more parents. This is the company union desk, right? Right! In or out? All emplo yees should join. I'd like to join the school French Club here. You hopping on? How long have you studied French? Can I come to your party this Friday? Of course! The more, the merrier. Aren't you going to stay with our group? Sorry, you have to count me out. Why don't you join our research group? I'm a solo act, sorry. You're leaving our department? Yeah. from now on you're on you're own. Why didn't you help carry our bags? Every man for himself. I've got no time to help you guys. You're leaving the company? Yeah. I'm jumping ship. I got a better offer. Is this the company bowling team? It sure is. Want in? Isn't this the local parents' group? It is. You signing up? We need more parents. This is the company union desk, right? Right! In or out? All emplo yees should join. I'd like to join the school French Club here.

Bonus 1 첫 대면부터 호감 가는 만문 질문 트기기본

International Conversation Starters and Conversation Killers

① 는 호감 가는 말, ② 는 너무 공식적이거나 교과서적인 말투로 들리는 경우

Greetings | 먼저 접근하면서 인사하기

① My name's 홍길동, and yours?
I'm sorry, I didn't catch your name.
I'm sorry, and you are...?

A : My name's Jin-seuk, and yours?
B : Tom Withers. Just call me Tom.

A : I'm sorry. I didn't catch your name.
B : I'm Sally Ralston.

② What's your name?
Can I have your name please?
Could you please tell me your name?

제 이름은 홍길동인데, 당신 이름은?
미안하지만 이름을 못 알아 들었어요.
실례지만 당신이 ~이신가요?

Starting conversations | 자연스럽게 대화 트기

① How do you like this weather?
Hot/cold/rainy, isn't it?
Did you catch the baseball/soccer/basketball game last night?
That's a nice jacket/shirt/suit you have on!

A : Hot, isn't it!
B : It sure is! I've never seen a summer like this!
A : You know, summers are always like this in Busan. I'm Gu-yeong, by the way...

이곳 날씨가 어떠세요?
덥죠/춥죠/비가 오네요?
어젯밤에 야구/축구/농구 봤어요?
당신 그 자켓/셔츠/양복 멋지군요!

① A : Hey, that's a sharp-looking pair of earrings you have on!
B : Thanks. I got them at the Seoul Department Store.
A : Really? In fact, I often go there myself. I'm Shin-a by the way...

② Excuse me, where are you from?
Where are you from? America?
Could you please tell me your name?
Are you Christian?

Yes and No | 거부감 들지 않게 No하기

① I'm afraid that's next to impossible.
That isn't normally done, I'm afraid.
I'm afraid not.
I wish I could, but it's not possible.
Maybe yes, maybe no.

A : Mr. Kim, would it be possible to ask the client to come in a day earlier?
B : I wish I could, but it's not possible, Mrs. Carter. He insists on coming on Friday instead.

A : So-yeon, can't we go to Gyeongbok Palace tomorrow?
B : I'm afraid not. It's closed tomorrow.

② Sure, but...(거부가 분명치 않게 들림)
Of course, but it would be very difficult.

좌송하지만 그건 거의 불가능합니다.
그건 일반적으로 안 되는 경우에요.
미안하지만 안 됩니다.
해 드리고 싶지만 안 됩니다.
글쎄요.

Getting Contact Information | 연락처 묻기

- How can I get in touch with you? 어떻게 연락 드릴까요?
- What's the best way to reach you? 가장 편리하신 연락 방법은요?
- Got a card? 명함 있으세요?

  A: How can I get in touch with you, Mr. Jones?
  B: You can ring my secretary at the office.

  A: Got a card, Mr. Walters?
  B: I sure do: here's one.

- Can I have/what's your phone number? (형식적이고 딱딱하게 들림)
  Please give me your business/personal card.

Personal Questions | 사적인 질문하기(나이/외모/결혼여부)

- When did you graduate? 언제 졸업했어요?
- How old are you?
- You have an impressive image. 인상이 좋으세요.
  Your sister is very attractive. 네 여동생은 아주 매력적이야.
- You're very handsome/beautiful. (직접적인 외모 칭찬은 좋지 않음)
- Have you changed something about yourself? 뭔가 변화를 주셨군요?
  I don't think you're overweight. 당신은 과체중 같지 않은데요.
- Have you lost some weight?
  You should lose weight.
- Are you here with your family? 이곳엔 가족과 함께 오셨나요?
  Still single, I bet! 아직 미혼 이시죠?

Invitations | 먼저 초대하기

- Here's my card. If you want … sometime, give me a ring.
  여기 제 명함입니다. ~이 필요하시면 전화주세요.
  Here's my cell phone number. If you ever want …. please give me a call.
  제 전화 번호입니다. 혹 ~이 필요하시면 전화주세요.

  A: Here's my card. If you want a tour of Namdaemun Market sometime, give me a ring.
  B: Thanks, I just might do that.

  A: Here's my cell phone number. If you ever want to see Daejeon Science Town, please give me a call.
  B: Thanks, I just might do that one day.

- Can I show you … one day?
  What about going to …?
  I want to take you to see …? How about it?

Invitations | 초면이 아닐 때

- Let's get together sometime. 언제 한번 만납시다.
  Let's meet for coffee(dinner/lunch/talks etc.) one day. 언제 차 한잔 해요.

  A: Let's get together sometime, Jason, and discuss business.
  B: Yes, Frank, let's do that.

  A: Let's meet for coffee one day, Melba.
  B: Sounds like a great idea.

- I want to meet you in the future. (너무 딱딱하게 들림)
  Let's meet in the future.

Are you married?
Why haven't you gotten married yet?
Do you have a girlfriend/boyfriend?

A: Jane, are you here with your family?
B: Oh, yes, with my husband.

Meetings | 회의 시작하기/질문하기/회의 끝내기

What about opening things up?　　시작해 볼까요?
Shall we start now?　　　　　　　지금 시작할까요?

A: It looks like everyone's here. So, what about opening things up?
B: Sounds great, Tom.

A: Anyone mind if we begin?
B: I don't think anyone does, Betty.

Let's start our meeting.
The meeting starts now.

Anyone want to contribute?　　　할 말 있으신 분 계세요?
Opinions? Questions?　　　　　　의견 있어요? 질문 있나요?

A: Anyone want to contribute?
B: Yes, would you mind if I asked you about a point you talked about?

A: Okay, I want to stop for a moment. Opinions? Questions?
B: Sure, Mr. Johnson, could I ask you about a term in the contract?

Give me your questions.
Please ask questions.

If there's nothing else, let's close it up.　　별다른 게 없으면 마치죠.
Okay, that seems to be everything.　　　　좋습니다, 다 끝난 것 같군요.

A: If there's nothing else, let's close it up.
B: Sounds good to us, Mr. Jackson.

A: Okay, that seems to be everything.
B: I think we all agree, Mrs. Ross.

Let's end our meeting.
The meeting is over.

Giving Opinions | 의견 제시 하기

If you don't mind my saying　　제 의견을 말해도 된다면
If you ask me　　　　　　　　제게 물어 보시니

A: If you don't mind my saying, you should wear a suit to the party tomorrow.
B: You really think so? Maybe I will, then.

A: If you ask me, you'd be better off if you came to work on time from now on.
B: You're right. I'd better do that.

Well, my opinion is ....
Let me give you my opinion.

Bonus 2 — 세대별로 다른 일상 말투 따라잡기

Phrases by Generation

화제	나이	14 〉 19	20 〉 34	35 〉 50	+ 50
Greeting 인사		What's Up?	How's it going?	How are you?	How do you do?
Personal States 개인상태		You cool?	You okay?	How do you feel?	Are you well?
Departures 출발		Let's bounce.	Let's shake.	Let's split.	Let's get out of here.
Dissatisfaction / Boredom 불만/지루함		This bites.	This sucks.	Wake me later!	Ho-hum.
Dancing 춤추기		You got moves?	Wanna hit the floor?	Wanna dance?	Shall we dance?
Music 음악		Check these tunes.	Check this song.	Listen to this.	Have a listen.
Smoking 흡연		Got any cigs?	Got some cigs?	Got smokes?	Got a cigarette?
Basketball 농구		Let's ball.	Let's shoot some hoops.	Let's hit the courts.	Let's play some round ball.
Fight Challenges 싸움/시비		Watch your back!	Want some of this?	Feel lucky!	You're cruising for a bruising.
Eating 먹기		Got any eats?	Let's grab something.	Anything to eat?	What's to eat?
Money 돈		Got any coin?	Carrying anything?	How much have you got?	How much do you have?
Video Games 비디오/온라인 게임		Let's do some vids.	Let's do some gaming.	Let's play online.	Let's play a round of …
Entertainer 인기 있는 사람		He's/She's right on time.	He's/She's hot.	He's/She's awesome.	He's/She's a looker.
Friends 친구		Who's in your crew?	Who do you hang with?	Who's your buddies?	Who're your pals?
Boy/girlfriend 남자/여자 친구		Is this your home girl/boy?	Is this your girl/man?	Is this your better half.	Is this the lucky guy/lady?
Agreement 동의 표시		Word!	Right on!	That's right!	Right!
Opposition 반대 의사		Not happening!	No way!	Not if I can help it.	Not on my watch.
Suggestions to inspect 점검 제안		Check!	Check this out!	Fix your eyes on this!	Have/Take a look!
Exposure 노출		You're cold busted!	Gotcha!	Bing-go!	Secret's out!
Foolishness 어리석음		You loco?	You lost your mind?	You lost your marbles?	You're plumb dumb.

Bonus 3 알아 두면 많이 되는 영어의 의례적인 인사말

Rhetorical Questions / Statements

생활 속에서 별 의미 없이 매일 매일 주고 받는 말들이 있죠.
상대방의 '바디랭귀지'를 통해 진짜 묻는 것인지 의례적인 인사인지 판단해야 할 때도 있습니다.

주제	의례적인 인사말	적절한 응답	피할 응답	노트
General Enquiry 인사	What's up?	Hey, what's up?	Nothing much.	Almost always rhetorical.
Gratitude 감사	Thanks.	It's nothing.	You're welcome.	"You're welcome" is possible under formal circumstances, but "It's nothing" is more natural.
Enquiry of Body Condition 건강안부	Feeling okay?	Sure.	Well, there are a few problems.	Sometimes, this question is not rhetorical. You have to judge according to each situation.
Enquiry of Personal Circumstances 개인적인 환경	How's life treating you?	Fine, thanks.	Recently, I managed to…	This question is rhetorical; speaker does not really want information.
Family Enquiries 가족안부	How're the wife/husband and kids?	They're great, thanks.	My first son just entered school.	Usually rhetorical, depending on circumstances.
Academic Enquiries 학업관련 안부	School okay?	Sure. No problem.	I'm having trouble in Math…	Usually rhetorical, depending on circumstances.
Social Activities Enquiries 사회활동	Up to anything nowadays?	The usual. Nothing much.	I'm actually planning…	Not always rhetorical, depending on circumstances.
Schedules 일정	Staying busy?	Yeah, pretty busy. Not too much.	Yes, I have several projects I'm working on.	This question is rhetorical; speaker does not really want information.